LIBRARY OF NEW TESTAMENT

662

Formerly the Journal for the Study of the New Testament Supplement series

Editor
Chris Keith

Editorial Board
Dale C. Allison, Lynn H. Cohick, R. Alan Culpepper, Craig A. Evans, Jennifer Eyl,
Robert Fowler, Simon J. Gathercole, Juan Hernández Jr., John S. Kloppenborg,
Michael Labahn, Matthew V. Novenson, Love L. Sechrest, Robert Wall,
Catrin H. Williams, Brittany E. Wilson

A Jewish Apocalyptic Framework of Eschatology in the Epistle to the Hebrews

Protology and Eschatology as Background

Jihye Lee

t&tclark

T&T CLARK
Bloomsbury Publishing Plc
50 Bedford Square, London, WC1B 3DP, UK
1385 Broadway, New York, NY 10018, USA
29 Earlsfort Terrace, Dublin 2, Ireland

BLOOMSBURY, T&T CLARK and the T&T Clark logo are trademarks of Bloomsbury Publishing Plc

First published in Great Britain 2022
This paperback edition first published in 2023

Copyright © Jihye Lee, 2022

Jihye Lee has asserted her right under the Copyright, Designs and Patents Act, 1988,
to be identified as Author of this work.

The Scripture quotations contained herein are from The New Revised Standard Version of the Bible,
Anglicized Edition, copyright © 1989, 1995 by the Division of Christian Education of the
National Council of the Churches of Christ in the United States of America, and are
used by permission. All rights reserved.

For legal purposes the Acknowledgments on p. ix constitute an extension of this copyright page.

Cover design: Charlotte James

All rights reserved. No part of this publication may be reproduced or transmitted in any form or by any
means, electronic or mechanical, including photocopying, recording, or any information storage or
retrieval system, without prior permission in writing from the publishers.

Bloomsbury Publishing Plc does not have any control over, or responsibility for, any third-party websites
referred to or in this book. All internet addresses given in this book were correct at the time of going
to press. The author and publisher regret any inconvenience caused if addresses have changed
or sites have ceased to exist, but can accept no responsibility for any such changes.

A catalogue record for this book is available from the British Library.

Library of Congress Cataloging-in-Publication Data
Names: Lee, Jihye, author.
Title: A Jewish apocalyptic framework of eschatology in the Epistle to the Hebrews :
protology–eschatology background of Heb 3:7-4:11 and 12:18-29 / by Jihye Lee.
Description: London ; New York : T&T Clark, 2021. | Series: The library of New Testament studies,
2513-8790 ; 662 | Includes bibliographical references and index. | Summary: "This book presents a
comparative study of the Urzeit-Endzeit eschatology in some Jewish apocalyptic literature for a fresh
understanding of the Epistle to the Hebrews"– Provided by publisher.
Identifiers: LCCN 2021016659 (print) | LCCN 2021016660 (ebook) | ISBN 9780567702876 (hardback) |
ISBN 9780567702883 (pdf) | ISBN 9780567702906 (epub)
Subjects: LCSH: Bible. Hebrews, III, 7-IV, 11–Criticism, interpretation, etc. | Bible. Hebrews, XII,
18-29–Criticism, interpretation, etc. | Apocalyptic literature–History and criticism. | Apocryphal books
(Old Testament) | Eschatology, Jewish. | Christianity and other religions–Judaism. |
Judaism–Relations–Christianity.
Classification: LCC BS2775.52 .L445 2021 (print) | LCC BS2775.52 (ebook) | DDC 227/.8706—dc23
LC record available at https://lccn.loc.gov/2021016659
LC ebook record available at https://lccn.loc.gov/2021016660

ISBN:	HB:	978-0-5677-0287-6
	PB:	978-0-5677-0305-7
	ePDF:	978-0-5677-0288-3
	ePUB:	978-0-5677-0290-6

Series: Library of New Testament Studies, volume 662
ISSN 2513-8790

Typeset by RefineCatch Limited, Bungay, Suffolk

To find out more about our authors and books visit www.bloomsbury.com
and sign up for our newsletters.

Contents

Acknowledgments ... ix

1 Introduction ... 1
   1.1 The Definition of *Urzeit-Endzeit* Eschatology ... 2
   1.2 Arguments for the Platonic Background in Hebrews ... 5
      1.2.1 James Thompson ... 5
      1.2.2 Wilfried Eisele ... 7
   1.3 Arguments on Various Grounds for a Dualism Between the Spiritual and the Material (and/or Between Heaven and Earth) in Hebrews ... 9
      1.3.1 Harold W. Attridge ... 9
      1.3.2 Stefan N. Svendsen ... 11
      1.3.3 Jared C. Calaway ... 13
   1.4 Arguments for Apocalyptic Backgrounds ... 15
      1.4.1 Lincoln D. Hurst ... 15
      1.4.2 Scott D. Mackie and Eric F. Mason ... 16
      1.4.3 David M. Moffitt ... 17

2 *Urzeit-Endzeit* Eschatology in Pre-70 Second Temple Literature ... 21
   2.1 Introduction ... 21
   2.2 1 Enoch ... 21
      2.2.1 The Book of Watchers ... 21
         2.2.1.1 1 Enoch 24-25 ... 21
         2.2.1.2 1 Enoch 10:16–11:2 ... 25
      2.2.2 The Book of Parables ... 27
      2.2.3 Summary ... 30
   2.3 Qumran Texts ... 30
      2.3.1 CD 3:12–4:4 ... 31
      2.3.2 4QpPs37 (4Q171) ... 35
      2.3.3 4QInstruction ... 39
      2.3.4 Summary ... 43
   2.4 Jubilees ... 44
      2.4.1 Imminent Possession of the Promised Inheritance ... 44

		2.4.2 The Time for Purification Before Entering the Sanctuary		45
		2.4.3 Covenant Renewal Based on the Filial Relationship Between Israel and God		50
		2.4.4 Summary		53
	2.5	*Liber Antiquitatum Biblicarum*		54
		2.5.1 The Connection Between the Historical and Eschatological Inheritances		54
		2.5.2 The Connection Among Eden, the Promised Land, and Paradise		55
		2.5.3 Other Elements of *Urzeit-Endzeit* Eschatology		57
		2.5.4 Summary		61
	2.6	Summary of Chapter 2		62
3	*Urzeit-Endzeit* Eschatology in Post-70 Second Temple Literature			63
	3.1	Introduction		63
	3.2	4 Ezra and 2 Baruch		63
		3.2.1 4 Ezra		64
			3.2.1.1 Hopeless Humanity and the Eschatological Hope	64
			3.2.1.2 The *Urzeit-Endzeit* Eschatology	66
			3.2.1.3 Summary	69
		3.2.2 2 Baruch		69
			3.2.2.1 The Promised Inheritance	70
			3.2.2.2 The Messianic Kingdom for the Restoration of Eden on Earth and Israel's Vindication	71
			3.2.2.3 The Messianic Era as a Bridge Between the Two Worlds	73
			3.2.2.4 Summary	75
		3.2.3 Summary of the Section on 4 Ezra and 2 Baruch		75
	3.3.	Revelation		76
		3.3.1 Christ's Redemption and the New Creation (chs. 4–5)		77
		3.3.2 The New Jerusalem (21:1–22:5)		79
		3.3.3 Summary		85
	3.4	Summary of Chapter 3		86
4	A Comparison of the Eschatological Visions			87
	4.1	Introduction		87
	4.2	The Pre-70 Eschatological Visions		87
		4.2.1 Gradual Transformation of the Earth (Jubilees)		88
		4.2.2 The New Creation at the Day of Judgment (The Book of Watchers, Qumran Texts, and *LAB*)		89
		4.2.3 Summary		91

	4.3	Post-70 Eschatological Visions		91
		4.3.1	The Coming World in 4 Ezra and 2 Baruch		92
			4.3.1.1	The Revelation of the Heavenly Paradise	92
			4.3.1.2	The Revelation of the Heavenly Zion	93
		4.3.2	The Coming World in the Book of Revelation		95
		4.3.3	Summary of Post-70 Eschatologies		97
	4.4	Summary of Chapter 4		97
5	God's Rest in Heb. 3:7–4:11		99
	5.1	God's Rest in Gen. 2:2		100
	5.2	God's Rest in Ps. 95		102
		5.2.1	Limitations of Some Scholarly Views		102
		5.2.2	The Wilderness Generation's Entrance into God's Rest in Heb. 3:7-19		105
			5.2.2.1	Failure of the Israelites in Num 14	105
			5.2.2.2	Failure of the Israelites in Num 20	106
				5.2.2.2.1 Heb. 3:7-14	107
				5.2.2.2.2 Heb. 3:15-19	109
		5.2.3	The Parallel Visions of the Eschaton in Some Apocalyptic Texts		111
			5.2.3.1	The Two Core Elements of God's Rest in the Present Passage	111
			5.2.3.2	Parallelism with the Eschatological Visions of Apocalyptic Texts	113
				5.2.3.2.1 The Continuity Between Israel's Rest in the Promised Land and the Eschatological Rest in Light of God's Presence	113
				5.2.3.2.2 The Change of Heart and the Renewal of Creation	115
		5.2.4	Summary		117
	5.3	Adam's Participation in God's Rest		117
		5.3.1	The Book of Watchers		119
		5.3.2	Qumran Texts		120
		5.3.3	Jubilees		121
		5.3.4	Pseudo-Philo		122
	5.4	Summary of Chapter 5		123
6	The Unshakable Kingdom		127
	6.1	Heb. 12:26-29		127
		6.1.1	The Usages of χρηματίζω and μετάθεσις		128

		6.1.2 The Quotations from the OT	130
		6.1.3 The Shaking Heavenly World	132
	6.2	The Warning from Esau's Example	135
		6.2.1 The Pivotal Role of Esau's Case	135
		6.2.2 Adam and Edom	136
	6.3	The Renewal of Creation	141
	6.4	Summary of Chapter 6	145
7	Conclusion		147

Bibliography	153
Index of References	169
Subject Index	183

Acknowledgments

This monograph represents a revised version of my dissertation submitted to the theological faculty of University of St. Andrews, UK in 2019. I must express my deep appreciation to my supervisor, Dr. David Moffitt, who was the most knowledgeable and encouraging mentor that I have ever met. This research could never have been completed without his tireless patience and insightful guidance. I would also like to thank Dr. T. J. Lang and Dr. Gordon Campbell for their constructive comments and suggestions. I wish to thank Dr. Aaron S. Son who has been always supportive in my steps of the way, providing invaluable encouragement. I hope I can be a good teacher following him who was not only teaching the class but making students actually feel the heart of the Apostle Paul in his NT class. The initial ideas for this work emerged during my master's courses. It is not coincidental that my approach reflects the influence of my teachers. I would like to thank Dr. John Walton for the opportunity to nurture my interests in the story of creation and Adam through his inspiring classes. I also want to thank Dr. Luke Timothy Johnson who guided me to expand my interests through the study of the book of Hebrews. My special thanks are due to my good friends, Janghoon Park, Euichang Kim, and Korean families in St. Andrews. Their support and fellowship were an invaluable blessing throughout my time in St. Andrews. I am indebted to the beloved friends, Harry and Rosalind, who provided thoughtful suggestions for this monograph and unforgettable memories to our family. My daughters would always miss the baking and game times with them in their lovely and warm house next door to us. I am deeply grateful to Sandra Peniston-Bird who carefully read the chapters and provided numerous comments and suggestions. This book is stronger because of her great work. I especially thank my parents-in-law, Jungwon Lee and Dongshim Kim, my parents, Sangkun Lee and Sukok Jun, and other family members. Their support and prayers made this long and demanding process possible. The biggest debt I accrued during the research for this monograph is to my husband. I gratefully dedicate this book to my husband, Min Su, who was always there to believe I could persevere even in the darkest point of the process. Our two daughters, Juha and Yuna, you have been a source of constant joy. Thank you.

To God alone be the glory!

1

Introduction

The epistle to the Hebrews does not mention Adam or Eden by name. This has not, however, kept scholars from positing that the letter has a particular interest in Adam, especially in the author's appeal to Ps. 8 in Heb. 2:6-10.[1] Psalm 8 is reminiscent of the creation account of Gen. 1:26-28, and scholars have argued that, by citing Ps. 8, the author of Hebrews demonstrates that Christ's humiliation and exaltation is a fulfilment of the original divine intention for Adam so that the sons of God may participate in the glory of Adam (cf. Heb. 2:9). Other than this, I am unaware of any full-scale study that explores further the existence of primordial themes interwoven into Hebrews' argument in the subsequent chapters of the book.

Hebrews 1:3 implies Jesus' nature as God's image: "the reflection of God's glory and the exact imprint of God's very being" (Heb. 1:3).[2] The combined concepts of sonship (esp. firstborn) and inheritance in Heb. 1:2 and the quoted text, Ps. 2:7, has an "Adamic ring" (cf. Col. 1:15-18).[3] The Adamic tone in ch. 1 is linked to the extensive quotation of Ps. 8, which presents an interpretation of Gen. 1:26-28. In Heb. 3:7–4:13, the author of Hebrews presents the hope of the eschatological rest as he exhorts his readers to enter it, first by drawing on the idea of Israel's entrance into the promised land from Ps. 95 and then by interpreting this act of entering the promised land, in light of Gen. 2:2, as the act of participating in God's own Sabbath rest after creation. Along with

---

[1] F. F. Bruce, *The Epistle to the Hebrews* (Grand Rapids: Eerdmans, 1990), 74; Philip Edgcumbe Hughes, *A Commentary on the Epistle to the Hebrews* (Grand Rapids: Eerdmans, 1977), 84; David Lewis Allen, *Hebrews*, New American Commentary 35 (Nashville: B & H Publishing Group, 2010), 228; George H. Guthrie, "Hebrews," in *Commentary on the New Testament Use of the Old Testament* (Grand Rapids: Baker Academic, 2007), 944–45. These scholars show a methodological limitation by finding the major support for their reading only in the theological category of New Testament (esp. Pauline Adam Christology).

[2] 1 Cor 11:7 describes humanity as "the image and glory of God (εἰκὼν καὶ δόξα θεοῦ)," implying a close connection between the expressions "the image of God" and "the reflection of God's glory." Colossians 1:15 shows the link between the two characteristics of Jesus, "the image of God" and "the firstborn."

[3] G. K. Beale points out indications that the discussion of sonship in Heb. 1 reflects an underlying Adam tradition. Gen. 5:1-4 implies that Adam's creation "in God's image" means that he was God's son because when Adam had a son, he was said to be the "father of [a son] in his own likeness, according to his image." According to Beale, Christ's sonship, demonstrated by his being "in God's image," is linked to the concept of Adamic sonship. G. K. Beale, *A New Testament Biblical Theology: the Unfolding of the Old Testament in the New* (Grand Rapids: Baker Academic, 2011), 444, 462–63.

his description of Jesus' priesthood in the heavenly sanctuary (e.g. Heb. 9:11) and the vision that believers will enter the holy of holies following the high priest (e.g. Heb. 4:16; 6:19; 10:19-22), the author envisages the eschatological kingdom which will involve the shaking of heaven and earth in ch. 12.

Is the eschatological inheritance of the believers, which the author describes in terms of God's rest, priesthood, and the temple, thought to be linked with Adam's glory and his authority over the creation that the Son restores? Can the themes of glory, firstborn, the sons' superiority to the angels, and resolution of the issue of death in Hebrews be comprehensively explained in this eschatological hope? My claim is that some Jewish apocalyptic texts provide a valuable eschatological framework, the so called *Urzeit-Endzeit* eschatology, in which the given notions of Hebrews are consistently understood in terms of inner relations among them, allowing a fresh reading of Hebrews' arguments, specifically the notions of God's rest in Heb. 3:7–4:11 and the unshakable kingdom in Heb. 12:26-29. When Heb. 3:7-4:11 is located in the context of the pattern that the apocalyptic texts show (i.e. the *Urzeit-Endzeit* eschatology), the author's citation and interpretation of Ps. 95 and Gen. 2:2 makes more sense than other scholarly views. The author of Hebrews envisions that, with the help of Jesus the high priest who serves in "the greater and perfect" sanctuary in the heavens, the eschatological generation will be restored to God's rest, something akin to what was available in Eden, which Adam lost through his sin, and which God intended the previous generations of Israel to obtain in their possession of the promised land. In this apocalyptic framework, the theme of God's promise with the citation of Haggai and Exodus passages in Heb. 12:26-29 is also more properly explained than the understanding of the passage with the idea of the destruction of the shaking creation. The author envisages the unshakable kingdom that will consist of the renewed creation and the revealed heavenly realms, which will be accomplished through "shaking."

In the present chapter, first, I present a definition of *Urzeit-Endzeit* eschatology as highlighting two essential elements of this eschatological framework, i.e. creation and Israel's history. Second, I show that the scholarly views which argue for an ahistorical and immaterial eschatological vision of Hebrews are incongruent with the text's argument. This group is divided into two categories, one of which claims a pure Platonic background of Hebrews and the other argues on various grounds for a dualism between the spiritual and the material (or/and heavenly and earthly) in Hebrews. Third, I list some scholars who hold the view that Hebrews shares an apocalyptic eschatological framework.

1.1 The Definition of *Urzeit-Endzeit* Eschatology

The expression, *Urzeit gleich Endzeit* ("primeval time corresponds to eschatological time") appears as early as 1895 in H. Gunkel's landmark book *Schöpfung und Chaos in Urzeit und Endzeit*. In this book, Gunkel shows how the Babylonian *Chaoskampf* myth moulded both the protological narrative of Gen. 1 and the eschatological narrative of Rev 12 and, thus, how the author of Revelation depicts the vision of the culmination of the primordial victory at the eschaton.[4] The *Urzeit-Endzeit* or protology-eschatology pattern refers, in general terms, to the conception that the eschaton should recapitulate the beginning, and it forms the basic structure of apocalyptic eschatological hope. D. Aune and E. Stewart point out that, in apocalyptic worldviews, "the imperfect present lies at the low point between the perfections of the distant past and the perfections of the imminent future."[5] Among the major concerns of Jewish apocalyptic theologies are the problem of evil and the solution projected into the eschatological future.[6] The perspective that the present world is hopelessly depraved and in need of divine reconstitution causes them to conceptualize the paradigmatic beginning to be the basis for the vision of the future as a restoration of the past.[7]

The term *Urzeit-Endzeit* used in Gunkel's work pertains to the concept of the eschaton, which is identical in most respects to the beginning of the creation.[8] Since Gunkel's study, however, there have been other scholars who do not agree that *Urzeit* is identical to *Endzeit* in the biblical traditions. B. S. Childs argues that, in Deutero- and Trito-Isaiah, the eschatological aspects entail not only the renewal of the primordial aspects but also "new things" which were hidden and unknown before.[9] W. Pannenberg similarly argues, "Es handelt sich nicht um eine einfache Rückkehr zum Anfang."[10] Concerning eschatological visions in apocalyptic texts, J. Jeremias states that only a few pre-Christian apocalyptic texts contain the idea that "the Paradise of the last age is identical with that of the first" (e.g. *Test. L.* 18:10 f; 1 En 25:4).[11] He points out that the

---

[4] Hermann Gunkel, Heinrich Zimmern, and Friedrich Hügel, *Schöpfung und Chaos in Urzeit und Endzeit: eine religionsgeschichtliche Untersuchung über Gen. 1 und Ap. Joh. 12* (Göttingen: Vandenhoeck und Ruprecht, 1895), 366–71. Gunkel et al. argue that the creation account in Gen. 1 as well as other OT texts modified the ancient Babylonian myth of cosmic and human creation to fit into their views of Yahweh. In turn, the author of Revelation not only went back to the OT concepts and their extension in Second Temple Judaism but also to the Babylonian tradition in his description of the eschaton. Revelation presents the revival of the cosmic power of chaos/evil after its defeat in the creation and its final and irrevocable destruction in the battle with the God of order/good, which allows the establishment of the eschatological kingdom.

[5] David E. Aune and Eric Stewart, "From the Idealized Past to the Imaginary Future: Eschatology Restoration in Jewish Apocalyptic Literature," in *Restoration: Old Testament, Jewish, and Christian Perspectives* (Leiden: Brill, 2001), 147.

[6] T. W. Willett analyzes the religious solutions for evil and death found in two late apocalyptic texts, 4 Ezra and 2 Baruch. 2 Baruch answers the issue of the theodicy with the promise of Israel's restoration under the Messiah's rule in Jerusalem, resurrection to eternal life, and entry into paradise along with retribution upon enemies. 4 Ezra focuses on the resolution of the sin problem through the mercy of God. Willet rightfully points out that, even though the solutions to the problem of theodicy in the two books are different, both books find their answers in the coming world in a similar fashion (p. 124). See T. W. Willett, *Eschatology in the Theodicies of 2 Baruch and 4 Ezra* (Sheffield: JSOT, 1989).

[7] Aune and Stewart, "From the Idealized Past to the Imaginary Future," 147.

[8] In his understanding of the biblical eschatology as myth, Bultmann similarly argues that eschatology "developed from the concept of the periodicity of the course of worldly events." He explains the course of the world in terms of the annual periodicity of nature: "as the seasons of the year follow each other, so do the corresponding periods in the course of the world, comprising the so-called 'year of the world' or 'the great world-year.'" Rudolf Bultmann, *History and Eschatology* (Edinburgh: The University Press, 1957), 23.

[9] Brevard S. Childs, *Myth and Reality in the Old Testament* (London: SCM Press, 1962), 77–80.

[10] Wolfhart Pannenberg, "Die weltgründende Funktion des Mythos und der christliche Offenbarungsglaube," in *Mythos und Rationalität* (Gütersloh: Gütersloher Verlagshaus Gerd Mohn, 1988), 116–17.

[11] Joachim Jeremias, "παράδεισος," *TDNT* vol.5, 767.

Urzeit-Endzeit eschatological vision in most apocalyptic texts does not describe a simple return *ad initium*. These scholarly discussions have made it clear that the *Urzeit-Endzeit* connection which some apocalyptic texts make is best conceived of in terms of the eschatological transformation or culmination of the world such that it will resemble in important ways the good things that existed at the beginning. There are important corresponding patterns between the primordial world and the eschatological world, but not simple identity.

N. A. Dahl helpfully provides some key types in the correlation between the first and the last things in Jewish and Christian texts: a relationship of analogy or parallelism in which the first and last things are to conform to one another (e.g. the idea of a new creation, a new heaven and earth); the idea of a restitution of creation, which has been laid under a curse; a transformation of the first things (the superiority of the new creation); an identity between the first and last things; a preservation of some of the first things for the end of the world (the inclusiveness of creation); the elimination of the powers of darkness.[12] Dahl's classification is criticized because he "tends to lump together texts from different time periods and diverse perspectives."[13] His study is, however, valuable in the sense that it provides some common elements in the eschatological visions which see the connection between the first and last things. Aune and Stewart provide some essential concepts that are observed in the *Urzeit-Endzeit* pattern in apocalyptic texts. On the one hand, they divide the apocalyptic texts into two groups, early and later, and note their different conceptions of the specific experiences of historical Israel.[14] On the other hand, they point out that even the later texts are related to "themes of general significance" for the concepts observed in the earlier texts.[15] The stereotypical features of apocalyptic *Urzeit-Endzeit* eschatology are listed in six points: the restoration of the land, the restoration of kingship (the Davidic messiah), national restoration (regathering the people), Jerusalem and the temple, regaining of the lost paradise, and the restoration of creation.

Of the features of Jewish apocalyptic *Urzeit-Endzeit* eschatology observed by some scholars, two points are worth highlighting. First, Jewish apocalyptic texts commonly envisage the restoration of creation. They do not believe that the debased creation will ultimately be destroyed; rather, they hope that evil, sin, and their consequence, i.e. the curse on creation, will be reversed at the end. Second, they share the recognition of the meaning of Israel's history; they hope that the land, kingship, and temple, which Israel historically retained, will be eschatologically regained in a transformed form. One might say these visions anticipate something like an Eden 2.0.

[12] N. A. Dahl, "Christ, Creation and the Church," in *the Background of the New Testament and Its Eschatology* (Cambridge: Cambridge University Press, 1956), 425–28.
[13] Harry Hahne, *The Corruption and Redemption of Creation: Nature in Romans 8.19-22 and Jewish Apocalyptic Literature* (London; New York: T&T Clark, 2006), 11.
[14] The two groups are as follows: five apocalypses originated from the late third century through the second century BCE (the Book of Heavenly Luminaries, the Book of Watchers, Daniel, the Epistle of Enoch, and the Book of Dreams) and five apocalypses originated from the early first century through the middle of the second century CE (the Similitudes of Enoch, 2 Enoch, 4 Ezra, 2 Baruch, 3 Baruch). Aune and Stewart, "From the Idealized Past to the Imaginary Future," 148–50.
[15] Aune and Stewart state that, particularly in the later apocalypses, such as 4 Ezra and 2 Baruch, there appear what to modern critics are "contradictory, inconsistent, disordered, missing and even paradoxical elements." Ibid., 148–50.

In sum, the *Urzeit-Endzeit* eschatology of Jewish apocalypses has at its core a concern for the fulfillment of God's creational intention for humanity and creation at the eschaton. This fulfillment was partially experienced in Israel's history, but anticipated its culmination at the eschaton. Before discussing the possibility that Hebrews shares a similar framework of *Urzeit-Endzeit* eschatology, I criticize, in the following two sections, the views that argue for an ahistorical and immaterial concept of the eschatological world in Hebrews, particularly by showing that these views cannot coherently explain Hebrews' logic.

1.2 Arguments for the Platonic Background in Hebrews

1.2.1 James Thompson

J. Thompson argues that, even though the author of Hebrews is not "a consistent Platonist," he employs Platonic categories of the transcendent/eternal and the earthly/mortal to interpret Christian existence in order to instruct believers that they should place their faith not in the visible world but in the world which is "invisible, unshakable, untouchable, and not of this creation."[16] Thompson insists that the author of Hebrews holds a worldview in which he uses the term "world" (κόσμος) "in a decidedly negative way."[17] Accordingly, in ch. 12, Hebrews contrasts the sense-perceptible and unstable character of the Sinai theophany and the unshakable and abiding character of the heavenly world, arguing that, when the material world disappears, only the untouchable world remains. Thompson states that "while there is a definite eschatology in Hebrews, it has been reshaped with metaphysical interest."[18] Thompson points out that in ch. 11 the author argues that knowledge of reality makes one "a stranger" to this world. His readers, all along with the heroes of faith, are on a journey toward the heavenly rest, and the exalted Christ has opened the way (2:20; 10:19-23). According to him, this theme of sojourning in the earthly region is familiar in Middle Platonism, particularly in Philo (*Conf.* 75-78; cf. *QG* 4.74; *Somn.* 1.181).[19] According to Thompson, this spiritual reality is ahistorical. Israel's historical inheritance, i.e. the promised rest in the land, is transformed in Heb. 3:7–4:11 into "a metaphor for the transcendent hope of ultimate salvation" through which the author "has provided an evocative image that has shaped Christian thought for centuries."[20]

---

[16] James W. Thompson, *Hebrews: Commentaries on the New Testament*, Paideia: Commentaries on the New Testament (Grand Rapids: Baker, 2008), 25. The influence of Philo of Alexandria on the author of Hebrews was first proposed by Eugène Ménégoz, *La théologie de l'épître aux Hébreux* (Fischbacher, 1894). C. Spicq suggests that Hugo Grotius was the first in modern times to argue the influence of Philo on Hebrews (Ceslas Spicq, *L'Épître Aux Hébreux*, Études Bibliques (Paris: Gabalda, 1952), vol. 1, 39.). Grotius presents some parallels between Philo and Hebrews rather than arguing for Hebrews' dependence on Philo. For this issue, see Philip Church, "Hebrews 1:10-12 and the Renewal of the Cosmos," *TynBul* (2016): 269–70, n.1.
[17] James W. Thompson, *The Beginnings of Christian Philosophy: the Epistle to the Hebrews* (Washington: Catholic Biblical Association of America, 1981), 76.
[18] Thompson, *Hebrews*, 52.
[19] James W. Thompson, "What Middle Platonism Has to Do with Hebrews," in *Reading the Epistle to the Hebrews: A Resource for Students* (Atlanta: SBL, 2011), 49–50.
[20] Thompson, *Hebrews*, 98.

One of the major bases of the argument for the Platonic background of Hebrews is the apparent similarity of vocabulary and ideas between Philo of Alexandria and the author of Hebrews.[21] The terms that the author applies to the earthly tabernacle, however, such as ὑπόδειγμα, σκιά, and ἀντίτυπος, are not self-evidently Platonic. The term σκιά is used in Platonic texts (e.g. Plato, *Rep.* 7.515 AB; Philo, *Leg. All.* 3.97-99; *Somn.* 1.188), but in Heb. 10:1 it is used in a non-Platonic way. The law is called "a shadow of the good things to come" (Σκιὰν ... τῶν μελλόντων ἀγαθῶν), and the contrast here is temporal: The law was foreshadowing what was to come.[22] L. D. Hurst points out that the term ὑπόδειγμα normally means "example" or "sketch," not "copy."[23] K. Schenck, who is otherwise sympathetic to the kind of conclusions Thompson draws, states that the term ὑπόδειγμα "is never used by any ancient author, let alone by Philo or Plato, in reference to a Platonic copy."[24] In 9:24, the author of Hebrews contrasts the true sanctuary with its "antitype" (ἀντίτυπος). As C. R. Koester aptly argues, it is not clear that the term has Platonic connotations in the book of Hebrews. In the third century, Plotinus used the word for "perceptible reality" (*Enneads* 5.3.6.17), but a similar usage does not appear in Plato, and Philo used it for what is "resistant."[25]

Thompson argues that, as the eschatological inheritance of God's people, the author envisions the spiritual and transcendent heavenly realm, which is "not made with hands, that is, not of this creation" (οὐ χειροποιήτου, τοῦτ᾽ ἔστιν οὐ ταύτης τῆς κτίσεως, 9:11) and "set up by the Lord, not by humans" (ἣν ἔπηξεν ὁ κύριος, οὐκ ἄνθρωπος, 8:2). As D. A. DeSilva points out, however, the author "does not oppose created to uncreated things, as would Plato, but rather two orders of created things—that which belongs to *this* creation and that which is not of this creation but rather of that better creation which is God's realm, 'heaven itself.'"[26] E. Adams aptly points out that, if the "anti-worldliness" of Hebrews is the case as Thompson argues, Hebrews is "at odds with mainstream Christian theology, which has traditionally emphasized the original goodness and ongoing worth of the created order."[27] Furthermore, the author repeatedly

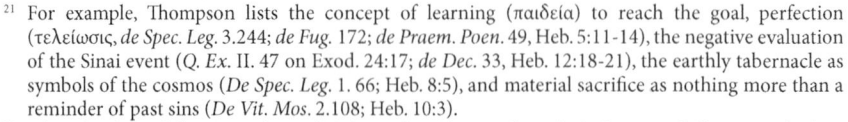

---

[21] For example, Thompson lists the concept of learning (παιδεία) to reach the goal, perfection (τελείωσις, *de Spec. Leg.* 3.244; *de Fug.* 172; *de Praem. Poen.* 49, Heb. 5:11-14), the negative evaluation of the Sinai event (*Q. Ex.* II. 47 on Exod. 24:17; *de Dec.* 33, Heb. 12:18-21), the earthly tabernacle as symbols of the cosmos (*De Spec. Leg.* 1. 66; Heb. 8:5), and material sacrifice as nothing more than a reminder of past sins (*De Vit. Mos.* 2.108; Heb. 10:3).

[22] Edward Adams, "The Cosmology of Hebrews," in *The Epistle to the Hebrews and Christian Theology* (Grand Rapids; Cambridge: Eerdmans, 2009), 132.

[23] L. D. Hurst, *The Epistle to the Hebrews: Its Background of Thought* (Cambridge: Cambridge University Press, 1990), 13–17.

[24] Kenneth Schenck, *A Brief Guide to Philo* (Louisville: Westminster John Knox Press, 2005), 84. E. Adams points out that if the author had in mind the Platonic ideal form and copy, it is reasonable to suppose he would have used μίμημα, the most obvious word for a Platonic copy (Adams, "The Cosmology of Hebrews," 133).

[25] Craig R. Koester, *Hebrews: A New Translation with Introduction and Commentary* (New York: Doubleday, 2001), 98.

[26] David Arthur DeSilva, *Perseverance in Gratitude: A Socio-rhetorical Commentary on the Epistle "to the Hebrews"* (Grand Rapids: Eerdmans, 2000), 29.

[27] Adams, "The Cosmology of Hebrews," 122. Adams states that Thompson misrepresents "the cosmological data of Hebrews themselves" and Philo's view as well. Adams presents how positive a view Philo has on the cosmos, mentioning "the most perfect of created things" (*De aeternitate mundi* 26, 50, 73, see also *De plantatione* 131; *De somniis* 1.207) and arguing that the created world is imperishable (*Aeternitate*, 19). Edward Adams, *Constructing the World: A Study in Paul's Cosmological Language* (Edinburgh: T&T Clark, 2000), 58–64.

shows his deep interest in the world's creation and in God as the Creator (1:2, 10; 2:10; 3:4; 4:3-4, 10; 9:26; 11:3). The idea that the author has a concept of the noetic heavenly realm is also undermined by the text. Consistently throughout the book, the author of Hebrews speaks of a concrete heavenly structure that corresponds to that of the earthly temple. He describes the true tent (σκηνή) and the holy places (ἅγια), in which Christ serves as the high priest (8:2), and which provide the τύπος for the tabernacle in the wilderness (8:5). Christ is said to have proceeded through "the greater and more perfect tent" (σκηνή, 9:11), entered within the veil (καταπέτασμα, 6:19) into the holy places (ἅγια), where he offered the sacrifice (9:23-26) and is seated with God upon the throne (θρόνος, 8:1).[28] The attempt to explain Hebrews only against a Platonic background has been hamstrung by a number of studies that highlight elements in Hebrews which cannot be derived from that religio-historical paradigm.[29] Thompson's argument for Hebrews' vision of nonmaterial and ahistorical heavenly reality against a Platonic background does not stand on firm ground.

1.2.2 Wilfried Eisele

W. Eisele follows E. Gräßer's idea presented in his article "Das wandernde Gottesvolk," i.e. that the question of *Parousia* in Hebrews has not yet been precisely determined. Eisele argues that, in Hebrews' basic dichotomy between the perceptible world and the transcendent principle, the *Parousia* is nothing other than the immediate judgment of each individual soul in heaven after death. For this argument, Eisele investigates Hebrews' passages that have been considered to contain allusions to the second coming of Christ (1:6; 9:27-28; 10:25, 36-39; 12:25-29). Through detailed analysis of these texts, Eisele claims that the traditional temporal tension between "the already" and "the not yet" is replaced with the spatial-ontological dichotomy between the "shakable" and "unshakable" world.[30] For example, the shaking of the created world in Heb. 12:26-27

---

[28] Scholars see a literal heavenly structure in Hebrews' argument. E.g. William L. Lane, *Hebrews 1–8* (Dallas: Word Books, 1991), 9–13; Lincoln D. Hurst, "Eschatology and 'Platonism' in the Epistle to the Hebrews," *SBLSP* 23 (1984): 48–55. J. A. Barnard states that the author connects Jesus' blood with the heavenly holy of holies in the same way that he connects the blood of animal sacrifice with the earthly holy of holies. Jody A. Barnard, *The Mysticism of Hebrews: Exploring the Role of Jewish Apocalyptic Mysticism in the Epistle to the Hebrews* (Tübingen: Mohr Siebeck, 2012), 105. D. M. Moffitt aptly points out that the way in which Hebrews describes Jesus' service in the heavenly tabernacle suggests that the author considers the analogical relationship between the high priest's entry into the sacred space of the earthly temple and Jesus' entry as the great high priest into the sacred space in the heavenly tabernacle. According to Moffitt, analogy, which is presented as a contrast to metaphor, "may stretch the meaning of the term by using it in a new way, but such usage does not generate a fundamentally new perspective or picture relative to the subject." David M. Moffitt, "Serving in the Tabernacle in Heaven: Sacred Space, Jesus's High-Priestly Sacrifice, and Hebrews' Analogical Theology," in *Hebrews in Contexts* (Leiden: Brill, 2016), 64.

[29] For further criticism of the views that Hebrews has a Platonic background, see E. F. Mason, "Sit at My Right Hand: Enthronement and the Heavenly Sanctuary in Hebrews," in *A Teacher for All Generations* (Leiden: Brill, 2012). Some scholars find some elements of new creation in Hebrews. See Andrew T. Lincoln, *Hebrews: A Guide* (London: T&T Clark, 2006), 100; Adams, "The Cosmology of Hebrews," 137.

[30] Eisele, *Ein unerschütterliches Reich: die mittelplatonische Umformung des Parusiegedankens im Hebräerbrief* (Berlin; New York: W. de Gruyter, 2003), 132.

refers to the transition of the individual from earth to heaven after death.[31] He also equates οἰκουμένη in Heb. 1:6 and 2:5 with the unshakable kingdom in Heb. 12:25-29, which, he thinks, refers to "eine eschatologische Wirklichkeit."[32] Eisele sees the connection between the citation of Hag 2:6 in Heb. 12:25-29 and Ps. 96:9-11. According to him, as Hag 2:6 describes the shaking of heavens, earth, sea, and dry land, i.e. the created world, the Psalm passage similarly presents the idea that the earth and the sea, with the things which fill them, will shake while "die Welt (ἡ οἰκουμένη), welche der Herr aufgerichtet hat, unerschüttert bleibt." In his analysis of some Middle Platonic texts, Eisele not only compares Hebrews with Philo, but also presents parallelism in Plutarch, Philo, and Hebrews concerning the question of theodicy and the nature of the soul (*Is. Os.* 53–57; *An. procr.* 5–10) or demonology (*E Delph.* 17–21; *Def. orac.*10–15).

Against Eisele's understanding of οἰκουμένη, D. M. Moffitt aptly points out that Ps. 96 (95 LXX) is to be understood within its context, as are Ps. 93 and 95, which contain the same term, οἰκουμένη. In these texts, the vertical cosmological stratification appears, i.e. earth as the human realm and the heavens as the divine realm, but it does not necessarily imply a dichotomy between material and spiritual realms. The author of Hebrews refers to God's promise to establish the Davidic kingdom through citing Ps. 97 in Heb. 1:6, implying a link of the heavenly realm to God's promise to establish the Davidic kingdom.[33] Furthermore, Ps. 96 identifies the unshakable realm with the heavenly sanctuary. In the context of the rebuilding of the temple (the superscription to Ps. 96), this psalm possibly implies the promise of the everlasting eschatological temple. In Hebrews' discussion of the inheritance of God's people, these correlated psalms suggest that the realm where God dwells is promised to his people as human habitation (cf. Heb. 2:5).[34] It is hard to say that the term οἰκουμένη refers to a spiritual and heavenly realm as Eisele argues along with other scholars.[35] Eisele argues that the structure of Heb. 9:27-28, i.e. placing the mention of death and judgment and the description of *Parousia* in tandem, is strong evidence of the understanding of Christ' second coming as "ein individuelles Gericht unmittelbar nach dem Tod des Menschen."[36] The structure, however, is not a concrete basis for the concept of an immediate postmortem judgment, which the author of Hebrews never mentions elsewhere in the text. It is hard to find other evidence that the second coming of Christ is other than a universal event, like his first coming with which it is parallel.

---

[31] Ibid., 428.
[32] Ibid., 59.
[33] The author of Hebrews highlights Jesus' identity as the Son, "heir of all things," and the ruler seated at the right hand of God, implying Jesus' royal and Davidic Messiahship.
[34] David M. Moffitt, *Atonement and the Logic of Resurrection in the Epistle to the Hebrews* (Leiden: Brill, 2011), 70–81.
[35] Albert Vanhoye, "L'οἰχουμένη dans l'épître aux Hébreux," *Bib* 45 (1964): 251; Thompson, *The Beginnings of Christian Philosophy*, 132.
[36] Eisele, *Ein unerschütterliches Reich*, 84.

1.3 Arguments on Various Grounds for a Dualism Between the Spiritual and the Material (and/or Between Heaven and Earth) in Hebrews

1.3.1 Harold W. Attridge

H. W. Attridge states that the overall discussion of Hebrews focuses on the exhortation to be faithful. On the one hand, the readers are recommended the qualities which maintain their Christian life. On the other hand, they are called to more dynamic virtue to move in various directions.[37] In doing this, the author of Hebrews draws upon the myths observed in apocalyptic Judaism and early Christianity, e.g. the imagery of the Messiah's victory over demonic forces used in Heb. 2:15, and interprets the categories in "existential terms."[38] The author provides an understanding of psychological factors in the human condition. For example, the parenthetical comment in Heb. 3:14 that believers are participants in Christ is grounded in philosophical concepts concerning "the conditional quality of the addressees" for relationship to Christ.[39] The exhortation in Heb. 3:7-4:11 based on the exodus generation's example is intended to provide psychological connotations: "The reality is not a natural, ontological affair, but something that is subject to human determination."[40]

In Attridge's view, Israel's history and earthly categories do not have a substantial significance in Hebrews' eschatology. He highlights the verses saying that God who spoke through the prophets has decisively spoken in the Son (1:2; 2:3) and points out that Christ provides the hermeneutical framework within which Hebrews interprets the OT passages. According to him, Hebrews' understanding of OT passages "as words of or oracles about Christ" involves a process of "decontextualizing" and "recontextualizing." In other words, the author's eschatological view grants meaning to the cited passage regardless of the text's historical context.[41] He also argues that his understanding of the categories of "heavenly" and "earthly" in Hebrews can be applied to Christ, i.e. his humanity as humiliation that leads to his exaltation to heaven (2:10). According to this understanding, Attridge suggests pastoral implications. Through the exposition in chs. 9-10, the category of "heavenly and true" becomes "equated with interior" so that this atoning event deals with what is at the depths of the inner lives of believers; Jesus made possible for believers "a life in touch with what is most true and real." He adds that these metaphysical categories of Hebrews are not dissonant with the contemporary assumption that "what is most objectively real is spiritual or noetic and hence found at the depths of the self."[42]

---

[37] Harold W. Attridge, *The Epistle to the Hebrews: A Commentary on the Epistle to the Hebrews* (Philadelphia: Fortress Press, 1989), 21–22.

[38] Ibid., 93. Concerning Hebrews' discussion of victory over the power of death, Attridge argues that the liberation from death's power is seen in Hebrews not as a literal release from Hades as Jewish apocalyptic texts or OT texts understand it but as a release from the fear of death, which is forcefully dealt with in Greco-Roman traditions and Philo.

[39] Attridge, *The Epistle to the Hebrews*, 117.

[40] Ibid., 118.

[41] Ibid., 24. Attridge presents 3:7 and 7:10 as occasional cases in which the author considers the historical context albeit in an "admittedly playful" manner.

[42] Ibid., 27.

As an example of Hebrews' decontextualizing and recontextualizing, Attridge looks at the citation of Ps. 110:4, which is interpreted with another text, Gen. 14:17-20, in Heb. 6:20–7:17. Nevertheless, this example shows the author's forceful intention to engage with the historical context of his citation rather than proving the author's interpretive tendency to take lightly the text's historical context in the focus on his own "eschatological oriented" or Christ-centered context. The author of Hebrews clarifies the meaning of the priesthood "according to the order of Melchizedek" in the cited passage, Ps. 110:4, through shedding light on a plausible historical background of Gen. 14 which connotes the superiority of Melchizedek priesthood to the Levitical priesthood. S. Docherty aptly points out that the author's interpretation of his citation is not motivated merely by his "theological or Christological presuppositions." His scriptural interpretation is derived from the "genuine exegetical questions" of the texts, and he is generally faithful to his source texts and their wider contexts.[43]

Attridge's understanding that the categories of earthly and heavenly in their respective connections to Jesus' death in humanity and his exaltation is incongruous with the text's presentation of the primary sign of Christ's exaltation: subjection of all things in creation (Heb. 2:8). The ideas that earthly categories belong only to the old covenant, which was valid only before Christ inaugurates the new covenant, and that, accordingly, he made possible for his followers "a life in touch with what is most true and real," which forms a parallel with a Platonic paradigm, do not align with Hebrews' emphasis on God the creator and the Son's inheritance of all things (e.g. 1:2, 10; 2:10; 3:4; 4:3-4, 10; 9:26; 11:3). Another example that shows the incongruity between Attridge's view and what Hebrews claims appears in his exegesis of Heb. 10:1-10. Attridge aptly recognizes that the consummation of Jesus' sacrifice happened in the heavenly realm. He interprets it in existential terms, however, saying, "yet, the reality of that sacrifice consists not simply in its physical quality, but in the willingness with which it is made. Hence, it is the interior disposition of the act which make it the heavenly or spiritual event."[44] He seems to collapse heavenly into earthly since it is a bodily sacrifice (σῶμα, Heb. 10:10). As Moffitt aptly argues, the major motif of the cited passage, Ps. 40 (i.e. the righteous sufferer's deliverance), suggests that the offering of Jesus' body in Heb. 10:1-10 refers to the idea of Jesus as "the delivered righteous sufferer *par excellence*," rather than to that of his death on the cross per se as many interpreters assume.[45] The author of Hebrews considers that Jesus went bodily into the heavenly realm and that his bodily sacrifice begun on earth thus continues in heaven. Attridge's approach does not appreciate Hebrews' deep and consistent interest in Israel's history and earthly categories and its extensive and detailed descriptions of them, which are better explained by their substantial continuity with the heavenly categories.

---

[43] Susan E. Docherty, *The Use of the Old Testament in Hebrews: A Case Study in Early Jewish Bible Interpretation* (Tübingen: Mohr Siebeck, 2009), 198–99.
[44] Attridge, *The Epistle to the Hebrews*, 269.
[45] Moffitt shows that the focus of Ps. 40 on the redemption of the righteous sufferer from the pit and the "internalization of God's Law" in the life of the righteous align with the logic of Heb. 10. This idea is well supported through the theme that appears consistently in two other Old Testament passages cited (Hab 2:3-4 LXX) or alluded to (Isa 26:20 LXX). Moffitt, *Atonement and the Logic of Resurrection in the Epistle to the Hebrews*, 230–56.

1.3.2 Stefan N. Svendsen

In the same scholarly endeavor to understand Hebrews as a combination of apocalyptic and Platonic backgrounds (e.g. G. W. MacRae and Gregory E. Sterling),[46] S. N. Svendsen claims that Hebrews adopts Philo's hermeneutical method, namely, allegorical interpretation, while he retains an apocalyptic metaphysical outlook. He challenges the common distinction between apocalypticism and Platonism depending on the fact that the former operates along a temporal axis with the concept of two worlds (present world and the world to come) and the latter operates along a conceptual axis from the phenomena of the immanent world to the ideas of the transcendent world. According to Svendsen, apocalyptic writers operate not only with a notion of temporal dualism but also with a notion of vertical duality.[47] He follows H. Tronier who argued that apocalyptic literature might be conceptualized as "an off-shoot of Platonic thought."[48] It is true that the spatial concept of the transcendent realities observed in apocalyptic texts is distinguished from a Platonic concept of a noetic structure of the transcendent world. Apocalyptic and Platonic worldviews both, however, "presume that two different worlds exist at one and the same time, one of which, the world of transcendence, is epistemologically inaccessible to most individuals."[49] Accordingly, Hebrews could adopt the allegorical interpretive method from Platonism while holding a concept of the heavenly world which exists as an actual place on top of the visible world.

Svendsen argues that the allegorical hermeneutics of Philo is accepted by the author of Hebrews with modifications. In his exegesis of Heb. 3–4, Svendsen compares Hebrews' unique use of allegory to that of Philo. In the treatise *De migratione Abrahami*, Philo allegorically interprets God's commandments for Abraham to depart from his land and enter the land which "I will show you" (Gen. 12:1, *Migr.* 1) as the divine wish to arrive at "full salvation" (σωτηρίαν παντελῆ) by departing from "the body, sense-perception and speech" (σώματος, αἰσθήσεως, λόγου, *Migr.* 1:2). Philo sheds light on the similarity between the symbol and its allegorical correlation. Allegorical meanings, i.e. the structures of the logos, exist in their counterparts, which Philo believes refer to Jewish culture alone.[50] In other words, the one that enters the promised land was also "*par excellence* the one that takes part in God's rest."[51] In Hebrews, in the opposite way,

---

[46] G. W. MacRae, "Heavenly Temple and Eschatology in the Letter to the Hebrews," *Semeia* 12 (1978): 190f; Gregory E. Sterling, "Ontology versus Eschatology: tensions between author and community in Hebrews," *SPhilo* 13 (2001): 210. Cf. E. Sterling, "The Place of Philo of Alexandria in the Study of Christian Origins," in *Philo und das Neue Testament. Wechselseitige Wahrnehmungen. I. Internationales Symposium zum Corpus Judaeo-Hellenisticum: Mai 2003, Eisenach/Jena* (Tübingen: Mohr Siebeck, 2004), 45.

[47] Stefan N. Svendsen, *Allegory Transformed: The Appropriation of Philonic Hermeneutics in the Letter to the Hebrews* (Tübingen: Mohr Siebeck, 2009), 60–61.

[48] Henrik Tronier, "The Corinthian Correspondence between Philosophical Idealism and Apocalypticism," in *Paul beyond the Judaism/Hellenism Divide* (Westminster: John Knox Press, 2001), 175.

[49] Svendsen, *Allegory Transformed*, 62. He argues that the Hebrews model in which the many human high priests are connected to one heavenly high priest also reflects the platonic presupposition that a single noetic idea can be reproduced an infinite number of times in the material world (pp. 59–60).

[50] Sterling terms this perspective "universal particularism." Sterling, "The Place of Philo of Alexandria in the Study of Christian Origins," 46.

[51] Svendsen, *Allegory Transformed*, 118.

the allegorical correlation highlights the contrast. On the one hand, in Hebrews, the promised land functions as a symbol of divine rest. On the other hand, the promised land "is an empty semantic shell whose sole purpose is to point beyond itself to what it signifies." Entrance into the land is not associated with participation in God's true rest.[52] Svendsen, accordingly, argues that the author of Hebrews draws on the allegorical hermeneutical interpretation developed by Philo and attempts to encourage his readers away from the Torah and to deprive Jewish identity markers of soteriological worth. He envisions that, when the visible world ends, the heavenly world, which does not have any substantial similarity with Israel's historical inheritance, will be given as the coming world.

In fact, the notion of the inaccessible world which exists contemporaneously with the immanent world on earth appears in some apocalyptic texts as well, such as 4 Ezra and 2 Baruch. In 4 Ezra, Jerusalem is described as a son of the mother, the heavenly Zion (4 Ezra 10:44-46). The earthly Zion can be destroyed by the gentiles, but the inaccessible Zion in heaven will be revealed at the eschaton, when evil and the unrighteous will be judged and removed (4 Ezra 13:35-36). 2 Baruch similarly presents the heavenly Zion, which has existed from the creation (2 Bar 4:1-3), and in the likeness of which the earthly sanctuary was made (2 Bar 59:4). In both texts, the transcendent world is physically inaccessible and exists at the same time with the immanent world. In these texts, the transcendent world allows the seers to understand the divine will that allows the disorder in the world "to enable people to grasp the true meaning of the phenomena," which Svendsen thinks is what Hebrews attempts to do by adopting the allegorical model.[53] Since Svendsen notes that Hebrews retains the apocalyptic metaphysical outlook, by understanding the transcendent world as an actual place which exists on top of the visible world, it is hard to explain why he would adopt a heterogenous framework of Platonism by transforming it to fit into an apocalyptic outlook. Furthermore, one should ask if the gap between a literal, spatial dichotomy and an ontological dichotomy can be simplistically overlooked by an author who has an apocalyptic outlook, based on the fact that they both have a vertical axis.

Svendsen's desire to understand Hebrews in light of Philonic hermeneutics leads him to make some illogical statements. In his exegesis of Heb. 3–4, he argues that, through connecting Ps. 95 and Gen. 2:2, the author indicates that the rest which the desert generation failed to enter, and the believers expect to enter refers to a Philonic concept, i.e. heavenly, spiritual, rest that has remained inaccessible to everyone up until the eschaton. He further claims that, unlike Philo, the author highlights that there is no essential similarity between the symbol (Israel's dwelling in the promised land) and its reality (participation in salvation/true rest). Nevertheless, the allegorical role of Israel's

---

[52] Ibid., 119. According to Svendsen, a similar difference between Philo and Hebrews is observed in their understanding of the tabernacle and priesthood. Through the description of the Jewish tabernacle, which was an exact copy of the noetic world, Philo emphasizes the value of the Jewish environment and explains the reason for Jewish reluctance to compromise loyalty to Jewish religion including the Mosaic Law. The author of Hebrews, on the contrary, uses the allegorical hermeneutics to stress the insignificance of the earthly sanctuary and its inferiority to its heavenly archetype (pp. 166–67).
[53] Svendsen, *Allegory Transformed*, 63.

historical situation solely to "point beyond itself to what it signifies" does not properly explain the fact that the situations of the readers of Hebrews and the Israelites are "not just parallel, they are also causally connected."[54] The author claims that the rest remains open because the previous generations failed to enter it (Heb. 4:6-9). Furthermore, the understanding that the rest which remains open is the heavenly rest that has remained inaccessible to people does not fit into the author's emphasis on Israel's disobedience and unbelief as the reason for their failure to enter the rest (Heb. 3:18-19). Svendsen asks the right question: "if that were all there was to it, one might ask why the author should go to such lengths to prove that eternal rest is still attainable" since it is conceivable that, in their shared framework of allegory, none of his readers would doubt or deny the feature of the heavenly rest. Svendsen's answer does not seem satisfactory though. Is this consistent emphasis of the author throughout the passage indeed simply "because it allows him to carry out the allegorical reading?" A similar logical stretch is observed in Svendsen's interpretation of Heb. 12:18-24. From the dichotomy of Mount Sinai and the heavenly Zion he draws the conclusion that the author argues for "the supersession of the Law." It is hard to say that the point of contrast between the two locations is materiality since, as he himself notes, the heavenly Zion is not explicitly characterized as intangible. Moreover, he makes a logical jump without concrete evidence from the text by arguing that the author seeks to denigrate the Law itself by "painting a bleak picture of the reception of the Law" in the framework of metaphysical dichotomy between the tangible and intangible worlds.[55] Svendsen's hybrid model, which fuses an apocalyptic worldview that negates its core understanding of Israel's history and creation and an allegorical hermeneutics removed from its root of ontological metaphysics in Platonism, is unlikely and not supported by the text.

1.3.3 Jared C. Calaway

J. C. Calaway argues that Hebrews appropriated the priestly framework of the Sabbath and the sanctuary from traditions in P and H that allow the land to have the characteristics of the sanctuary and be linked to its own "Sabbath" and modified it in a way that resembles contemporary models observed in the *Songs of the Sabbath Sacrifice*, which made the Sabbath the temporal alignment between heaven and earth as the entrance into heavenly realities. He then suggests that Hebrews reconfigured the framework similarly with a post-war emergent Christian worldview that sees the earthly cult as transcended by Jesus' death so that Jesus' sacrifice is the only way to enter the Sabbath rest and the sanctuary, i.e. God's presence.

Calaway claims that through the "intra-textual interrelationship between 3:7–4:11 and 11:1–12:2," the author formulates the interrelationship between time and space, i.e. between Sabbath rest and the heavenly city.[56] Depending on a corollary of the Sabbath-sanctuary relationship and polyvalent usages of the term "rest" in LXX, Hebrews 3:7–4:11

---

[54] Ibid., 109.
[55] Svendsen, *Allegory Transformed*, 233.
[56] Jared C. Calaway, *The Sabbath and the Sanctuary: Access to God in the Letter to the Hebrews and Its Priestly Context* (Tübingen: Mohr Siebeck, 2013), 96.

transforms the spatial land-as-rest tradition into a temporal Sabbath rest of God, i.e. the age to come. In the connection to Gen. 2:2, Hebrews reinterprets rest "by disassociating it from the land."[57] While the sacred land has been temporalized into the Sabbath, the Sabbath has obtained spatial dimensions as Hebrews connects entering into the rest to entrance into the heavenly homeland (11:13-16, 39-40). This link between the two passages allows Calaway to suggest a spatiotemporal concept of the eschatological inheritance: the eschatological Sabbath, which is an enduring state of access to God's presence in the heavenly reality. Based on the connection between Sabbath and sanctuary in the *Songs of the Sabbath Sacrifice*, Calaway argues that this text evokes the heavenly sanctuary through a weekly Sabbath observance. Hebrews, by way of contrast, equates these two entities: one can experience the sanctuary only by following Jesus and entering the Sabbath rest in an eschatological scheme launched by Jesus' unique priesthood in the heavenly sanctuary; this rest is only accessible in Hebrews "today," through the perfected perfecter of faith, Jesus.[58] Calaway introduces another spatiotemporal reworking of Hebrews related to the sanctuary. Both the *Songs of the Sabbath Sacrifice* and Hebrews draw upon biblical priestly traditions and realign the Sabbath and the sanctuary as interpreting the "pattern" Moses saw as an "enduring heavenly reality" that the community can enter and experience.[59] Yet, they present the communal experience of the heavenly realities in different ways: the experience in the *Songs* aims to catalyse the heavenly sacrifice, while for Hebrews, Christ's sacrifice is the means by which the community can enter the heavenly realities.

By identifying the rest of the wilderness people as the eschatological rest, Calaway misses the main line of the text's rhetorical flow. He assumes a task that the author of Hebrews does not consider: in his words, "the homilist must explain not only the failure of the desert generation to enter, but the failure of all who followed, even the faithful."[60] Calaway aptly notes that Hebrews presents a causal relationship between the past failure and present opportunity: "because 'they shall not enter my rest,' there is now an opportunity to enter it."[61] Yet, he misses the fact that the text's focus is on the reason for their failure, nothing else but their disobedience. The disobedience and unbelief of Israel is presented not only as a type that provides a paradigm, but, more importantly, as the key cause of their failure and the rest that remains open for later generations. Furthermore, contrary to Calaway's argument, Hebrews' attribution of the psalm to David does not seem to provide a reason to omit this key point of the author's exhortation. Hebrews' mention of David would appear to highlight the fact that, because of disobedience, "not only did the desert generation fail, but so did all who came after it."[62]

Calaway's failure to grasp Hebrews' logic in 3:7–4:11 leads him to connect the text to Heb. 11:1–12:2. The idea of Heb. 3:7–4:11, Calaway argues, is that everyone (not only

---

[57] Ibid., 75. Calaway insists that, in this process, the author highlights the entry requirement to obedience and faith of Christ and to Christ (p. 26).
[58] Ibid., 63.
[59] Ibid., 138.
[60] Ibid., 71.
[61] Ibid., 73.
[62] Ibid., 73.

the disobedient desert generation but also all who came after it) failed to enter the rest, and that this aligns with the list of faithful people who could not enter the heavenly city "apart from us" in 11:1–12:2. According to Calaway, through these two passages, which share the themes of promised land, faithfulness, and obedience, the author argues that "neither the disobedient (3:7–4:11) nor the obedient (11:1–12:2) could enter the heavenly Sabbath rest/city 'today,' 'apart from us.'"[63] Calaway, however, loses the distinction, which the author makes in the text, between the rest that the Israelites could enjoy by entering the promised land (3:7–4:11) and the heavenly city that the Israelites who had entered the promised land were still waiting for (11:1–12:2).

1.4 Arguments for Apocalyptic Backgrounds

I have pointed out some weaknesses of the scholarly views which argue for an ahistorical and immaterial concept of eschatological inheritance in Hebrews. In the present section, I introduce some scholars who alternatively suggest Jewish apocalyptic frameworks as a plausible background of Hebrews' eschatology. Some of their limitations will be dealt with together at the end of the section.

1.4.1 Lincoln D. Hurst

L. D. Hurst is one of the most adamant advocates of the Jewish apocalyptic background of Hebrews. He insists that a dichotomy in which a "horizontal" (temporal) framework is Jewish and a "vertical" (cosmological) framework is Platonic is "oversimplified," and that spatial and temporal eschatologies are mutually coherent in the Jewish apocalyptic worldview. According to him, the vertical dimension in Hebrews cannot be an undoubtable indication of Platonism.[64] After examinations of the possibility of the Platonic background of Hebrews, he concludes that a few points in Hebrews that could be said to show Philonic influence can equally be explained by "influences within the apocalyptic tradition."

Hurst reviews the interpretations of the Platonic view on some key texts concerning the reference of "the true tent." For example, the statement that Jesus entered "heaven itself" in Heb. 9:24 is commonly used as proof that the heavenly tent in Hebrews is identical to heaven. Hurst aptly points out that the phrase does not define what the tent is, but it indicates "the general realm in which Christ ministers as opposed to the earthly priest."[65] In another text, Heb. 9:11, the true tent is understood by some scholars as a symbol for the upper regions, which comes close to Philo's "cosmic allegorizing of

---

[63] Ibid., 26.
[64] Hurst, *The Epistle to the Hebrews*, 22. Hurst states that the "vertical" language exists in the OT (cf. Gen. 11:5; 28:12; Ps. 24:4; 102:19, etc.) and the idea of a heavenly sanctuary is well attested in apocalyptic sources.
[65] Ibid., 28. In the passage, the author is most likely looking back to his earlier statement in 8:4, "Now if he were on earth he would not be a priest." According to Hurst, on earth and heaven itself are thus a synecdoche, in which the whole (earth, heaven) is presented for the part (the earthly and heavenly sanctuaries).

the temple." According to them, the outer part represents the sense-perceptible world and the holy place is the ideal, heavenly world. Hurst argues for the possibility that διά in the present verse is used not in the sense of location, but instrumentally – Christ enters the presence of God by means of the true tent – and subsequently points out that Heb. 9:11 cannot be a firm ground for arguments either for apocalypticism or for Platonism in Hebrews.[66]

Hurst also presents weaknesses in Thompson's interpretation of the unshakable kingdom in Heb. 12:28 as "the Platonic intelligible realm." He claims that the realm that cannot be "touched" (12:18, 22) does not denote a Platonic dualism but the fact that "it is essentially future" (13:14), reflecting the widespread Jewish-Christian understanding of the future realm that the people can receive through faith (Acts 7:48, 17:24; cf. 2 Cor 5:1). After highlighting Hebrews' OT citations which carry the texts' contexts with them, Hurst points out that the context of the cited passage of Haggai does not describe the end of history, i.e. cosmic catastrophe as the result of shaking. He also highlights that what makes the heavenly tent superior to the earthly one is not the fact it is uncreated (as observed in Platonism), but that it is made by God not humans (8:2; 11:10).

Hurst alternatively suggests the apocalyptic interpretation of the true tent as an actual tent in heaven. In Heb. 8:2, the heavenly tent is described as being "pitched" (πήγνυμι, cf. Num 24:6 LXX) by God, and it dismisses the idea that the heavenly tent is "uncreated eternal archetype." Jubilees 1:17, 28 states that God will build the new temple in Zion, while in *Sib Or* 3:290 and Isa 53:5, it is built by the Son of Man or the Messiah. According to Hurst, this hope for a new temple combines with an interest in a heavenly temple. Some OT texts such as Isa 6 and Ezek 1 describe God in his own temple in heaven. 4 Ezra envisions the new Jerusalem which will come and be manifest to all men, as prepared and built (13:36; cf. also 8:52). Similarly, 2 Baruch presents the hope that a heavenly Jerusalem appears to be "the Jerusalem to come" (4:1-7, 32:4). These apocalyptic texts suggest a process in which the statements of some OT texts, i.e. that the tabernacle was built according to a pattern, are used to imply "the existence of a heavenly archetype," i.e. "pre-existent heavenly Jerusalem."[67]

1.4.2 Scott D. Mackie and Eric F. Mason

S. D. Mackie and E. F. Mason also make strong cases for apocalyptic backgrounds in Hebrews. Mackie claims that apocalyptic two-age eschatology is Hebrews' controlling conviction: the age of the eschaton had already been inaugurated in the author's time by the sacrifice and exaltation of Christ. The believers are living in the "last days" (Heb. 1:2) and "the powers of the age to come" (Heb. 6:5).[68] According to him, Thompson's claim that the Hebrews' use of μένω in Heb. 12:27 is "exclusively for the non-material world" is incorrect in light of the non-metaphysical usages of the term in Hebrews to describe the impermanent priesthood of Levitical priests (7:24) or to exhort the readers

---

[66] Hurst, "Eschatology and 'Platonism' in the Epistle to the Hebrews," 1984, 52.
[67] Ibid., 56–57.
[68] Scott D. Mackie, *Eschatology and Exhortation in the Epistle to the Hebrews*, Wissenschaftliche Untersuchungen Zum Neuen Testament 223 (Tübingen: Mohr Siebeck, 2007), 6.

"let brotherly love continue" (13:1).⁶⁹ He also points out that the unshakable kingdom cannot be understood as a timeless, pre-existent sphere since it is described as a future reality, "as attested by the temporal language (μέλλω) that denotes its impending manifestation (2:5; 13:14)."⁷⁰ Mackie states that the cultic approach of the heavenly sanctuary through the instrumentality of a perfected conscience, particularly through Christ the forerunner, indicates that the author's exhortation is based not on the difference between the sense-perceptive world and the pure reality, but on the difference between holiness and sin.⁷¹ For him, the heavenly sanctuary is not a "sustained metaphor" but the place where Jesus' sacrifice, which began at the cross, is completed.⁷²

Mason examines "apocalyptically influenced texts,"⁷³ especially Qumran texts that contain the notions of Melchizedek as an angelic figure. These texts (4Q401, 11Q17, 4Q544, and esp. 11Q13) provide plausible conceptual backgrounds against which Hebrews portrays Jesus as the heavenly high priest (i.e. a messianic priest and a heavenly Melchizedek), notwithstanding Philo's remarks in *Alleg. Interp.* 3.82.⁷⁴ Following Mackie and Hay, Mason emphasizes that Hebrews' concept of Jesus' priesthood is connected to the notion of Jesus' enthronement at God's right hand. After pointing out that the idea of the throne of God is "a hallmark of apocalyptic thought," while Platonic readings say little about the notion, Mason concludes that Hebrews' interpretation of Ps. 110 in its discussion of Jesus as the exalted Son indicates an apocalyptic cosmology which includes the conceptions of heavenly liturgical setting and throne.⁷⁵

1.4.3 David M. Moffitt

D. M. Moffitt argues that, in Hebrews, Jesus' presentation of his perfected humanity, i.e. his entering into the heavenly sanctuary with his resurrected blood and flesh, opens the way for other sons to enter into God's presence. Concerning the meaning of οἰκουμένη in Heb. 1:6 and 2:5, Moffitt challenges the interpretations that understand the term in the earthly/spiritual dichotomy and asserts that both verses refer to the same entity, the eschatological realm where humans will be able to dwell in God's presence with their

---

⁶⁹ Ibid., 69.
⁷⁰ Ibid., 71.
⁷¹ Ibid., 120.
⁷² Ibid., 159.
⁷³ Mason claims that the Dead Sea Scrolls contain relatively few texts that are defined as displaying apocalyptic genre, but the Qumran sect can be called "an apocalyptic community" because of its ideas such as the dualism between good and evil, the final war between spiritual forces, the interest in angels, and the hope of messianic figures and eternal life. Eric F. Mason, "Cosmology, Messianism, and Melchizedek: Apocalyptic Jewish Traditions and Hebrews," in *Reading the Epistle to the Hebrews: A Resource for Students* (Atlanta: SBL, 2011), 53.
⁷⁴ Eric F. Mason, *You Are a Priest Forever: Second Temple Jewish Messianism and the Priestly Christology of the Epistle to the Hebrews* (Leiden; Boston: Brill, 2008), 161–63. Mason argues that the presentation of a heavenly Melchizedek at Qumran contributed to the presentation of Jesus as superior to angels in Hebrews.
⁷⁵ Eric F. Mason, "Sit at My Right Hand: Enthronement and the Heavenly Sanctuary in Hebrews," in *A Teacher for All Generations: Essays in Honor of James C. Vanderkam* (Leiden; Boston: Brill, 2012), 911.

bodies. He supports the idea with some second temple texts which envision the eschatological promised land which will be transformed and encompass the whole earth. Moffitt also argues for an underlying Adamic tradition in Heb. 1–2, based on the author's exposition of Ps. 8 and some related Second Temple and Rabbinic texts.[76] Through careful analysis of the textual context of Heb. 2 and of the historical background of certain phrases and concepts in Ps. 8, he undercuts a false dichotomy between the anthropological and the christological interpretations of the citation of Ps. 8 in Heb. 2. In this passage, Hebrews presents Christ as the one who fulfills what was intended for humanity as their representative.[77] Moffitt rightly highlights the on-going

---

[76] Marcus examines two apocryphal texts, *The Life of Adam and Eve* (LAE) and *The Cave of the Treasures* 2:10-14, as examples of a "more developed form" of the biblical account of Adam. These two texts unfold a narrative of Adam's creation in God's image, Satan's jealousy and refusal to worship him, the punishment of Satan, and Satan's revenge by leading Adam to death. Marcus suggests that Heb. 1–2 and the temptation story in the gospel of Mark show the influence of this Adamic tradition within early Christianity. Concerning Heb. 1–2, he argues that specific aspects of these chapters, such as the divine command that angels worship God's "first-born" (Heb. 1:6), are hard to understand without the background of this Adamic tradition. Marcus, "Son of Man as Son of Adam: Exploring an Adamic Eschatology within the Pre-Gospel Jewish-Christian Tradition," *RB* 110 (2003): 54–55. Silviu N. Bunta, F. F. Bruce, and G. K. Beale also recognize similarities between Heb. 1–2 and Adamic traditions in Jewish literature. Bunta thinks the presentation of God's firstborn to the angels and their worship of the Son in Heb. 1:6 closely parallels the creation of Adam and angelic veneration of him, an opinion fully expressed in the *Life of Adam and Eve*. Bunta argues that Hebrews' use of Ps. 8 in 2:5-9 is also best comprehended within a Jewish tradition that associated Adamic narratives with the angelic opposition to humanity (cf. the superiority over the angels and the angelic worship, which has already been introduced in ch.1). Silviu N. Bunta, "The Convergence of Adamic And Merkabah Traditions in the Christology of Hebrews," in *Searching the Scriptures: Studies in context and intertextuality* (London: T&T Clark, 2015), 279. However, Bunta's major argument connecting the Adamic notion specifically with *merkabah* mysticism does not seem likely. Some features of Hebrews, such as the throne of God and the Son's enthronement and his entering into the holy of holies (1:3, 8, 13; 4:16; 8:1; 10:12), are not specific enough to be defined as markers of *merkabah* mysticism. Furthermore, *merkabah* mysticism comes rather late to have had a comparative value for New Testament texts. The oldest Jewish mystical work, *Hekhalot*, dates from the second or third century CE. (See Ithamar Gruenwald, *Apocalyptic and Merkavah Mysticism*, 2nd ed. (Leiden; Boston: Brill, 2014), 142; R. Bergmeier, "Quellen vorchristlicher Gnosis?," in *Tradition und Glaube: das frühe Christentum in seiner Umwelt* (Göttingen: Vandenhoeck & Ruprecht, 1971), 200–220). Concerning this description, Bruce also highlights the tradition of Adam's creation and angelic worship in *The Life of Adam and Eve* which could explain Hebrews' particular description of the angelic worship of God's firstborn son, when he is introduced to the world. Bruce, *The Epistle to the Hebrews*, 57. G. K. Beale argues that Heb. 1:2–2:9 describes Christ's sonship by allusion to Adam's sonship. Such an allusion is supported by the presence of shared concepts, such as being in the image of God, the firstborn and inheritance. In order to support this argument, Beale discusses some early Jewish traditions that link the idea of Adam's sonship to his being "in God's image" (*LAE* 35:2-3; Philo, *Mos.* 2.65). Beale also notes the link between Heb. 1 and the citation of Ps. 8 in Heb. 2:5-9. Beale states that "Psalm 8 is the clearest and most elaborate interpretation of Gen. 1:26-28 in all of the OT, and its application to Christ explicitly makes him the fulfillment of the ideal end-time Adam." Beale, *A New Testament Biblical Theology*, 444–48.

[77] Moffitt provides compelling evidence for this conclusion. Hebrews emphasizes Jesus' humanity through several representative notions in the first two chapters such as the Son's peers, his brotherhood with human beings, and his tasting death on behalf of "many sons." In Heb. 1:9, the author depicts the Son's anointment above his peers, which, Moffitt argues, refers to human beings. Moffitt points out that if the Son's peers here are angels as many interpreters believe, the author's emphatic claim that no angel has been called Son or invited to sit at the right hand of God is undermined. Some first century Jewish texts also reflect the idea that the Son of man or Messiah is the representative of God's people (e.g., 1 En 37-31; Dan 7:13, 27). Moffitt, *Atonement and the Logic of Resurrection in the Epistle to the Hebrews*, 123–27.

contrast between angels as spiritual beings and the Son as human, and the significance of this contrast for understanding Christ's role as the representative of humanity in Heb. 2—an understanding often ignored by Christocentric interpretations of the citation of Ps. 8. Following Marcus, Moffitt further clarifies that this picture of Christ's vocation very likely corresponds to a certain Adamic tradition in some Jewish literature: Adam's creation and the angels' worship of him as described in the *Life of Adam and Eve*. Moffitt helpfully clarifies that Jewish apocalyptic literature does not provide a single account of eschatology, but the different accounts envision a common hope for "a transformation of humanity and the corruptible world," which provide valuable analogies for the eschatological vision of Hebrews.

The scholars above demonstrate that the logic of Hebrews is not coherently explained by the views which argue that Hebrews envisions an ahistorical and immaterial reality in a dualism between material/earthly and spiritual/heavenly, and they alternatively attempt to understand Hebrews in an apocalyptic framework. Some of the scholars, such as Moffitt, especially highlight the parallelism between Hebrews' eschatology and apocalyptic eschatologies that envision the eschaton in terms of protological language, i.e. *Urzeit-Endzeit* eschatology. It has been observed in the beginning of this chapter that apocalyptic eschatologies envisage the eschatological restoration of Israel's historical entities such as land, kingship, temple, and priesthood, which will be regained in a culminated form. As a resolution of their major concerns about the problem of evil in the present world, they hope for an eschatological status which is reminiscent of the primordial bliss in Eden. Some apocalyptic texts explicitly state that the primordial status or bliss of Adam in Eden will be regained at the end in a transformed form.[78] Moffitt aptly points out that, although each text formulates a respective eschatology in its own contexts and theological focuses, the eschatologies of these apocalyptic texts share common patterns. Israel's history is placed in between the corresponding beginning and end of the creation; at the end, the divine intention for the creation and humanity, historically experienced by the chosen people, Israel, will be accomplished in a culminated form.

The scholars who show how this *Urzeit-Endzeit* eschatological framework operates in Hebrews open the possibility of reading Hebrews from a new angle, which has not been sufficiently pursued even among the scholars who argue for apocalyptic backgrounds of Hebrews. Nevertheless, these studies have the limitation that most of them focus primarily on a discussion of Heb. 1–2. The emphasis that these scholars place on certain elements of apocalypticism suggest possible *Urzeit-Endzeit* categories in the rest of Hebrews.

I propose, therefore, a fresh reading of Hebrews' homily in Heb. 3:7–4:11 and 12:26-29 in these categories. The author of Hebrews envisions not the spiritual or noetic reality through the notion of God's rest, but the eschatological rest, something in many ways similar to what Adam enjoyed in Eden, and which is the culmination of what the Israelites could experience in their possession of the promised land. He envisages the unshakable kingdom not as the transcendent realm of heaven abstracted from the material creation,

---

[78] See especially the discussion of Marcus and others in n. 77 above.

but as the eschatological inheritance that consists of the renewed creation and the revealed heavenly sanctuary as the culmination of an Eden-like world and the promised land. I use the language of *Urzeit-Endzeit*, qualified above, as a useful shorthand to refer to the logic of this sort of eschatological vision, a vision similar in some respects to those of apocalyptic texts roughly contemporary with Hebrews. In Chapters 2–4, I examine these other *Urzeit-Endzeit* eschatological visions, which the relevant apocalyptic texts share even in their different socioreligious contexts and subsequent rhetorical focuses, and then, in Chapters 5–6, I suggest some fresh understandings of Hebrews dependent on their noticeable parallelism with Hebrews' vision of the eschatological inheritance of God's people.

2

Urzeit-Endzeit Eschatology in Pre-70 Second Temple Literature

2.1 Introduction

In the previous chapter, I discussed the weaknesses of some views which argue that Hebrews envisions an ahistorical and immaterial inheritance at the eschaton and, as an alternative background of Hebrews, suggested Jewish apocalyptic eschatologies, particularly an *Urziet-Endzeit* eschatological framework often observed in apocalyptic visions of the eschaton. In the present chapter, I investigate how relevant apocalyptic texts envisage the eschatological world for the chosen people of God. In particular, this chapter deals with some pre-70 texts which were arguably composed before 70 CE and thus, consider the restored land of Canaan and the Jerusalem temple in it as the chosen people's eschatological inheritance. I examine the eschatological visions of the Book of Watchers, the Book of Parables, some Qumran texts (CD, 4QpPs37, 4QInstruction), Jubilees, and Pseudo-Philo.

2.2 1 Enoch

2.2.1 The Book of Watchers

1 Enoch is a collection of Jewish apocalyptic traditions composed between the fourth century BCE and the turn of the Common Era.[1] In the first section of 1 Enoch, the Book of Watchers (chs. 1–36), readers find an eschatological vision that presents the transplanting of the life-giving tree to the temple (1 En 24–27) and the renewal of the world (1 En 10–11).

2.2.1.1 1 Enoch 24–25

In ch. 25, the text states that at the end days of judgment, God would transplant the life-giving tree from the midst of the seven mountains to the 'Holy Place beside the

---

[1] George W. E. Nickelsburg, *1 Enoch. 1, A Commentary on the Book of 1 Enoch, Chapters 1–36; 81–108*, Hermeneia—a Critical and Historical Commentary on the Bible (Minneapolis, MN: Fortress Press, 2001), vii.

temple of the Lord' in Jerusalem (1 Enoch 24–25). The identity of the seven mountains in chs. 24–25, which revisits the vision of 18:6-16, has been a matter of some discussion in relation to the "other mountains" in ch.32 where the Garden of Eden is placed.[2] Scholars have different views on whether the seven mountains in chs. 18 and 24–25 can be identified with the Garden of Eden in ch. 32 and thus whether the life-giving tree in ch. 24 refers to the Tree of Life.[3]

K. C. Bautch argues that only the garden in ch. 32 refers to Eden and the seven mountains of chs. 18 and 24–25 are to be identified with Mount Sinai.[4] According to her, the life-giving tree refers to the Torah, and the transplanting of it represents "the locus of religious activity shifting from the scene of the exodus to that place where God chooses to make his name dwell." This view, however, has the following two weaknesses. First, the comment on the tree in v. 4 (i.e., that "not a single human being has the authority to touch it until the great judgment") cannot be applied to the Torah, which Moses received in order to hand over to Israel. Second, as G. W. E. Nickelsburg aptly notes, the Sinaitic covenant and the Torah do not explicitly appear in 1 Enoch except for once in the Apocalypse of Weeks (ch. 108).[5] The identification of the life-giving Tree in chs. 24–25 as the Torah seems unlikely.

V. Bachmann argues that the tree symbolizes wisdom, similarly denying the link of the location of chs. 18 and 24–25 with paradise in ch. 32.[6] She points out that 1 En 25:6 which states that the righteous will gain a long life from the tree does not correspond with Gen. 3:22 which states that the tree of life gives human beings an eternal life. As a key passage for the interpretation of the life-giving tree, Bachmann highlights the mention of wisdom in 1 En 5:8 where, she suggests, wisdom is said to become accessible after the judgment day. She also presents a parallel connection between the tree of life and wisdom in Prov 3:18 in which wisdom is designated as the tree of life. L. Doering properly evaluates Bachmann's claim that long life in the present text is distinctive from eternal life in Gen. 3:22 as "most probably overdrawn" particularly in light of the "this-worldly eschatology" of the Book of Watchers.[7] Another weakness of Bachmann's

---

[2] The expression, "seven mountains" occurs instead in Ethiopic mss and Gr^pan.
[3] These disagreements have been caused by two conflicting elements of the present passage. On the one hand, in the midst of the mountains of chs. 24–25, a life-giving tree appears that is reminiscent of the Tree of Life in Eden. On the other hand, the text nowhere identifies the mountains as being in the Garden of Eden, nor does it explicitly connect them with the Garden of righteousness in ch. 32, which clearly refers to the Garden of Eden.
[4] Kelley Coblentz Bautch, *A Study of the Geography of 1 Enoch 17–19: "No One Has Seen What I Have Seen,"* Supplements to the Journal for the Study of Judaism, v. 81 (Leiden; Boston: Brill, 2003), 112–13, 124–25.
[5] George W. E. Nickelsburg, *1 Enoch. 1, A Commentary on the Book of 1 Enoch, Chapters 1–36; 81–108*, Hermeneia—a Critical and Historical Commentary on the Bible (Minneapolis, MN: Fortress Press, 2001), 50.
[6] V. Bachmann, "Rooted in Paradise? The Meaning of the 'Tree of Life' in 1 Enoch 24–25 Reconsidered," *JSP* 19, no. 2 (2009): 99–104.
[7] Doering states that in the this-worldly eschatology of the Book of Watchers "long life would be an appropriate effect of the tree's life-giving properties." Lutz Doering, "Urzeit-Endzeit Correlation in the Dead Sea Scrolls and Pseudepigrapha," in *Eschatologie-Eschatology* (Tübingen: Mohr Siebeck, 2011), 39. For the this-worldly eschatology of the Book of Watchers, Nickelsburg highlights the eschatological focus on the transformation of the earth in 1 Enoch. George W. E. Nickelsburg, "Where Is the Place of Eschatological Blessing?" in *Things Revealed: Studies in Early Jewish and*

view is found in her argument that "wisdom is the gift provided for the righteous, Jerusalem and its temple being the center from where she unfolds her blessing." In 1 En 5:8, however, wisdom is given to the chosen people as a help through which they might not return again to sin, while 1 En 25:5 indicates that the fruit of the tree will be given to "the righteous and the pious," implying its feature as a reward for the chosen people's pious life according to wisdom. Furthermore, as Bachman herself admits, even her key passage 1 En 5:8 does not show any connection between wisdom and Jerusalem.[8]

In an effort to harmonize the conflicting evidence, P. Grelot argued for the existence of two paradises in the Enochic corpus.[9] According to Grelot, the mountains in ch. 32 refer to the Garden of Eden designed as the earthly counterpart of the heavenly paradise (i.e., the northwest paradise in chs. 18 and 24–25) and the life-giving tree in chs. 24–25 refers to the Tree of Life which was transplanted once in Eden and will be transplanted again in the New Jerusalem at the eschaton. While Grelot's thesis was initially popular, it has faced criticism. This view of the two paradises "is not explicit in the text and cannot be based upon contemporaneous data."[10]

Meanwhile, some scholars such as Black,[11] Doering[12] and Nickelsburg argue that 1 Enoch reflects two different traditions about the Garden of Eden. They think that the

---

Christian Literature in Honor of Michael E. Stone (Leiden: Brill, 2004), 53–56. For similar understandings of this-worldly eschatology of the Book of Watchers, see Günter Stemberger, *Der Leib der Auferstehung: Studien zur Anthropologie und Eschatologie des palästinischen Judentums im neutestamentlichen Zeitalter (Ca. 170 v. C[h]r.-100 N. Chr.)*, Analecta Biblica 56 (Rome: Biblical Institute Press, 1972), 38; Kelley Coblentz Bautch, "Situating the Afterlife," in *Paradise Now: Essays on Early Jewish and Christian Mysticism* (Atlanta: Society of Biblical Literature, 2006), 249–64.

[8] Bachmann, "Rooted in Paradise?" 99.

[9] According to him, God temporarily transplanted the Tree of Life from the northwestern Paradise where God dwells to its earthly counterpart in the northeast, but after the Fall of man, he brought it back to the northwestern paradise. On the day of judgement, God will transplant the Tree of Life to the new Jerusalem. Pierre Grelot, "La Géographie Mythique d'Hénoch et Ses Sources Orientales," *RB* 65, no. 1 (1958): 43.

[10] Eibert J. C. Tigchelaar, "Eden and Paradise," in *Paradise Interpreted: Representations of Biblical Paradise in Judaism and Christianity* (Leiden; Boston; Köln: Brill, 1999), 47. Following the theory of some OT scholars, Tigchelaar argues that 1 Enoch 32 reflects an original tradition of Eden which contains only the Tree of Knowledge. Nevertheless, the source-critical assumption that he depends on is also open to question. For the view of a paradise narrative with originally only one special tree, see Eberhard Witte, *Untersuchungen zur Machtverteilung im Unternehmen*, Sitzungsberichte der Bayerische Akademie der Wissenschaften. (München: Bayerische Akademie der Wissenschaften, 1978), 79–87; Henrik Pfeiffer, "Der Baum in der Mitte des Gartens: zum überlieferungsgeschichtlichen Ursprung der Paradieszählung (Gen. 2,4b–3,24)—Teil I: Analyse," *ZAW* 112, no. 4 (2000): 487–500. For the opposite view on this issue, see H. N. Wallace, "Tree of Knowledge and Life," in *Anchor Bible Dictionary*, vol. 6, 1992, 656–60; Jutta Krispenz, "Wie viele Bäume braucht das Paradies? Erwägungen zu Gen. II 4B–III 24," *VT* no. 3 (2004): 301.

[11] Black believes that each of the two different traditions (eastern paradise in ch. 32 and western paradise in chs. 24–25 and 77) is respectively from the Jewish idea of the western Illyssium and the Hellenistic eastern Eden idea (Black and VanderKam, *The Book of Enoch or 1 Enoch*, 17). It is not a huge logical leap to conclude that the cultural background of each tradition is only based on the location of each paradise.

[12] Doering suggests a tradition that links Eden, Sinai and Zion as observed in the Book of Jubilees (Jub 4:26; 8:19). Doering presents LAB 11:15 as a parallel connection between the tree of life and Sinai. But it is hard to find textual evidence of that connection in the present passage (Doering, "Urzeit-Endzeit Correlation in the Dead Sea Scrolls and Pseudepigrapha," 41).

mountains of chs. 18 and 24–25 refer to the Garden of Eden, but not as one of two paradises that Grelot argued. According to these scholars, the chapters reflect a tradition about Eden that differs from the tradition observed in ch. 32 which itself reflects Gen. 2. Nickelsburg highlights the fact that the mountains in 1 En 18 and 24–25 are an allusion to the portrayal of Eden in the book of Ezekiel.[13] In Ezek 28, the rebellion of the prince of Tyre is described as an attempt to seize God's throne on the holy mountain, that is, the Garden of Eden. This text shows the geographical juxtaposition of the mountain throne of God and the pits of destruction, which is strongly reminiscent of the depiction of God's throne on the mountain in 1 En 18 and 25 and the pit of punishment for the stars and the powers of heaven in 1 En 18. The image of flaming fire on God's mountain also appears in both the text of Ezekiel ("the stones of fire", Ezek 28:14, 16) and that of 1 Enoch 18 ("a flaming fire", 1 En 18:9). The precious stones of each venue in Ezek 28 and 1 En 24:2 are another noticeable parallel.

Another possible connection of the portrayal of 1 Enoch 24–25 to a biblical text can be found in Isaiah. In the present context of 1 Enoch, the author states that the tree of life will be transplanted into the house of God in Jerusalem and the people of God will gain new lives through its fragrance which penetrates their bones. In Trito-Isaiah, the prophet envisions the New Jerusalem in which the people of God are nourished and their "bones shall flourish like the new grass" (Isa 66:14). Significantly, in the context of the Isaiah text, the holy mountain on which the New Jerusalem will be built is described with a clear image of Eden (Isa 65:25).[14] Considering the impressive parallelism between the present 1 Enoch text and the biblical texts observed above, the most reasonable conclusion is that the book of 1 Enoch shares a common tradition about Eden with these prophetic texts. If this is correct, the two different locations of the mountains in 1 Enoch can be understood as evidence of two different traditions about Eden. The mountains of God in 1 En 18 and 24–25 reflect the tradition that links Eden with Zion (e.g. Ezekiel and Isaiah), whereas 1 En 32 presents the Eden tradition attested in Gen. 2.

The identification of the mountains in 1 En 18 and 24–25 as Eden is further supported by other elements in the texts. In 1 En 25:3, the high mountain is portrayed as the throne of God where he sits "when he descends to visit the earth with goodness." In early Jewish texts, God's visitation often refers to his judgment as in 1 Enoch 1:4f.[15] However, God's visitation "with goodness" in ch. 25 is distinguishable from the judgment that 1:4 describes with its language of "marching" and "emerging from heaven with a mighty power." Nickelsburg suggests the possibility that the high mountain in the present text rather alludes to God's visitation of the Garden of Eden in Gen. 2–3.[16] Additionally, the inaccessibility of the specific tree until the eschaton

---

[13] Nickelsburg, *1 Enoch 1–36; 81–108*, 285–86, 326–27.
[14] John Oswalt, *The Book of Isaiah. Chapters 40–66*, The New International Commentary on the Old Testament (Grand Rapids; Cambridge: Eerdmans, 1998), 661.
[15] George W. E. Nickelsburg, *1 Enoch. 1, A Commentary on the Book of 1 Enoch, Chapters 1–36; 81–108*, Hermeneia—a Critical and Historical Commentary on the Bible (Minneapolis, MN: Fortress Press, 2001), 314; *TDNT* vol. 2, 601, 606–7.
[16] Nickelsburg, *1 Enoch 1–36, 81–108*, 315.

(see 1 En 25:4) is a significant theme in later literature (e.g. Life of Adam and Eve and T. Levi 18:10-11). In these later texts, the tree is certainly placed in the Garden of Eden.

Given the identity of the life-giving tree and the mountains in chs. 24–25, certain implications follow. First, the transplanting of the essential tree of Eden implies that the eschatological sanctuary of Jerusalem signifies the restoration of Eden.[17] Second, the fact that the place to which the tree is transplanted is the sanctuary plausibly implies that Eden, where the tree was originally located, was a sacred place. The status of Eden as a sacred place accords with the depiction of the high mountain, Eden, as the throne room for "the Holy and Great Lord of Glory, the Eternal King" (25:3). 1 En 25:6 describes the eschatological scene of the people of God gaining long life by entering into the sanctuary with the Tree of Life: "Then they shall be glad and rejoice in gladness and they shall enter into the holy (place); its fragrance shall (penetrate) their bones..." Here, then, we observe an *Urzeit-Endzeit* typology. In the eschaton, the righteous people will enter the holy place and enjoy long life by eating from the tree of life like the first human beings in the sanctuary of Eden. That is to say, the primordial blessing in Eden will be restored in the eschatological sanctuary. A possible connection between the present text and Isaiah's depiction of the New Jerusalem in terms of Edenic language, as suggested above, corresponds well with this typology. Third, the present eschatological vision implies a connection between the eschatological inheritance of God's people and the blessings of the forefathers that they enjoyed in the promised land. The text of 1 En 25:6 states that the people who will gain life from the tree will "live on earth" as their "fathers lived in their days."

2.2.1.2 *1 En 10:16–11:2*

1 Enoch 10:16–11:2 shows a link between the postdiluvian restoration and the eschaton, and this link illuminates the *Urzeit-Endzeit* pattern with the allusion to Trito-Isaiah's eschatological vision. In the text, the angels inform Noah about the coming Flood. This passage can be divided into two subsections of 10:16-19 and 10:20–11:2 which share the same structure.[18] The passage does not explicitly mention the relationship between the two sections, but the following evidence suggests an inference of the relationship. As readers move from the first section to the second, they find that the range of recipients of the divine blessing is expanded: from "the plant of righteousness and truth" (a reference to Noah's descendants) to "all the children of the people" who will

---

[17] The identity of "the holy place" in the present passage as Jerusalem where the holy mountain, Zion, becomes explicit in ch. 26 (cf. Isa 27:13; 56:7; 57:13; 65:11; 66:20; Dan 9:16; Joel 2:1; 4:17; Obad 16; Zech 8:3).

[18] Nickelsburg analyses the structure as follows:

Michael to purge the earth	16a	20
Regarding the righteousness	16bc, 17	21
"All the earth"	18a	22
Blessing/fecundity	18b-19	11:1-2

(Nickelsburg, *1 Enoch 1-36; 81–108*, 224. Also see Doering, "Urzeit-Endzeit Correlation in the Dead Sea Scrolls and Pseudepigrapha," 25.)

become righteous.[19] Also, the purification from defilement becomes more intensive, moving from God's commandment to destroy "injustice from the face of the earth" and "every iniquitous deed" to the divine commandment to cleanse the earth from "all injustice, all defilements, all oppression, and all sin." The pattern seen in the relationship between the two sections suggests that the author/editor of this passage connects the accounts of the Flood (the first section) with the eschatological vision (the second section).

This connection is also observed in allusions to Trito-Isaiah that appear in both sections. In the first section, the combination of the longevity of young and old (v. 17), as well as planting vines and obtaining fruit from them (v. 19) are most likely adopted from the vision of the new heaven and earth in Isa 65:20-23.[20] The account of the flood and the renewal of the world is, in other words, described in eschatological language. The second section contains another allusion to Trito-Isaiah: the worship of God by all nations in Isa 66:20-23.[21] Parallelism of the two sections implies that the author interprets the eschatological promise for the righteous, i.e., the new beginning after the destruction by the last judgment, in light of the renewed earth that Noah and his sons received after the flood (Gen. 9). Trito-Isaiah envisages the eschaton as the new creation in which the new heaven and earth will be like the Garden of Eden (Isa 51:3; 65:25). By drawing on these texts, the author develops an understanding of the eschatological restoration of creation, i.e. the renewal of creation. Another point to be noted is that the author understands this eschatological restoration is a culmination of the postdiluvian restoration of creation.[22]

A similar connection between the eschatological restoration of the Edenic blessings and the blessings in the promised land appears in other places in the Book of Watchers as well. The eschatological vision in 1 En 11:1 adopts the language of Deut 28:12: "And in those days, I shall open (ἀνοίγω) the storeroom of blessing which is in the heavens (ἐν τῷ οὐρανῷ), so that I shall send them down upon the earth, over the work (τὰ ἔργα) and the toil of the children of man."[23] Furthermore, the language of the

---

[19] The identification of "the plant" as the descendants of Noah in 1 En 10:3 suggests that "the plant of righteousness and truth" also refers to Noah's progeny. The Greek text of Syncellus reads: "Teach the righteous one what he should do, the son of Lamech how he may preserve himself alive and escape forever. From him a plant will be planted, and his seed will endure for all the generations of eternity." (So Nickelsburg, *1 Enoch 1*, 215).

[20] Nickelsburg, *1 Enoch 1-36; 81-108*, 226; Doering, "Urzeit-Endzeit Correlation in the Dead Sea Scrolls and Pseudepigrapha," 28.

[21] Some scholars recognize that a link with Noahic in the second section suggests the interwoven themes of Noahic flood and the eschaton. In 11:2, the eschatological blessing that will "descend upon the earth" forms an implicit contrast to the waters of the flood. Lars Hartman, "'Comfort of the Scriptures'—an Early Jewish Interpretation of Noah's Salvation, 1 En 10:16–11:2," *SEÅ* 41-42 (1977): 92; Nickelsburg, *1 Enoch 1-36; 81-108*, 228; Doering, "Urzeit-Endzeit Correlation in the Dead Sea Scrolls and Pseudepigrapha," 28.

[22] Nickelsburg states that Noah's account functions as a prototype of the eschaton. (George W. E. Nickelsburg, "Apocalyptic and Myth in 1 Enoch 6–11," *JBL* 96, no. 3 (1977): 388f.)

[23] Hartman, "Comfort of the Scriptures," 92; Black and VanderKam, *The Book of Enoch or 1 Enoch*, 141; Nickelsburg, *1 Enoch 1-36; 81-108*, 228. Deuteronomy 28:12 LXX states: "The Lord will open (ἀνοίγω) for you His good storehouse, the heavens (τὸν οὐρανόν), to give rain to your land in its season and to bless all the work (τὰ ἔργα) of your hand" (NASV). The Eth. version supports ἐπὶ τῆς γῆς as in Deut 28:8 LXX.

eschatological blessings in 1 En 10:16–11:2—longevity, progeny, fertility of the land (esp. of vine and olives)—appears in Deut 28 as the divine blessings in the promised land. Some scholars see a similar connection between an eschatological vision and the exodus in 1 En 51.[24] In 1 Enoch's illustration of the eschatological scene of the resurrection of the dead and the enthronement of the Elect One, the author draws on the images of exodus that appear in Ps. 114:4: "In those days, mountains shall dance like rams; and the hills shall leap like kids satiated with milk." The joyful dance of the creation, which Ps. 114 depicts as having happened in the exodus, is applied to the eschatological deliverance of the righteous people of God. The authors of these texts envision the renewal/restoration of the creation at the eschaton: consequences of Adam's sin such as defilement, sin, oppression, infertility of the land, and shortened lifespan will be reversed, and God's people will enjoy the Edenic status (e.g. fertility, progeny, and longevity). He also indicates that this eschatological restoration means the completion of the divine blessing which the Israelites could enjoy temporarily in the postdiluvian restoration and also in the promised land.

2.2.2 The Book of Parables

Although the Book of the Watchers does not (apart from ch. 32) explicitly discuss Eden, the Book of Parables (chs. 37–71)[25] contains mentions of a "garden" that is described as a dwelling place for God's people. In 1 En 60:23, a "garden of the righteous" appears, and within the same chapter "the garden of Eden" is introduced: it is the place "wherein the elect and the righteous ones dwell, wherein my grandfather (Enoch) was taken, the seventh from Adam, the first man whom the Lord of the Spirits created" (60:8).[26] A link between Eden and "the garden of the righteous" in this text is implied by their common feature as a habitat for the righteous. Related to this link, the account of the two monsters in the present chapter suggests a background which is worth investigating. The depiction of two monsters, Leviathan and Behemoth is highly reminiscent of a tradition in two other apocalyptic texts 4 Ezra and 2 Baruch (4 Ezra 6:49-52; 2 Bar 29:4). These two texts describe the creation of these monsters on the fifth day. One is sent to the sea (Leviathan), the other to the dry land (Behemoth), and both ultimately become food for God's people at the eschatological

---

[24] August Dillmann, ed., *Das Buch Henoch* (Leipzig: Fr. Chr. Wilh. Vogel, 1853), 166; Siegbert Uhlig, *Das äthiopische Henochbuch*, jüdische Schriften aus Hellenistisch-Romischer Zeit, Lfg. 6 (Gütersloh: Mohn, 1984), 186; Nickelsburg, VanderKam, and Baltzer, *1 Enoch. 2*, 186.

[25] The Book of Parables is notoriously difficult to date. Some scholars argue for a late date because these chapters are not found in Qumran. For example, Milik dates it 270 CE. (Józef T. Milik and Matthew Black, eds., *The Books of Enoch: Aramaic fragments of Qumrân Cave 4* (Oxford: Clarendon Press, 1976), 91–98.). Knibb proposes a date near 100 CE. (M. A. Knibb, "The Date of the Parables of Enoch: A Critical Review," *NTS* 25, no. 3 (1979): 345–59.) However, the absence of the text in the Qumran collection proves nothing about its date since not every Jewish apocalyptic work composed before 68 CE is included in the Qumran collection. For further discussion of the date of the Book of Parables, see George W. E. Nickelsburg, *Jewish Literature between the Bible and the Misnah: A Historical and Literary Introduction*, 2nd ed. (London: SCM Press, 1981), 254–56.

[26] Jubilees 4:23 states that Enoch was led into the Garden of Eden.

banquet.[27] Notably, the account of the two monsters reflects a part of the texts' *Urzeit-Endzeit* eschatology. In 2 Baruch, the account of the two monsters belongs to the unit of chs. 21–34 which deals with the question, how God will complete the work which he has begun in creation despite its corruption. In the context of the two monsters in 4 Ezra 6, the text offers the assurance of eschatological blessings for the chosen people of God by highlighting the divine plan written at creation and ultimately fulfilled at the eschaton.[28]

1 Enoch 60 closely parallels these two texts: the names and respective habitats of the two monsters are the same, their separation from each other is discussed in all three works,[29] and the reference to their association with food in the eschaton occurs in each one of these texts.[30] In light of the level of similarity between these three apocalyptic texts, one may plausibly suppose that these texts share a common tradition which reflects an *Urzeit-Endzeit* link presented in terms of the creation of the two monsters and their ultimate consumption.[31] The *Urzeit-Endzeit* eschatology, which most likely underlies the envisioning of ch. 60, is resonant with the link of the garden of righteousness (as the eschatological habitat for the righteous) to Eden in the present context.

In ch. 61, another garden reference appears, "the garden of life." This garden is also described as the place where all the elect ones dwell (61:12). Chapter 61 describes angels making measurements, but the object which is measured is not immediately obvious. The text only implies that the object of the measurement is connected to the righteous by stating that the measurements "shall be given to faithfulness" and "shall strengthen righteousness" (61:4). The passage also implies that the measurements will have significance for the forefathers at the time of their resurrection at the eschaton

---

[27] Nickelsburg and VanderKam interestingly argue that Behemoth's location near the garden of the righteous makes it "a convenient pantry for those participating in the eschatological banquet." Nickelsburg, VanderKam, and Baltzer, *1 Enoch. 2*, 242.

[28] K. William Whitney, *Two Strange Beasts: Leviathan and Behemoth in Second Temple and Early Rabbinic Judaism*, Harvard Semitic Monographs, no. 63 (Winona Lake, IN: Eisenbrauns, 2006), 38–39.

[29] 4 Ezra and 2 Baruch describe the monsters' separation at the time of creation. In 1 Enoch, there is a tension within the text between a reading in which the separation will be a sign of the eschaton (v. 7) and one in which the separation has already happened (v. 9). Whitney persuasively argues that the primordial reading is preferred. Whitney, *Two Strange Beasts*, 50.

[30] In fact, the last words of 1 En 60:24 are textually ambiguous. The textual witnesses are divided into two readings, i.e., a passive or middle form of the verb (meaning "they will be fed" or "they will feed themselves") and an active form of the verb (meaning "they will feed [to]" or "they will provide [themselves as] food"). Nickelsburg, VanderKam, and Baltzer, *1 Enoch. 2*, 241.

[31] Some scholars also argue that the three texts of the Second Temple period (i.e. 4 Ezra 6:49-52; 2 Bar 29:4; 1 En 60:7-10) represent a single tradition. Concerning the accounts of the two monsters in 4 Ezra and 2 Baruch, R. H. Charles and P. Bogaert claim that the relationship between the two tests are not one of dependence, rather these texts represent a single tradition upon which both authors drew. Robert Henry Charles, ed., *The Apocalypse of Baruch: Translated from the Syriac, Chapters I–LXXVII from the Sixth Cent. Ms. in the Ambrosian Library of Milan: And Chapters LXXVIII–LXXXVII–The Epistle of Baruch from a New and Critical Text Based on Ten Mss. and Published Herewith* (London: Adam & Charles Black, 1896), 53, n. 4; Pierre Bogaert, ed., *Apocalypse de Baruch*, Sources Chrétiennes, no. 144, 145 (Paris: du Cerf, 1969), 2, 63. Whitney also similarly argues for a single tradition in the three texts. According to him, "the combat-banquet" sequence in the tradition has been developed from the divine warrior myth in early ancient Near Eastern texts (e.g. Mesopotamian *Enuma Eliš*, Ugaritic *Ba 'l-Yamm*). Whitney, *Two Strange Beasts*, 31, 168-69.

(61:5). In 1 En 70:3, the object the angels measured becomes clear. The angels are said to have taken a cord to measure "the place for the elect and righteous ones." Enoch continues, "And there I saw the first (human) ancestors and the righteous ones of old, dwelling in that place." The place which is measured by the angels in ch. 61 most likely refers to "the garden of life" in 61:12 where the righteous dwell.

Nickelsburg and VanderKam call attention to some Old Testament and early Christian parallels of the idea of angels' measuring (Zech 2:1-5; Ezek 40:1-4; Rev 21:10-21). In these texts, the object being measured is the New Jerusalem and the new temple in it.[32] Notably, the New Jerusalem of these texts has distinct Edenic features. All three texts describe the eschatological city/temple as having life-giving rivers flowing out of it. In Ezekiel 47, the stream coming out of the temple makes the water of the sea "become fresh" and every living creature "live" (Ezek 47:8-9). There is little doubt that this vision of Ezekiel has been influenced by Gen. 2:10-14.[33] Revelation shares with Ezekiel the portrayal of the life-giving river, flowing out of the eschatological temple, and the trees whose leaves are used for healing. Specifically, in Rev 22:2, the trees are called "the tree of life." In Zechariah, the eschatological day of the Lord, when the rivers will flow out of Jerusalem temple,[34] is depicted with the imagery of Gen. 1 (i.e. God's setting up the sequence of day and night, Zech 14:17-18).[35] 1 Enoch does not present the concept of the river which comes from the city, but the vision of the seven mountains in ch.24 contains the concept of trees which "never wither forever," a concept which appears in the descriptions of the New Jerusalem and its river in Ezekiel and Revelation. The parallel texts in the OT and NT support the idea that the garden of life that angels measure in 1 En refers to the eschatological temple. The Edenic features of the eschatological temple in the parallel texts further suggest an *Urzeit-Endzeit* link in the Book of Parables: "the garden of life" where the righteous will dwell is the restoration of the first sanctuary, Eden.

In conclusion, in the uses of the term "garden" in the Book of Parables observed above, readers can see an implicit but reasonably deducible connection between the eschatological dwelling place for the righteous and Eden. We can also see that this idea of a garden in the text is interwoven in broader backgrounds of the idea of *Urzeit-Endzeit* and the concept of the New Jerusalem as the restoration of Eden. Unlike, the Book of Watchers, the Book of Parables conceives of eternal life. The text describes the resurrection of the dead (51:1). All flesh shall glorify God's name "forever and ever" (61:12; 39:6); they will inherit eternal life (40:10). The location of the eternal inheritance is not explicit, but there are some hints. The Book of Parables envisions the coming of Elect One when all evil kings and sinners will be judged (46:4), and the earth will be

---

[32] Nickelsburg, VanderKam, and Baltzer, *1 Enoch 2*, 245.
[33] Daniel Isaac Block, *The Book of Ezekiel*, The New International Commentary on the Old Testament (Grand Rapids: Eerdmans, 1997), 696.
[34] The object of the angels' measuring in Zechariah is not explicitly indicated as the Temple. Yet, Zechariah emphasizes God's presence in the eschatological Zion with the holy people (2:10; 14:5) and transformation of the whole city as "the City of Truth" and "the Holy Mountain" (8:3). These elements most likely indicate that, as Ezekiel and Revelation, Zechariah similarly envisions the eschatological Temple with the image of measuring.
[35] John Walton, *Zondervan Illustrated Bible Backgrounds Commentary* (Grand Rapids: Zondervan, 2009), vol. 5, 225.

transformed (45:4). On the one hand, the people of God will dwell in the eschatological sanctuary upon the transformed earth (51:5). On the other hand, the text states that the dwelling places for the righteous will be "with the holy angels" (39:5), implying an emerging idea of the inclusion of the heavenly realm in the eschatological inheritance.

2.2.3 Summary

In the Book of Watchers, the *Urzeit-Endzeit* connection appears in two ways. First, the author conceives of the eschaton as the new creation. The Noahic blessing after the flood and the eschatological blessings are interwoven with the eschatological imageries of the new creation in Trito-Isaiah. Second, the eschatological sanctuary is portrayed as the restoration of Eden, the first sanctuary. The text envisages that the Tree of Life will be transplanted in the eschatological sanctuary. The consequent bliss of a long life expressed with the language of flourishing bones reflects Trito-Isaiah's vision of the restoration of Eden in the New Jerusalem. Noticeably, in the Book of Watchers, the eschatological inheritance appears in the connection to the bliss in the promised land. The chosen people's "long life" in the eschatological inheritance is described as the recapitulation of their fathers' life "in their days" (25:6). The text also envisions that the blessings, which Israel could enjoy in the promised land (Deut 28), will be ultimately consummated at the eschaton (1 En 10–11).

Eschatology informed by protological elements appears also in the Book of Parables. In the text, an eschatological place for the righteous, which is called a garden of righteousness (60:23) or a garden of life (61:12), is implicitly identified with Eden in the context (60:8). The account of two monsters in the context, also reflected in parallel *Urzeit-Endzeit* traditions in 4 Ezra and 2 Baruch, supports this connection of the eschatological inheritance and Eden. Moreover, the eschatological place appears together with the imagery of angels' measuring that reflects a clear *Urzeit-Endzeit* pattern in some OT and early Christian texts. Apparent parallels between the Book of Parables and the OT and Christian texts further suggest the vision of the eschatological sanctuary in the Book of Parables, which will restore the first sanctuary, Eden, and will be granted to the righteous as their eternal dwelling place. The Book of Parables conceives of resurrection and eternal life, and the eternal inheritance shows both earthly and heavenly elements.

2.3 Qumran Texts

In this section, I shall focus on three Qumran texts, the Damascus Document, 4QpPs37, and 4QInstruction to analyse how they envisage the eschaton and find some common elements to shed light on the eschatology of the Qumran community.[36]

---

[36] The "Groningen Hypothesis" suggests that the Qumran texts are not "a disparate collection of loose elements without any connection" but they form "a unity that we can describe as a religious library" that reflects the views and interpretations of a distinct group of Qumran. F. García Martínez and A. S. van der Woude, "A 'Groningen' Hypothesis of Qumran Origins and Early History," *RevQ* 14, no.

2.3.1 CD 3:12–4:4[37]

Ever since Schechter's publication in 1910,[38] scholars have commonly divided the Damascus Document into two sections, admonitions and law. The first section of CD, i.e., columns 1-8 of the texts of MS A and Col. 19 of MS B, includes three admonitions and scriptural interpretations.[39] These three admonitions present an eschatology that draws on the account of Genesis 1–3: the remnant of Israel (first admonition) fulfill the Adamic vocation under God's sovereignty that controls all events from the beginning to the end of the world (second admonition); the knowledge of Israel's history will be given only to the remnant, and consequently, the obedient people will enjoy the reversal of the consequence of Adam's sin, that is, "everlasting life and all the glory of Adam" (third admonition).

In the first admonition (CD 1.1–2.1), the author places the identity of the chosen people in the larger historical context of Israel. Although the sinfulness of Israel has provoked God's anger and been tragically punished by exile, God's steadfast love allowed the existence of remnants, called "a root from Israel and from Aaron" (1.7). In the second admonition (CD 2.2–2.13), God's intent for this remnant is witnessed as follows: "so that there would always be survivors on the earth, replenishing the surface of the earth with their descendants" (2:11-12).[40] Interestingly, the terms used to describe the vocation of the chosen people, i.e., ארץ ("earth"), מלא ("to fill"), פנה ("the face" of the earth), are highly reminiscent of Gen. 1:27-28. The text states that God intended the chosen people and their descendants (זרע) to fill the face of the earth as He had intended Adam to do. It suggests the possibility that the community considered themselves as the chosen people to succeed the vocation of the forefathers and initially that of their first ancestor, Adam. Additionally, this identity of the eschatological community is buttressed in the text's highlighting of God's sovereignty over history from the beginning to the end of the world.

---

    4 (56) (1990): 522. I agree with the idea that the Qumran texts reflect somewhat unified views of a particular group. For some critical assessments of the hypothesis and García Martínez's response to them, see Gabriele Boccaccini, ed., *Enoch and Qumran Origins: New Light on a Forgotten Connection* (Grand Rapids: Eerdmans, 2005).

[37] The first noticed witnesses to the Damascus Document (CD) were the two medieval manuscripts discovered in the Cairo Genizah. MS A, dated in the tenth century, contains CD 1-16 and MS B dated to the twelfth century contains CD 19-20. Among Dead Sea scrolls, scholars identified ten Damascus Document manuscripts (4Q266-73, 5Q12, and 6Q15). For the texts from cave four, see Joseph M. Baumgarten et al., eds., *Discoveries in the Judaean Desert. 18, Qumran Cave 4, XIII, The Damascus Document (4Q266-273)* (Oxford: Clarendon Press, 1996). For the texts from caves five and six, see Joseph Baumgarten and Michael Davis, "Cave IV, V, VI Fragments," in *Damascus Document, War Rule, and Related Documents* (Tübingen: Mohr Siebeck, 1995), 59–79.

[38] Solomon Schechter, *Fragments of a Zadokite Work* (Cambridge: Harvard University Press, 1910).

[39] Each of the three admonitions in the first section begins with the call for attention of the covenantal group with the phrase, "now listen" (ועתה שמעו). Maxine L. Grossman, *Reading for History in the Damascus Document: A Methodological Study*, Studies on the Texts of the Desert of Judah, v. 45 (Leiden ; Boston ; Köln: Brill, 2002), 90.

[40] Unless otherwise stated, the translation of CD is from Michael Owen Wise, Martin G. Abegg, and Edward M. Cook, eds., *The Dead Sea Scrolls: A New Translation*, 1st ed. (London ; San Francisco: HarperSanFrancisco, 1996).

The third admonition (CD. 2.14–4.12a) is devoted to an extended presentation of Israel's history.[41] According to the author/editor of CD, the knowledge of what God has done and of how human beings are supposed to live—which is the initiative and essential element of God's salvation[42]—is revealed only to the chosen people (4Q268 Frag. 1.7-8). In this admonition, the way in which he delivers the knowledge to his reader is nothing other than a review of the history of Israel from the beginning to the eschatological completion.[43] The highlighted significance of Israel's history related to the eschatological redemption of the chosen people carries two implications, which will be undergirded by following discussions below. First, the author understands that what Israel forfeited through their transgressions, i.e. the divine blessings in the promised land and the temple, will be ultimately granted to the chosen community at the end (CD 3.7, 10; 4:1). Second, the author does not present the examples of Israel's failure randomly but aims to show how the wrecked beginning is restored at the end of time.

In fact, the passage begins to unfold the history of Israel from the account of Gen. 6 omitting the account of Adam. Specifically, at first glance, the account of fallen angels in CD 2:8 seems to demonstrate an understanding of the origin of sin congruous to the Enochic view. The present passage, however, clearly differs from the Enochic presentation in light of the fact that in CD, the initial cause of the depravity actually stemmed from human beings.[44] Angels' coming down happened while human beings "walked in the stubbornness of their hearts," and they were ensnared "for they did not heed the precepts of God" (2:18). Even though the text does not explicitly mention Adam, it implies that the first human beings' choice of doing what was "in their willful heart" initiated the pervasive sin that continues in the subsequent history of Israel (in terms of following "their own will" or living "by their willful heart," 2.21; 3.5; 3.6; 3.7; 3.11; 3.12).

This view of the origin of sin corresponds well to the author's understanding of the eschatological restoration for the chosen people as the reversal of the consequence of

---

[41] Scholars have presented different views on the boundary of this section, M. Grossman's unit, 2:14–3:16, ignores the clear continuity of the discussion in 3:17 from the previous verses. Grossman, *Reading for History in the Damascus Document*, 91. The unit of 2:14–4:12a argued by Campbell and Davies seems reasonable in terms of the coherence of the content. Ibid., 91; Jonathan G. Campbell, *The Use of Scripture in the Damascus Document 1-8, 19-20*, Beihefte zur Zeitschrift für die Alttestamentliche Wissenschaft, Bd. 228 (Berlin; New York: W. de Gruyter, 1995), 67–88; Philip R. Davies, *The Damascus Covenant*, Journal for the Study of the Old Testament 25 (Sheffield: JSOT Press, 1983), 52–53.

[42] P. R. Davies summarizes the sequence of the renewed covenant in CD as follows: 1) the revelation; 2) the human response; 3) the divine forgiveness; 4) the making of the 'sure house.' Davies, *The Damascus Covenant*, 83–90.

[43] Murphy O'Connor argues that the admonition, which he thinks in 2:14–6:1, is a "Missionary Document' directed to non-members of the Essene community." J. Murphy-O'Connor, "Essene Missionary Document: CD II, 14-VI, 1," *RB* 77, no. 2 (1970): 201–29. However, as Davies rightly points out, there is no evidence that the material is specifically redirected from its original readers towards non-members. Davies, *The Damascus Covenant*, 77.

[44] J. J. Collins notes that in CD, the fall of the Watchers is not the origin or source of human sinfulness; it is rather paradigmatic to show the pattern of human sin repeated throughout history. John Joseph Collins, *Apocalypticism in the Dead Sea Scrolls*, The Literature of the Dead Sea Scrolls (London ; New York: Routledge, 1997), 36.

Adam's sin.[45] The third admonition continues to highlight God's grace in delivering his people from the desperate situation: even despite all their rebellions, he would forgive the transgression of his chosen people and ultimately provide them with an eternal place with glory. Those who belong to God would receive "everlasting life and all the glory of Adam" (3:20). Concerning the issue of the life span, CD 10:7-9, where the author explains qualifications for judges, states, "no one above the age of sixty shall hold the office of judge of the nation, because when Adam broke faith, his life was shortened."[46] The author recognizes that human beings' shortened life span is a consequence of Adam's sin. Thus, the combination of the blessing of longevity, which is clearly reminiscent of Gen. 3:16-19 in the present text, and the mention of Adam's glory suggests that the eschatological status of the covenantal people is linked to the concept of the reversal of the Adamic curse at his fall.

Noticeably, in CD, the eschatological restoration observed above is closely linked to the temple and priesthood. The text states that those, to whom the everlasting life and Adam's all honor will be granted, are designated as the priests and the sons of Zadok as the prophet Ezekiel foretold. The author quotes Ezek 44:15 and interprets the passage as a reference to the community:

> God promised them by Ezekiel the prophet, saying, "The priests and the Levites and the sons of Zadok who have kept the courses of My sanctuary when the children of Israel strayed from Me, they shall bring Me fat and blood" (Ezek 44:15). "The priests": they are the repentant of Israel, who go out of the land of Judah and the Levites are those accompanying them; "and the sons of Zadok": they are the chosen of Israel, the ones called by name, who are to appear in the Last Days.
> CD 3:21-4:4

This passage envisages that the chosen people shall stand before God as the Levites and sons of Zadok "in the Last Days"—which marks the passage of lines 2–7, which correspond to eschatological events.[47] The quoted verse from Ezek 44 clearly highlights the priestly vocation of sons of Zadok, which is to offer sacrifices, and it implies the venue of the cults, i.e., the sanctuary, even though there is no explicit mention of the temple in the current context. Furthermore, Ezek 44 belongs to the wider context of Ezek 40–48 which deals with the vision of the eschatological temple. From this, it seems plausible to infer that the author is describing here the vision that God's people will serve as priests by offering sacrifice in the eschatological temple.

This understanding of the passage fits well with CD's focus on the temple. The community's participation in the temple cult at the present time is ambiguous in the

---

[45] Wise interestingly notices the word-play between הָאָדָם of the Leviticus quotation (Lev 18:5 in 3.15) and in line 20. According to Wise, the author is apparently arguing for "a connection between proper worship and the glory of Adam." Michael O. Wise, "4QFlorilegium and the Temple of Adam," *RevQ* 15, no. 1–2 (1991): 126, n.79.
[46] Translation is from Wise, Abegg, and Cook, *The Dead Sea Scrolls*, 71.
[47] Ben Zion Wacholder, *The New Damascus Document: The Midrash on the Eschatological Torah of the Dead Sea Scrolls: Reconstruction, Translation and Commentary*, Studies on the Texts of the Desert of Judah 56 (Leiden: Brill, 2007), 182.

CD text, but it includes some passages which recognize the efficacy of proper sacrifice supposing participation in the Jerusalem cult (CD 6.17-18; 9:14; 11:18-19; 12:1-2; 16:13).[48] More importantly, the adherents of the new covenant are exhorted to live in the land of Damascus finding their existential basis in the temple.[49] The defilement of the temple is a major concern of the author of CD for the covenantal community; the readers are taught to avoid behaviors that would cause the defilement of the temple. The author of CD presents three main traps at the present time, by which Belial endangers the community: fornication, wealth, and defiling the sanctuary (CD 4:17-18). In the following explication of the fornication issue, there are interesting aspects which link it to the defilement of the temple: "They also defile the sanctuary, for they do not separate clean from unclean according to the Law, and lie with a woman during her menstrual period. Furthermore, they marry each man the daughter of his brother" (CD 5.6-8).[50] Concerning the trap of "wealth," CD discusses it with regard to the oaths and vows which one makes with sacrifices and offerings (CD 6.15-16) along with the sins against the poor, orphans, and widows. In other words, the failure to observe these prohibitions results in the defilement of the temple. The author's exhortation concerning the three issues above ultimately aims for the community's life to protect the temple from defilement.

In light of the emphasis of the life which protects the temple from defilement, the text of CD 6:11-14 is illuminating:

> None who have been brought into the covenant shall enter into the sanctuary to light up His altar in vain; they shall "lock the door," for God said, "Would that one of you would lock My door so that you should not light up my altar in vain" (Mal 1:10) *unless they are* careful to act according to the specifications of the Law for the era of wickedness.[51]

Some scholars understand this passage as aiming to exhort the readers to avoid the temple cult in Jerusalem.[52] In support of this view, Wacholder argues that CD 6:14 refers to the authorities in charge of the temple rather than the chosen community. As J. Kampen rightly points out, however, this is not the major concern of the passage.[53] The author declares that the passage of Malachi will be fulfilled—the door of the

---

[48] Marianne Dacy, "Attitude to the Temple in the Damascus Document and the Temple Scroll," *AJJS* 4 (2009): 44.

[49] John Kampen, "The Significance of the Temple in the Manuscripts of the Damascus Document," in *Dead Sea Scrolls at Fifty: Proceedings of the 1997 Society of Biblical Literature Qumran Section Meetings* (Atlanta: Scholars Press, 1999), 190.

[50] A similar link of the fornication issue to the temple defilement appears in the Temple Scroll as well (11Q 66:15-17).

[51] The italics mark my translation in light of the phrase, אם לא. Both Wise, Abegg Jr. and Cook and Martinez and Tigchelaar interpret the phrase as obligatory ("must" "should").

[52] J. M. Baumgarten and D. R. Schwartz, *The Dead Sea Scrolls, Volume 2: Damascus Document, War Scroll, and Related Documents*, ed. James H. Charlesworth (Tübingen; Louisville: Westminster John Knox Press, 1996), 7; Wacholder, *The New Damascus Document*, 222-23.

[53] Kampen, "The Significance of the Temple," 194.

temple will be locked—"unless" the chosen people are "careful to act according to the specifications of the Law for the era of wickedness." The phrase, "according to the specifications of the Law (כפרוש התורה)" was used to demonstrate the righteous life of the "priests" and "sons of Zadok" who are called by name in CD 4.8. Furthermore, the regulations following the citation of Mal 1:10 in 6:14, such as "separating from corrupt people," "avoiding filthy wicked lucre" or "distinguishing between defiled and pure," are also congruous with the ways by which the covenantal group should live during the wicked time (cf. 4.17-18). Hence, the present passage likely envisions that the covenantal group who live the life which protects the holiness of the temple according to the specification of the Torah will gain access to the eschatological temple without the need to lock the door of the temple; they will "light up His altar" properly and not "in vain." In CD 3:1, the author has mentioned that when Israel rebels against God, God "turns away from Israel and from His sanctuary." This breach between God and his people resulting from the defiled temple will ultimately be healed in the eschatological temple.

The Damascus Document demonstrates an understanding of an *Urzeit-Endzeit* eschatology. In God's sovereignty over the whole history of humanity, he chose the covenantal group as the people who will ultimately fulfills the Adamic vocation. These people who were delivered from the wicked age in God's grace are described as regaining the glory and longevity that Adam forfeited through his transgression. The eschaton is envisioned as the restoration of what Adam lost. Interestingly, CD further links this eschatological restoration to the ideas of the temple and priest. Unlike their forefathers who followed Adam's example by rebelling against "the creator", the chosen people would bring God "fat and blood" in the sanctuary. Even though the text does not provide an explicit mention, the worldview of *Urzeit-Endzeit* and the eschatological restoration in terms of priesthood and temple allow an adequate inference of CD's comprehension of Adam in Eden as a priest in a sanctuary. At the eschaton, the covenantal people will be restored to the privileged status of God's priests in the eschatological temple which might be related to the expression of the glory of Adam.

2.3.2 4QpPs37(4Q171)

In his interpretation of Psalm 37, the author of 4QpPs37 believes that the members of the covenantal community and their leader, the Teacher of Righteousness, represent the righteous of the psalm, while their enemies, all those who belong to the Wicked Priest and the Man of the Lie represent the wicked. Through the psalm's clear dichotomy between the salvation of the righteous and the destruction of the wicked, the author of 4QpPs37 encourages his readers to endure the time of suffering at the present time and wait for God's eschatological vindication of them.

The author specifically compares the current status of the community with Israel's situation, i.e., expecting to enter the promised land at the end of the forty years of wandering in the wilderness. This description of the community's status is particularly illuminated by two other parallel biblical and Qumran texts. In 4QpPs37 F1-2ii.5-8, the pesherist presents an eschatological vision as follows:

⁵ועוד מעט ואין רשע
⁶ואתבוננה על מקומו ואיננו. פשרו על כול הרשעה לסוף
⁷ארבעים השנה אשר יתמו ולוא ימצא בארץ כול איש
⁸ר[ש]ע

In a short time, there will be no wicked man. I will pay attention to his place, but he will not be there. It refers to all the wicked at the end of the forty years when they will be *destroyed/exterminated,* and no wicked man will be found on the earth.[54]

A similar idea of the period of forty years at the end of which the enemies of the chosen community are destroyed appears in the Damascus Document (CD 20:13b-15a):[55]

ומיום
¹⁴האסף יורה היחיד עד תם כל אנשי המלחמה אשר שבו
¹⁵עִם איש הכזב כשנים ארבעים

And from the day of the assembling[56] by the Unique Teacher until the *destruction* of all the warriors who returned to the Man of the Lie will be about forty years.[57]

These two texts are reminiscent of Deut 2:14 in that all three passages mention the forty years before the wicked people "perish" using the same verbal root,[58] תמם:

והימים אשר־הלכנו מקדש ברנע עד אשר־עברנו את־נחל זרד שלשים ושמנה שנה עד־תם
כל־הדור אנשי המלחמה מקרב המחנה כאשר נשבע יהוה להם

And the length of time we had traveled from Kadesh-barnea until we crossed the Wadi Zered was thirty-eight years, until the entire generation of warriors had *perished* from the camp, as the LORD had sworn concerning them (NRSV).

The Deuteronomy passage describes the death of the rebellious generation of the wilderness before Israel enters the promised land. The Damascus Document most likely equates the situation of the wilderness generation with that of the people who do not join those assembled by the Teacher in Damascus and thus will perish after forty

---

[54] My translation and emphasis.
[55] Concerning the connection between the Damascus Document and 4QpPs37, I will discuss this below.
[56] Scholars have considered the term to mean ingathering, i.e., euphemism for death, see S. Schechter and Anan ben David, eds., *Documents of Jewish Sectaries* (Cambridge: The University Press, 1910); Chaim Rabin, ed., *The Zadokite Documents* (Oxford: Clarendon Press, 1954); Wise, Abegg, and Cook, eds., *The Dead Sea Scrolls*. Wacholder, however, rightly suggests that the term means "gathering." In the OT texts, the term, פְסָאה, is never used alone to express the idea of death but is always followed by "to your people" or "to his people" or used together with the expressions such as "and he expired" or "and he died" (Gen. 25:8,17; 35:29; 49:33; Num 20:24; 27:13; Deut 32:50). Ben Zion Wacholder, "The Teacher of Righteousness Is Alive, Awaiting the Messiah: פְסָאה in CD as Allusion to the Siniatic and Damascene Covenants," *HUCA*, 1999, 78–79.
[57] My translation and emphasis.
[58] Wacholder, *The New Damascus Document*, 164–65.

years. In light of these parallel texts, the author of 4QpPs37 probably considers the chosen community to be promised that at the end of "a time of trial" (F1-2 ii.18), which is considered as the time in "the wilderness," they will receive the inheritance as Israel expected to receive the promised land (F1-2 ii.24-25). In addition to this, the parallel text, the Damascus Document, suggests how to understand the relationship between the wilderness period and the present time of the chosen community. It is drawn not because of the symbolic meaning of Israel's wilderness wandering (i.e. a general principle of obtaining divine blessing), but because of the same inheritance that the wilderness people and the present community share after the transitional time of wilderness. For the author of 4QpPs37, the eschatological redemption of the covenantal community is the ultimate fulfillment of the patriarchal promise of the land. This idea is further supported by the discussions below.

In iii.1-2, the author concretizes the identity of the inheritance for the chosen people who endure the time in the wilderness. Interestingly, a similar combination of longevity and the inheritance of Adam appears as presented in the Damascus Document: "Those who have returned from the wilderness, who will live for a thousand generations, in salva[tio]n; for them there is all the inheritance of Adam, and for their descendants forever" (4Q171 iii.1-2). The connection between the two documents, CD and 4QpPs 37 is shown by some distinct elements: "Man of the Lie" (4Q171 F1-2 i.18; CD 1.14-15; 8.13; 19:26), "return to the Law" (4Q171 F1-2 ii.2-3; CD 15:9, 12; 15:1-2, 4-5), "snares"/ "traps" of Belial (4Q171 F1-2 ii.9-10; CD 4:15) and "forty years" for evil people (4Q171 F1-2 ii.7; CD 20:15).[59] These similarities between the two documents support the possibility that they project a common eschatological vision in terms of Adam's privilege, i.e., his inheritance/glory and longevity.

The following illustration of this inheritance in 4QpPs37 demonstrates a further interesting similarity to the eschatological vision of the Damascus Document. In the following verses of iii.8-12, the reference to "the inheritance of Adam" in particular becomes clearer: "Its interpretation concerns the congregation of the poor [to whom is] the inheritance of the whole ... They will inherit the high mountain of Isra[el and] delight [in his] holy [mou]ntain. «But those who are [curs]ed by him will be cut off" (3.10-11). In his explication of the eschatological inheritance of the righteous, the author equates "the inheritance of Adam" with "the high mountain of Israel."[60] The phrase, "the high mountain of Israel" appears only three times in the Old Testament, all in Ezekiel (17:23; 20:40; 34:14).[61] Scholars recognize here one of the exegetical techniques, *gezerah shawah,* that the Qumran pesherists use.[62] The pesherist of 4QpPs37 employs allusions by using particular words that lead the reader to interpret them in light of the biblical

---

[59] D. Pardee recognizes the shared concepts in the Damascus Documents and 4QpPs37. Dennis Pardee, "Restudy of the Commentary on Psalm 37 from Qumran Cave 4," *RevQ* 8, no. 2 (1973): 172–74.

[60] In light of the uses in vv. 9-10 along with the uses in the rest of the text (4QpPs37 F1-2 iv.10-12; 4Q173 F1. 7), obviously the two terms נחל and ירש are used interchangeably in this pesher. The inheritance (נחלת) of Adam can be equated with the high mountain that Israel would possess (ירש).

[61] Wise, "4QFlorilegium and the Temple of Adam," 128.

[62] For the use of this technique in 1QpHab and 4Q174 see Bilha Nitzan, *Pesher Habakkuk: A Scroll from the Wilderness of Judaea (1QpHab)* (Jerusalem: Bialik Institute, 1986), 61–79. For the same technique in 4Q171, see David Katzin, "'The Time of Testing': The Use of Hebrew Scriptures in 4Q171's Pesher of Psalm 37," *HS*, no. 1 (2004): 121–62.

corpus in which they appear. D. Katzin points out that in the current case, the terms used by the pesherist are "rare or otherwise conspicuous" so that the readers can easily recognize the related biblical corpus.[63]

The possibility of a shared tradition in these two texts of 4QpPs37 and Ezekiel is also supported by the distinctive feature of the mountains. In both the present Qumran text and the book of Ezekiel, the high mountain of Israel is called God's "holy mountain." 4QpPs37 refers to the high mount as "His holy place" while Ezekiel especially contains the vision in which the eschatological temple of God is erected on the high mountain of Israel (chs. 40–48). The prophet explicitly describes the role of the holy mountain as the sanctuary, i.e., the place of offerings to God (20:40). In 4QpPs37, the pesherist depicts the eschatological destiny of the chosen people similar to CD's: they will inherit Adam's heritage and longevity, and the inheritance is nothing else but the holy mountain of God, which most likely includes the idea of the sanctuary on the holy mountain.

Noticeably, this concept of the holy mountain is closely linked to the image of Eden in Ezekiel, while it is identified as the inheritance of Adam in 4QpPs37. In chs. 40–48, Ezekiel depicts a river that would flow from the threshold of the temple, through the whole city, and on to the Dead Sea. The eschatological temple which is the source of the river which brings healing and vitality echoes the four rivers which flowed from Eden.[64] A more explicit connection between the mountain and Eden appears in Ezek 28:13-15 where the prophet describes the king of Tyre who is in the holy mountain of God:

> You were in Eden, the garden of God; every precious stone was your covering: The ruby, the opaz, and the diamond; the beryl, the onyx, and the jasper; the lapis lazuli, the turquoise, and the emerald; and the gold, the workmanship of your settings and sockets, was in You. On the day that you were created they were prepared. You were the anointed...You were on the holy mountain of God....
>
> Ezek 28:13-14

In this passage, the king of Tyre is described adorned in the jewels which are strongly reminiscent of the ephod of a high priest (Exod 28:17-20). This priest is on the holy mountain of God, which is said to be Eden. Moreover, the priestly figure in Eden reminiscent of Adam is also intriguing.[65]

The author of 4QpPs37 envisions the eschatological inheritance of the chosen community with primordial languages, i.e. Adam's inheritance and longevity. The plausible link to Ezekiel's vision suggests a clearer understanding of this bliss. The chosen people will inherit Zion, the Mount of the temple at the eschaton. The Edenic vision of Ezekiel, the explicit statement of "Adam's inheritance" along with longevity, and the similar concepts in the parallel text, CD, all suggest that 4QpPs37 demonstrates

---

[63] Katzin, "'The Time of Testing,'" 122.
[64] Donald W. Parry, *Temples of the Ancient World: Ritual and Symbolism* (Salt Lake City, UT: Deseret Book Company, 1994), 129–30.
[65] The view that this passage is formulated in terms of primeval Adam is well known. See Walther Zimmerli, Frank Moore Cross, and Klaus Baltzer, *Ezekiel: A Commentary on the Book of the Prophet Ezekiel*, Hermeneia: A Critical and Historical Commentary on the Bible (Philadelphia: Fortress Press, 1979), 2:81-95.

an *Urzeit-Endzeit* connection: the people of God will enjoy the eschatological restoration of the primordial sanctuary, Eden. This eschatological picture is most likely the reason for the emphasis of the particular way of life in 4QpPs37: The people who live in the way which keeps the sanctity of the temple during the present time of evil are properly qualified to enjoy their existence in the eschatological sanctuary. To that extent, he places the present time in tandem with Israel's wilderness wandering for 40 years. The eschatological restoration of Eden is the fulfillment of the promise of the land given to the wilderness generation of Israel.

2.3.3 4QInstruction

4QInstruction is distinct from traditional sapiential literature in terms of its eschatological perspective while the text shows characteristics of the broader wisdom tradition.[66] In 4QInstruction, eschatology buttresses ethical exhortation by promising the eschatological judgment and rewards which will be sustained during the eternal time.[67] In this framework of eschatology, the author of 4QInstruction places the present and eschatological status of the chosen people intriguingly in parallel with Adam's status. In this section, I investigate the affinity in three points, i.e., the knowledge of good and evil, dominion over inheritance, and longevity.

First, Adam and the believers are similar in their possession of the knowledge of good and evil. In 4Q417 F1 i.13-18, the author presents the contrast between the spiritual people and the fleshly spirits/carnal spirits. The spiritual people and אנוש are granted the "vision of insight" while the fleshly spirits are not since they do not have the knowledge of good and evil. Concerning the term אנוש, there have been different interpretations. Some understand it as humanity.[68] It is indeed one of the common terms for man in the Dead Sea Scrolls (e.g. CD 3:17; 1QH 9:25; 4Q381 46.5). This specific meaning of the term is, however, not in accord with the context in which the author of 4QInstruction divides humanity into two groups: that of *Enosh* and the other. Some other scholars understand the term to refer to the biblical patriarch, Enosh.[69] A. Lange especially argues that this interpretation is confirmed by the

---

[66] For the characteristics of 4QInstruction as wisdom literature, see Daryl F. Jefferies, *Wisdom at Qumran: A Form-Critical Analysis of the Admonitions in 4QInstruction* (New Jersey: Gorgias Press, 2002), 54–57.

[67] Matthew J. Goff, *The Worldly and Heavenly Wisdom of 4QInstruction*, Studies on the Texts of the Desert of Judah, v. 50 (Leiden ; Boston: Brill, 2003), 168–71; Robert L. Cavin, *New Existence and Righteous Living: Colossians and 1 Peter in Conversation with 4QInstruction and the Hodayot*, Beihefte Zur Zeitschrift Für Die Neutestamentliche Wissenschaft, Band 197 (Berlin: De Gruyter, 2013), 210–12; García Martínez, "Wisdom at Qumran: Wordly or Heavenly?," in *Wisdom and Apocalypticism in the Dead Sea Scrolls and in the Biblical Tradition* (Leuven: University Press, 2003), 9–10.

[68] So, Torleif Elgvin, "An Analysis of 4QInstruction" (Hebrew University of Jerusalem, 1997), 93; Daniel J. Harrington, *Wisdom Texts from Qumran* (London ; New York: Routledge, 1996), 56; A. Caquot, "Les Textes de Sagesse de Qoumrân (Aperçu Préliminaire)," *RHPR* 76, no. 1 (1996): 18.

[69] See, e.g., J. Strugnell, D. J. Harrington, and T. Elgvin, *Qumran Cave 4. XXIV: 4QInstruction (Musar LeMevin): 4Q415 Ff. (DJD 34)* (Oxford: Clarendon, 1999), 165; Armin Lange, *Weisheit und Prädestination: weisheitliche Urordnung und Prädestination in den Textfunden von Qumran*, Studies on the Texts of the Desert of Judah, v. 18 (Leiden; New York: Brill, 1995), 87; George J. Brooke, "Biblical Interpretation in the Wisdom Texts from Qumran," in *Wisdom Texts from Qumran* (Leuven: Leuven University Press, 2002), 213.

mention of "the children of Seth" in line 15 of the fragment. According to him, the text depicts the generation of Enosh ("the children of Seth") as the object of God's punishment while Enosh and the spiritual people form a chosen remnant.[70] As J. J. Collins rightly points out, it is hard to find a parallel tradition of this depiction of Enosh over against the "children of Seth."[71] Furthermore, in second temple writings, it is difficult to find an illustration of the biblical patriarch Enosh as a recipient of revelation.[72]

A plausible reading of the term is to see it as referring to the biblical Adam.[73] For the usage of the term אנוש for this reference to Adam, we can find another Qumran text: "He created Adam (אנוש) to rule over the world" (1QS 3:17-18). Here, the reference of the term to Adam is supported by the immediate context of creation (vv. 15-17) and the existence of certain term for general humanity, i.e., "all sons of man (איש)" (v.13). More importantly than this parallel Qumran text, in the current context of 4QInstruction, the focus on the knowledge of good and evil undergirds an allusion to Adam.[74] 4QInstruction does not present the idea of prohibition from eating from a certain tree in the Garden. Rather, Adam (Enosh) and the people of spirit are illustrated as the recipients of the heavenly knowledge. This same interpretation appears in Ben Sira's creation account as well: God filled the first couple with knowledge and understanding and showed them good and evil (Sir 17:7). Ben Sira's parallel concept of the knowledge of good and evil is particularly worth noting in light of the similarities between the two texts, Sirach and 4QInstruction.[75]

---

[70] Lange, *Weisheit und Prädestination*, 88.

[71] John J. Collins, "Likeness of the Holy Ones," in *The Provo International Conference on the Dead Sea Scrolls: Technological Innovations, New Texts, and Reformulated Issues* (Leiden; Boston ; Köln: Brill, 1999), 612. The later rabbinic tradition mentions "the wickedness of the children of Seth" which begins in the generation of Enosh (Gen. Rab. 23:6).

[72] Elgvin, "An Analysis of 4QInstruction," 88. In a similar vein, Steven Fraade points out that Enosh was viewed in the pre-Rabbinic Jewish sources (Sir 49:16; Jub 4) as "part of a "chain" of such righteous antediluvians." Steven D. Fraade, *Enosh and His Generation: Pre-Israelite Hero and Historyin Postbiblical Interpretation*, Society of Biblical Literature Monograph Series, no. 30 (Chico, CA: Scholars Press, 1984), 27.

[73] Collins, "Likeness of the Holy Ones," 612; Grant Macaskill, *Revealed Wisdom and Inaugurated Eschatology in Ancient Judaism and Early Christianity*, Supplements to the Journal for the Study of Judaism 115 (Leiden; Boston: Brill, 2007), 83.

[74] Matthew J. Goff, *4QInstruction*, Wisdom Literature from the Ancient World, no. 2 (Atlanta: Society of Biblical Literature, 2013), 163; Shane Berg, "Ben Sira, the Genesis Creation Accounts, and the Knowledge of God's Will," *JBL* 132, no. 1 (2013): 156.

[75] Since the publication of 4QInstruction, a number of scholars have recognized the similarities between this sapiential work and Ben Sira. D. G. Harrington, "Two Early Jewish Approaches to Wisdom: Sirach and Qumran Sapiential Work A," in *The Wisdom Texts from Qumran and the Development of Sapiential Thought*, BETL 159 (Leuven: Leuven University Press, 2002), 263–75; B. G. Wright, "The Categories of Rich and Poor in the Qumran Sapiential Literature," in *Sapiential Perspectives: Wisdom Literature in Light of the Dead Sea Scrolls, Proceedings of the Sixth International Symposium of the Orion Center for the Study of the Dead Sea Scrolls and Associated Literature* (Leiden: Brill, 2004), 101–25; Goff, *The Worldly and Heavenly Wisdom of 4QInstruction*, 117. J. Rey presents some forceful common features of the two texts: Rey notes common terminology including the formula "Do not do this...lest..." (18 times in Ben Sira and 19 times in 4QInstruction); He also points out the connection between honoring ones parents and honoring God in both texts (4Q416 2 iii 15-19 and Sir 3:1-16). Jean-Sébastien Rey, *4QInstruction: sagesse et eschatologie*, Studies on the texts of the desert of Judah, v. 81 (Leiden; Boston: Brill, 2009), 18, 183–226.

Second, the usage of the term משל ("rule") indicates the connection between Adam and the chosen group of 4QInstruction. With regard to the Garden of Eden, 4QInstruction declares to the addressee:

> [...] every fruit of the crops and every pleasant tree "that is desirable to make one wise" (Gen. 3:6), is it not the garden [...] [...desirable] to make one [very] wise, and he *made you ruler* (המשילכה) over it to till it and keep it. [...] [..."the land] will sprout thorns and thistles for you" (Gen. 3:18), and "it will not yield its strength to you" (4:12) [...] [...] when you fall away.
>
> 4Q423 F 1-2 1-4

Here the author of 4QInstruction emphasizes that the addressee possesses Adam's stewardship over Eden which requires work to keep and till it.[76] In 4QInstruction, the obtaining of wisdom is attained by the study of revealed mysteries, and the people who have the wisdom are required to behave in an ethical manner. The author of 4QInstruction compares this way of life of the chosen people with Adam's stewardship in Eden.[77] 4QInstruction encourages its addressees with the statement that, through this diligent life, they will obtain the culmination of their already given status to rule over God's inheritance at the eschaton. They will enjoy their inheritance "full in truth" (4Q418 F88 8).

One thing to note in 4Q418 F 81 is that this concept of God's granting his people rulership is linked to the priesthood (4Q418 F 81 1-5):[78]

> Open your lips as a spring to bless the holy ones, and give praise like an eternal spring [...] He has separated you from every carnal spirit; so you, be separate from everything He hates, and abstain from every abomination of the soul, for He made everything and bestowed on each his inheritance. And He Himself is "your portion and inheritance" (Num 18:20) among the human race, and He *made you ruler* (המשילמה) over His inheritance. So honor Him by this when you consecrate

---

[76] Throughout 4QInstruction, the verb המשיל is used to refer to the elect status of the chosen group. "He has made you sit among the nobility, and he has *made you master* (המשילכה) of a glorious inheritance. Seek His will always" (4Q416 F 2 iii 11-12).

[77] Goff persuasively argues that 4Q423 F 1 3 reformulates God's curse on Adam as the result of the addressee's failure in their stewardship. This interpretation is supported by the usage of the concept in Hodayot. In this text, the teacher claims that he has the power to ruin the Garden (1QH 2:25-26). Goff, *4QInstruction*, 296.

[78] Some scholars argue that this section, 4Q418 81 1-14, is specifically for the priestly sub-group (Crispin H. T. Fletcher-Louis, *All the Glory of Adam: Liturgical Anthropology in the Dead Sea Scrolls*, Studies on the Texts of the Desert of Judah 42 (Leiden ; Boston ; Köln: Brill, 2002), 184; Strugnell, Harrington, and Elgvin, *Qumran Cave 4. XXIV: 4QInstruction (Musar LeMevin): 4Q415 Ff. (DJD 34)*, 20.). It is hard to explain, however, why the author isolates this passage devoted solely to priests in the middle of his exhortation for the whole chosen community. The author exchanges the phrase, "all the sons of Israel" in the quoted passage from Num 18:20 for "among sons of Adam" which refers to humankind in 4QInstrcution (4Q418 F55 11; 4Q418 F77 2). Furthermore, readers easily find a number of expressions used in the exhortations to the whole community, such as their nature contrary to the fleshly spirit/carnal spirit's (lines 1-2; cf. 4Q417 F 1 i 17), God making them rulers over His inheritance (line 3; cf. 4Q416 F 2 iii 12), their existence among angels (line 4; cf. 4Q418 F 69 ii 15), increased honor (line 5; cf. 4Q418 F 69 ii 14) and their status like a firstborn son (line 5; cf. 4Q416 F 2 ii 13).

yourself for Him, just as he has made you a Holy of Holies [for all] the world, and among [di]vin[ities] He has cast your lot and greatly increased your honor and has made you like a firstborn son for Him [...]

In the context of the chosen people's rulership over God's inheritance, the author of 4QInstruction defines the chosen people's identity as priests.[79] The chosen people's identity is not explicitly stated, but their distinctive and specially separated status allows the readers to infer their identity. They were separated from abomination. The passage about priests' inheritance in Num 18:20 is applied to them. The author states that God chose the people as "a Holy of Holies" for the world and among the angels. The holiness of the chosen community is highlighted in other passages in 4QInstruction as well: they have a "holy spirit" that is more valuable than money (4Q416 2 ii 6-7); they have a "holy seed" (4Q415 1 ii and 2 i), an "inheritance of holi[ness]" (4Q418 236 3; cf. 4Q423 9 3), and a "ho[ly] heart" (4Q418 236 3; cf. 4Q423 9 3).[80] This suggests a parallelism with the eschatological visions in the other two Qumran texts that describes the inheritance of Adam's glory related to the priesthood. The rulership of Adam in 4QInstruction, which the chosen people take in their moral life and will obtain its culmination at the eschaton, refers to nothing else than Adam's priesthood in the first sanctuary, Eden. Additionally, it is also noticeable that, in the present passage, the author of 4QInstruction describes the special status of the chosen people with their increased honor/glory (כור) and their identity as the firstborn son of God.

Thirdly, readers can find the possible link between the community and Adam in 4QInstruction's discussion of longevity. The eternal life of the people in the community is not mentioned explicitly, but it can be reasonably inferred. In 4Q417 F2 i 10-12, the author encourages his addresses to mourn in their hardship so that they may enjoy the "eternal joy" which will be granted to the mourners. In 1QS 4:7, the eternal joy (ושמחת עולמים) is clearly linked to everlasting life while the eternal pit (לשחת עולמים) in v. 12 refers to the eternal status of the wicked. 4QInstruction uses the same expression, the eternal pit (ולשחת ולם) for the eternal destination of the wicked (4Q418 F69 ii 6). Accordingly, it can be inferred that the expression of eternal joy refers to the eternal life as in 1QS. The affinity between the angels and the chosen people in 4QInstruction reinforces the idea that in the eschatological vision, the people of God enjoy eternal life with the angels.[81] Other parallel Qumran texts that often describe the longevity of God's people as one of the Adamic blessings also support the interpretation of longevity in 4QInstruction as an Adamic blessing.

4QInstruction posits two kinds of humanity. One is associated with flesh and the other with spirit. The spiritual people in the chosen community are described as enjoying Adam's privilege: They have the knowledge of good and evil through which they can realize the divine mystery. The chosen community is required to fulfill its

---

[79] Although it is true that 4QInstruction does not dedicate much of the text to the theme of the temple or priests, there are references to cultic issues in 4QInstruction (4Q423 3 4-5; 4Q416 2 iv 7-10; 4Q418 103 ii 6-9). Goff, *4QInstruction*, 247.

[80] Goff, *The Worldly and Heavenly Wisdom of 4QInstruction*, 107–8.

[81] Goff, *4QInstruction*, 17–18. 4QInstruction confirms the eternal life of the angels (4Q418 F69 ii 12-13).

Adamic vocation, to till and keep the Garden so that the thorns and thistle do not sprout over its inheritance; in other words, the people need to be diligent in learning and meditating on the knowledge of good and evil (4Q417 F1 i 4-5). Based on this Adamic identity of the chosen people, 4QInstruction presents an *Urzeit-Endzeit* eschatology. When they do not exchange their inheritance for material fortunes even in their poverty and hardships (4Q416 F2 ii17-18), in other words, when they follow the way of life according to the revealed mystery, they will obtain the eternal culmination of their Adamic privilege. They will enjoy the longevity and glory as God's priests and his firstborn son. They will restore Adam's privilege as God's priest in the first sanctuary, Eden.

2.3.4 Summary

The three Qumran texts reflect a similar *Urzeit-Endzeit* eschatological perspective in three points. First, the chosen community is said to fulfill Adam's tasks in Gen. 1. The Damascus Document indicates that what God intended Adam to do, i.e. to "fill the earth" (Gen. 1:27-28), is accomplished by the remnant and their descendants. 4QInstruction states that the chosen people are carrying out Adam's stewardship over Eden through their diligent life that follows the way of life revealed to them in the heavenly wisdom. Second, the chosen people will obtain the restoration of longevity that Adam lost by his transgression. CD explicitly states that the shortened life span of humanity is caused by Adam's sin. All three texts contain the idea of the eternal life that the chosen people will enjoy in the eschaton. Third, the chosen people will restore Adam's priesthood in the first sanctuary, Eden. The chosen people will possess Adam's glory and inheritance, and each bliss is related to priesthood and the sanctuary. Adam's glory is directly connected to the chosen people's identity as the sons of Zadok (CD 3.20-21). The inheritance of Adam refers to the holy mountain (4QpPs37 3.8-12), and the inheritance for the people of Adam (*Enosh*) is linked to the inheritance of the priests in Num 18:20 (4Q418 F 81 1-5).

These texts suggest that the Qumran community replaced the cult of the Jerusalem temple, which they regarded as invalid (1QS 8:5-6), by participating in the liturgy of the heavenly world (1QH 11:21-3; 4Q400 f2; 1QS 11:7-8).[82] After the time of "the wilderness," i.e. the time of testing and cleansing, the chosen community will regain the temple of Zion that originally belonged to Adam. The temple has been defiled by Israel's transgression, but, at the eschaton, it will eventually be perfected through the community who has been keeping its responsibility as holy priests of God and

---

[82] Hodayot 11:21-3 says, "the corrupt spirit you have purified from great sin so that it may take its place with the host of the holy ones and enter into communion with the congregation of the sons of heaven... that it may praise your name together in celebration and tell of your wonders before all your works" (cf. 1QH 3:21-3). George W. E. Nickelsburg, *Resurrection, Immortality, and Eternal Life in Intertestamental Judaism*, Harvard Theological Studies 26 (Cambridge: Harvard University Press, 1972), 144-69. The Songs of the Sabbath Sacrifice, specifically, similarly portray the community's communal experience of the divine liturgy (cf. 4Q401 f14.1.8). The chosen people praise God's glory with the divine beings (line 1), and they are honored in all the camps of the divine beings (line 2).

experience the restoration of the primordial glory in the present fellowship with the heavenly beings. What Israel possessed in the promised land only temporarily will be culminated in this eschatological temple forever more.

2.4 Jubilees

According to the prologue, Jubilees' narrative framework is the situation of Exod 24:12-18 in which the Sinaitic Covenant has just been established, and Moses has ascended Mount Sinai to receive the tablets of the Law. Instead of reproducing the laws about the tabernacle and cult, which Exodus 24–31 contains, Jubilees illustrates Israel's future rebellion, punishment, and repentance and also reviews in great detail the history of Israel's patriarchs. Nevertheless, the laws of the Sabbath in the final chapter of Jubilees are interestingly reminiscent of the way in which Exodus 31 concludes its section.[83] Here, a question that could be raised is what role this specific frame serves for the message of Jubilees.[84] In the discussion that follows, I discuss this in three points: imminent possession of the promised inheritance, the wilderness period for purification, and covenant renewal. And particularly, I highlight a worldview that is consistently observed underneath the framework.

2.4.1 Imminent Possession of the Promised Inheritance

Chapter 50 is a good place to observe the first element of Jubilees' intention in the framework. In this chapter, the author proclaims that the forty years which belong to the last Jubilee of Jubilees shall pass before Israel crosses over the shore of the promised land. Then, he adds the following:

> And Jubilees will pass until Israel is purified from all the sin of fornication, and defilement, and uncleanness, and sin and error. And they will dwell in confidence in all the land. And then it will not have any Satan or any evil (one). And the land will be purified from that time and forever.
>
> Jub 50:5

---

[83] James C. VanderKam, "The Scriptural Setting of the Book of Jubilees," *DSD* 13, no. 1 (2006): 64. There is a view that 50:1-6 was inserted by a later editor or copyist. An attempt to find a rhetorical coherence in a text, however, does not contradict a literary-critical approach to it. For a discussion of the interpolation of 50:6-13, see Liora Ravid, "The Relationship of the Sabbath Laws in 'Jubilees' 50:6-13 to the Rest of the Book," *Tarbiz* (2000): 161–66; Menahem Kister, "Two Formulae in the Book of Jubilees," *Tarbiz*, (2001): 297; Michael Segal, *The Book of Jubilees: Rewritten Bible, Redaction, Ideology and Theology*, Supplements to the Journal for the Study of Judaism, v. 117 (Leiden ; Boston: Brill, 2007), 19–21; James L. Kugel, *A Walk through Jubilees: Studies in the Book of Jubilees and the World of Its Creation*, Supplements to the Journal for the Study of Judaism 156 (Leiden ; Boston: Brill, 2012), 204.

[84] VanderKam correctly notices that the author reapplies the biblical narrative to a new setting. As an example, in ch.1, Moses does not plead for his contemporaries as witnessed in Exodus, but for the generations to come. James C. VanderKam, *The Book of Jubilees*, Guides to Apocrypha and Pseudepigrapha (Sheffield: Sheffield Academic Press, 2001), 27.

The author juxtaposes the situation of the wilderness generation with the eschatological promise for his readers: after the time of purification, Israel will enter the promised inheritance and enjoy it forever while Israel's first generation was expecting to enter the promised land after the time in the wilderness. One can observe a similar parallelism in v. 11:

> This work ("to offer incense and to bring gifts and sacrifices before the Lord for the days and the Sabbaths") alone shall be done on the day of the Sabbath in the sanctuary of the Lord your God so that they might atone for Israel (with) continual gift day by day for an acceptable memorial before the Lord. And so that he might accept them forever, day by day, just as he commanded you.

In the regulation of the Sabbath which Israel shall observe in the promised land, the author evokes the eschatological scene of the acceptable sacrifice that will be offered forever in the sanctuary of the Lord. In previous passages, Jubilees declares that Israel's first generation would fail to maintain the divine inheritance along with the eschatological hope for restoration: after entering the promised land, Israel will turn from God by defiling themselves with sins and idolatry and consequently will receive punishment by virtue of their rebellion; but ultimately, God's great mercy will cleanse and restore Israel so that they enjoy their relationship with God and the inheritance forever (ch. 1; 4:26; ch. 23). In light of this clear vision of Israel's future events, in ch. 50, the author is most likely highlighting the fact that the eschatological inheritance is the accomplishment of the promise for the first generation of Israel, a promise they forfeited in their rebellion and thus remained for coming generations to restore. If this is correct, then we can say that in this understanding of the eschatological restoration, the author of Jubilees transports his readers to the critical moment at the border of the promised land where they look forward to obtaining the divine inheritance, which they will enjoy forever in God's grace.

2.4.2 The Time for Purification Before Entering the Sanctuary

The framework of Exod 24 could be understood from the second rhetorical angle, the wilderness period. Jubilees' intentional juxtaposition of the wilderness generation with the eschatological generation in ch. 50 suggests that the period in the wilderness is being used to understand the time of the final generation. If he compares the purified Israel's eternal dwelling in the land with the wilderness generation's entering into the promised land, it is highly reasonable to think that the 40 years of wilderness wandering forms a parallelism with the present time of "purification" for the eschatological generation. Furthermore, the period of forty years is particularly designated as the time "to learn the commands of the Lord" (50:4). The existence in tandem of these two concepts, purification and learning God's commandments, in the section containing the eschatological vision (1:22-25), reinforces the connection between the time in the wilderness and the present time of purification. Through the given time frame, the author of Jubilees specifically highlights that his readers are facing the time of purification in the wilderness. In other words, the author encourages his readers by letting them know that the present time of suffering and transgression is like the time which the people of God are supposed to pass through before obtaining the promised inheritance.[85]

The concept of purification before entering the promised land is reminiscent of the forty days of purification of the first human being (Jub 3:9). In ch.3, the time of purification before Adam's entrance into Eden is explained with the postpartum time of purification before the woman may enter into the temple. I am not attempting to argue that the two periods of purification of forty years for Israel and forty days for Adam share the same meaning. Adam's purification in ch. 3 refers to cultic necessity while the purification in ch. 50 involves moral issues as well. Nonetheless, a point worth noting is the common feature of Eden and the promised land as holy places and, as such, people must be pure before they may enter them.

In further investigations of the two sacred places of Eden and the promised land, deeper connections between them can be identified related to Jubilees' eschatological vision. Before examining the relation between the two entities, it is necessary to look closely at one of the dominant depictions of Eden—as a sanctuary of God. The Garden of Eden is said to be "more holy than any land" (Jub 3:12); it belongs to the Lord as one of the four sacred places upon the earth (Jub 4:26); it is called "the holy of holies and the dwelling of the Lord" (Jub 8:19).[86] These explicit comments correspond to Jubilees' respective portrayals of the garden. As we mentioned briefly above, the author of Jubilees facilitates a link between the entrance of the parturient into the temple and the entrance of Adam and Even into the garden. This connection between the postpartum entrance into the temple and the entrance of Adam and Eve into the garden is observed in a Qumran text 4Q265 as well. The portrayal of the garden in this text explicitly indicates that the garden is a holy sanctuary. While the Genesis account does not describe all the trees of Eden as sacred, this Qumran writer attributes sanctity to all its trees (cf. 1QH 8:10-13), explicitly mentioning the holiness of the Garden of Eden in line 14:[87] "she [h]ad no [holiness] until she was brought t[o him in the Garden of Eden after eighty days] [because] the Garden of Eden is holy, and every growing thing in its midst is holy." Accordingly, J. M. Baumgarten correctly concludes:[88]

> ... both 4Q265 and Jubilees view the purifications required of a parturient after the birth of a male or female child before being allowed access to the Temple as

---

[85] Cf. Moses' intercession for the people of God in the time of suffering and God's promise of restoration in 1:19-25.
[86] The characteristic of Eden as the sanctuary is well recognized by scholars. See J. van Ruiten, *Primaeval History Interpreted: The Rewriting of Genesis 1-11 in the Book of Jubilees*, Supplements to the Journal for the Study of Judaism, v. 66 (Leiden ; Boston: Brill, 2000), 85–86. Cf. Joseph M. Baumgarten, "Purification after Childbirth and the Sacred Garden in 4Q265 and Jubilees," in *New Qumran Texts and Studies* (Leiden: Brill, 1994), 3–10; Beate Ego, "Heilige Zeit—Heiliger Raum—Heiliger Mensch : Beobachtungen zur Struktur der Gesetzesbegründung in der Schöpfungs- und Paradiesgeschichte des Jubiläenbuches," in *Studies in the Book of Jubilees*, eds. Matthias Albani, Jörg Frey, and Armin Lange (Tübingen: Mohr, 1997), 211-15; C. T. R. Hayward, "The Figure of Adam in Pseudo-Philo's Biblical Antiquities," *JSJ* 23 (1992): 1–20.
[87] Baumgarten, "Purification after Childbirth and the Sacred Garden in 4Q265 and Jubilees," 6.
[88] Ibid., 9–10.

patterned after the respective preparatory periods of Adam and Eve before their entrance into the garden of Eden. This etiology is clearly based on the concept of Eden as a sanctuary.

The idea of Eden as a sanctuary also causes the author of Jubilees, by rewriting the biblical account, to highlight that the sexual relationship of Adam and Eve took place outside the Garden. It is observed that God commanded the Israelites not to go near to a woman for three days before they received his revelation on Mount Sinai (Exod 19:15). The book of Leviticus mentions that, by virtue of a man's uncleanness after having intercourse, he is prohibited from eating holy things until the evening (Lev 15:18; 22:4-7). Some Qumran texts contain a strict application of these passages: after sexual relationships, they are not permitted to enter the city of the temple for three days (11QT^a 45:11-12; CD 11:21-12:2; 4Q274). In Jubilees, Adam and Eve meet one another before their entry into the garden, and their initial sexual encounter ("he knew her") happens outside the garden (Jub 3:6).[89] Their second sexual relation occurs only in the second jubilee after they left the garden (Jub 3:34).[90]

The relationship between Eden the primordial sanctuary and the promised land, which is hinted by the shared concept of a purification period, is clarified in other parts of Jubilees. Jubilees indicates that Eden is located in the midst of the land of Canaan (8:16 and 10:31-34). Consequently, obtaining the promised land from the Canaanites means for Israel to restore Eden. An even more specific relationship between the two entities appears, however, in Jubilees' presentation of the idea of "the new creation" (1:29). The focus of the restoration in the new creation is on the rebuilding of the sanctuary among the people of God in Jerusalem: "Then he said to an angel of the presence, 'Dictate to Moses (starting) from the beginning of the creation until the time when my temple is built among them throughout the ages of eternity'" (Jub 1:27). The *eschaton* is even defined as the "time when the temple of the Lord will be created on Mount Zion" (Jub 1:29). Concerning the focus of eschatology on God's sanctuary, Enoch's entering into the Garden of Eden in Jub 4 is also quite insightful.[91] Immediately after Enoch's offering of the incense in the Garden of Eden, v. 26 continues to state the four sacred places on earth which include the Garden of Eden and Mount Zion (Jub 4:26).

> For there are four places on earth that belong to the Lord: The Garden of Eden, the mountain of the East, this mountain on which you [sc. Moses] are today—Mt.

---

[89] Gary Anderson, "Celibacy or Consummation in the Garden? Reflections on Early Jewish and Christian Interpretations of the Garden of Eden," *HTR* 82, no. 2 (1989): 129; J.T.A.G.M. van Ruiten, "Eden and the Temple: The Rewriting of Genesis 2:4–3:24 in the Book of Jubilees," in *Paradise Interpreted: Representations of Biblical Paradise in Judaism and Christianity* (Leiden, Boston, Köln: Brill, 1999), 77.

[90] Anderson emphasizes that these descriptions of the sexual relations of the first couple are not coincidence. According to him, the idea of their sexual relations outside the garden which is the temple is well consistent with Jubilees' prohibition of sexual activity on Sabbath: "The sabbatical experience and the Temple experience are one. The first represents sanctity in time, the second, sanctity in space, and yet they are somehow the same." Anderson, "Celibacy or Consummation in the Garden?," 129–30.

[91] Enoch's role as a prototype of the priesthood of the restoration will be dealt with in detail later in this chapter.

Sinai—and Mt. Zion (which) will be sanctified in the new creation for the sanctification of the earth. For this reason, the earth will be sanctified from its uncleanness into the history of eternity.

Jub 4:26

Given that this passage follows the account of Enoch's offering incense in Eden, the author suggests that Enoch's priestly function in the Garden of Eden is analogous to what will be accomplished in the temple on Mount Zion.[92] Consequently, along with the fact that Israel restores Eden by obtaining the promised land, the common focus of eschatology and protology on God's sanctuary well draws the synthesis as follows: The eschatological establishment of the temple on Mount Zion is the restoration of Eden, the first sanctuary. In sum, after the investigations above, we can reach a comprehensive portrayal of the relationship among Eden, the promised land and the eschatological sanctuary on Zion. The author of Jubilees presents the *Urzeit-Endzeit* understanding of Israel's history. The first generation of Israel failed to restore the primordial sanctuary of Eden by maintaining its possession of the promised land, and the eventual restoration of the temple in the divine land is accomplished in the eschaton.

Regarding the *Urzeit-Endzeit* connection, the readers find a similar line of presentation in Jubilees' depiction of Israel's identity. Scholars notice that Jubilees seeks to show that Israel's identity and their law originated not merely from the time and the person of Moses but from the primordial time, as a result of the eternal divine will.[93] The author of Jubilees highlights the connection between Israel and Adam by presenting Israel as the descendants of the first priest Adam. The text clearly places Israel in the genealogical line starting from Adam. In Abraham's blessings for Jacob, it reads: "And in his seed (Jacob's seed) my name will be blessed and the names of my fathers Shem and Noah, and Enoch, and Mahalalel, and Enos, and Seth, and Adam" (19:24).[94] The connection of Israel and Adam is further seen in their unique status as priests.

---

[92] J. M. Scott points out that Enoch's offering incense in the Garden of Eden forms "a typological trajectory from *Urzeit* to *Endzeit*." James M. Scott, *On Earth as in Heaven: The Restoration of Sacred Time and Sacred Space in the Book of Jubilees*, Supplements to the Journal for the Study of Judaism 91 (Leiden ; Boston: Brill, 2005), 58–59. For the identification of the temple on Mount Zion without mention of the temple in this passage, see Jub 1:29 "the temple of the Lord will be created in Jerusalem on Mt Zion."

[93] James C. VanderKam, "The Origins and Purposes of the Book of Jubilees," in *Studies in the Book of Jubilees* (Tübingen: Mohr Siebeck, 1997), 21; William K. Gilders, "The Concept of Covenant in Jubilees," in *Enoch and the Mosaic Torah: The Evidence of Jubilees* (Grand Rapids: Eerdmans, 2009), 181.

[94] Jubilees indicates that Eden belongs to Israel in its detailed demonstration of the division of the earth to each son of Noah. Noah re-divided the earth into lots after his sons' attempt to divide the earth "in an evil (manner) among themselves" (Jub 8:9). In this division, Shem's portion was assigned "the middle of the earth," which corresponds with Ezekiel's illustration of the land of Israel ("the center of the world" in *NASB*, Ezek 38:12). Notably, his portion includes the three sanctuaries on earth where God was present, Eden, Mount Sinai, and Mount Zion (Jub 8:19). This specific portion for Shem is confirmed as the divine will by Noah's blessing over Shem, foretold beforehand: "...may the Lord dwell in the dwelling place of Shem" (Jub 8:18). Jubilees emphasizes that this portion was assigned "by lot" to Shem "forever for his generations forever" (8:17). For Jubilees, Israel who is in the line of Shem, is the right heir of Eden that belonged to Adam. The account of division of the earth in Jubilees has the general purpose to legitimize Israel's possession of Canaan. But at the same time, it suggests Jubilees' understanding of Israel's status as a rightful heir of what had belonged to Adam.

Along with the concept of the garden as a sanctuary, the author of Jubilees sees Adam as a priestly figure. He burns incense at the gate of the Garden of Eden: "On that day, as he was leaving the Garden of Eden, he burned incense as a pleasing fragrance in the early morning when the sun rose at the time he covered his shame" (Jub 3:27). The burning of incense is one of the prerogatives of the priests, and the incense is burned in front of the Holy of Holies (Exod 30:7-8, 34-38; Num 16:39-40; 2 Chron 26:16-20; *Ant* 9.223-27).[95] Another piece of evidence is the covering of his nakedness, which is a condition for offering. The author indicates this idea by mentioning that Adam offered to God "from the day when he covered his shame" (Jub 3:27).[96] In the OT, the priests were to cover their nakedness in their service (Exod 20:26; 28:42). Exod 20:26 mentions that the priests are clothed, among other elements, in "coats" (כתנת). Here in Jubilees, Adam who is clothed in "coats of skins" (כתנות עור cf. Gen, 3:21) offers an incense offering "in the morning with the rising of the sun" when God "covered his shame" (Jub 3:28).[97] This is indicative of Jubilees' interest in Adam's priesthood.[98]

In light of Jubilees' highly schematic chronology in which the beginning and the end of human history correspond, the specific depiction of the Garden of Eden and Adam described above suggests an inference of the identity of the eschatological space and that of God's people in it. This idea is observed in Jub 4. Jubilees envisions that what Adam lost at his expulsion from the sanctuary would be restored in the eschatological consummation. In this chapter, Enoch is brought to the Garden of Eden by angels for "greatness and honor" (4:23), and he offers incense to God in the Garden of Eden. Immediately after describing Enoch's offering, Jubilees establishes the connection between the Garden of Eden and the eschatological temple on Zion in its list of holy places and implies that Enoch's offering incense in the Garden is analogous to what will be established on Mount Zion.

The uniqueness and significance of the figure of Enoch appears at several points. The expanded section on Enoch in Jub 4:17-26 is placed at the focal point of a carefully constructed passage (Jub 3:32–4:33).[99] In congruity with the biblical account, Jubilees introduces Enoch in a manner distinct from the formulaic pattern of the genealogies of other patriarchs (e.g. the report of his firstborn, the age of the father at the birth of his son, or mention of other sons and daughters). Jubilees presents Enoch as "the

---

[95] John R. Levison, *Portraits of Adam in Early Judaism: From Sirach to 2 Baruch*, Journal for the Study of the Pseudepigrapha 1 (Sheffield: JSOT, 1987), 93–95; J. van Ruiten, *Primaeval History Interpreted: The Rewriting of Genesis 1-11 in the Book of Jubilees*, Supplements to the Journal for the Study of Judaism 66 (Leiden: Brill, 2000), 88; Scott, *On Earth as in Heaven*, 56–57.

[96] Nakedness of males is considered as an offence to the sacred. See Ruiten, *Primaeval History Interpreted*, 2000, 106–7; Ego, "Heilige Zeit - Heiliger Raum - Heiliger Mensch," 215–16; Michael L. Satlow, "Jewish Constructions of Nakedness in Late Antiquity," *JBL* 116, no. 3 (1997).

[97] Levison notices the connection between covering of nakedness and priestly service in 2 Macc 4:12-14 which criticizes the priests for participating in the practices of gymnasium where public nudity was expected (cf. *Ant.* 12.237-41). Levison, *Portraits of Adam in Early Judaism*, 94–95.

[98] S. N. Lambden also considers covering the nakedness and offering incenses in Jubilees as the indication of Adam's priesthood. Stephen N. Lambden, "From Fig Leaves to Fingernails: Some Notes on the Garments of Adam and Eve in the Hebrew Bible and Select Early Post biblical Jewish Writings," in *Walk in the Garden: Biblical, Iconographical and Literary Images of Eden* (Sheffield, England: JSOT, 1992), 82.

[99] For a structure analysis of Jub 3:32-4:33, see Ruiten, *Primaeval History Interpreted*, 117–18.

human source of the calendar and chronology that are foundational to the cultus."[100] Through Enoch's testimony, the basic chronological framework is known to human beings (v. 17) and Enoch fills the chronology with the historical events both past and future until the day of judgment (v.19). Enoch's activity lasts until the end of human history (v.24). This unique status of Enoch supports Enoch's special role in Jubilees' account as a prototype of the priesthood of the restoration when God rebuild his temple on Zion. Significantly, this priestly role of Enoch is highlighted with his activity in the Garden of Eden. In other words, through the account of Enoch, Jubilees implies that the eschatological restoration would achieve the reverse of Adam's expulsion from the Garden of Eden, i.e., the restoration of a priest to the sanctuary as it was designed at the beginning. In fact, Jubilees does not extensively discuss of Israel's priesthood. Yet the following idea is clearly observed in the text. Just as Adam is the first priest of Israel, Israel is called a priestly people constituting the holy line from Adam: "a holy nation to the Lord" and "a nation of priests" (Jub 33:20).[101]

This depiction of Israel in terms of Adam's priestly identity is strongly resonant with Jubilees' illustration of the restoration of what Adam lost, particularly in its dealing with the longevity issue. The author demonstrates that Adam's death at the age of 930 (Gen. 5:5) was the fulfillment of God's warning, "on the day that you eat of it, you will die" (Gen. 2:17) because 1000 years are "one day in the testimony of heaven" (Jub 4:30, based on Ps. 90:4).[102] This decrease in human lifespan began with Adam and continues as a result of the perpetuation of sin by the successive generations of humanity (Jub 23:15). For the author of Jubilees, this shortened human lifespan is restored to its original length of 1000 years or more (Jub 23:27) only after Israel repents and returns in the eschaton.[103] As J. M. Scott contends, in Jubilees' framework, "*Endzeit* should completely recapitulate *Urzeit*, that is, restore the world to its original, pristine condition before the fall of Adam."[104]

2.4.3 Covenant Renewal Based on the Filial Relationship Between Israel and God

We turn, then, to the third points noted above regarding Jubilees' framework reflecting Israel's situation in Exodus 24–31, covenant renewal. In the specific framework of Jubilees, readers are placed at the moment when the covenant with God was just established. Covenant is a key theme of Jubilees which shows the special relationship between God and his people.[105] On the one hand, the Mosaic covenant where the

---

[100] Scott, *On Earth as in Heaven*, 40–41.
[101] In Jubilees, the patriarchs behaved like priests (3:27; 4:25; 6:1-2; 14:19: 31:12-17). See Segal, *The Book of Jubilees*, 10–11.
[102] Kugel, *A Walk through Jubilees*, 51; Scott, *On Earth as in Heaven*, 228.
[103] By quoting Ps. 90:10, Jubilees mentions the destiny of sinful humanity: "But behold, (as for) the days of our lives, if a man should extend his life seventy years or if he is strong (for eighty years, then these are evil" (Jub 23:15).
[104] Scott, *On Earth as in Heaven*, 8. See chart 6 on p. 152.
[105] Concerning the significance of covenant as a key theme, see James C. VanderKam, "Covenant and Biblical Interpretation in Jubilees 6," in *The Dead Sea Scrolls* (Jerusalem: Israel Exploration Society, 2000), 92; Gilders, "The Concept of Covenant in Jubilees," 178.

readers are located is the most significant moment when the covenantal relationship between Israel and God reaches its complete form.[106] On the other hand, in Jubilees, only one, eternal covenant serves for this relationship.[107] The respective covenants are not new agreements but earthly iterations of the divine decision made at the creation. All the covenants—Noahic (6:1), Abrahamic (14:1, 20), Mosaic (6:11)—are established in the third month.[108] This common date of the three covenantal events is said to be derived from the fact that the date had always been important from the creation: at this date, the festival of *Shebuot* had been celebrated in heaven from the time of creation (6:18). There are different views about the reference of the festival of *Shebuot*.[109] One thing is clear, however, that the festival has been the time in which the covenant between God and Israel is remembered and renewed "year by year" (6:17). In two other places in Jubilees, the festival of *Shebuot* appears as the context of covenant establishment (6:17 for the Noahic covenant; 15:1 for the Abrahamic covenant). The basic idea derived from these texts, therefore, is the concept of the covenants simply as occasions for renewal of the divine decision made in the creation.

In 1:18, the author of Jubilees proclaims that despite Israel's rebellions, God has been faithful to the covenant and will be so until he ultimately ensures the eternal maintenance of the covenant through purifying Israel. The author, then, by locating his readers on the foot of Mount Sinai, powerfully witnesses that the divine will for the covenant with his people, which began from the beginning of the world, has not been given up even with the rebellion of the wilderness generation and is waiting to be accomplished through the eschatological generation.

In Jubilees, this unfailing divine commitment is said to be based on a more fundamental fact than the covenant made on Mount Sinai. It depends on the filial relationship God established with his people:[110]

> I shall be a father to them, and they will be sons to me. And they will be called "sons of the living God." And every angel and spirit will know and acknowledge that they are my sons and I am their father in uprightness and righteousness. And I shall love them.
>
> Jub 1:24-25

---

[106] Concerning the Sinai covenant's role in shaping Jubilee's conception of the covenant, see Gilders, "The Concept of Covenant in Jubilees," 182–83.

[107] VanderKam, *The Book of Jubilees*, 13.

[108] William K. Gilders, "Blood and Covenant: Interpretive Elaboration on Genesis 9.4-6 in the Book of Jubilees," *JSP* 15, no. 2 (2006): 95.

[109] Concerning the reference of the festival of *Shebuot*, there are different views due to the double meaning of the Hebrews *sbwt*, that is, "weeks" (*shabuot*) or "oaths" (*shebuot*). Some scholars interestingly argue that the reference of the festival is the festival of the covenant instead of the festival of Weeks which takes several weeks and thus does not fit into Jubilees' account which is particularly sensitive to chronology. S. Zeitline, *The Book of Jubilees: Its Character and Its Significance* (Pennsylvania: University of Pennsylvania, 1939), 6; Isac L. Seeligmann, *Studies in Biblical Literature* (Jerusalem: Magnes, 1992), 438–39. Seeligmann considers it to be the festival of the covenant since the name of the festival is derived from the word, "oath (*Shabuot*)." However, the Hebrew consonants *sbwt* were more probably intended to maintain the double meaning instead of favoring one meaning over the other. For the same interpretation, see James H. Charlesworth, ed., *The Old Testament Pseudepigrapha*, Anchor Bible Reference Library (New York: Doubleday, 1983), vols. 2, 67.

[110] Gilders correctly points this out. Gilders, "The Concept of Covenant in Jubilees," 180.

A significant point is that the designation of sons of Jacob as the firstborn son of God is accomplished at the culmination of creation. In Jub 2:23, Jacob, the twenty-second generation from Adam, is said to be specially sanctified and blessed since twenty-two kinds of works were completed in creation (before the seventh day of creation). God proclaims as follows:

> Just as I have sanctified and shall sanctify the Sabbath day for myself thus shall I bless them (Israel)… And I have chosen the seed of Jacob from among all that I have seen. And I have recorded him as my firstborn son, and have sanctified him for myself forever and ever.
>
> Jub 2:19-20

In other words, the covenant is based on the filial relationship between God and Israel which is established in their creation. The Mosaic covenant and the other two covenants (Noahic and Abrahamic) are simply the confirmation of Israel's eternal relationship with God the Father which began from the creation. And even with Israel's continuous rebellion, God will finally restore them by purifying his "firstborn" Israel (Jub 2:20).[111]

In Jubilees, we can find two other prominent features of this sonship of Israel in comparison with the angels. First, Israel's identity as the firstborn son of God allows them to join the heavenly assembly. Jub 2:20 says that the Sabbath was granted to Israel who was sanctified as God's firstborn son. Israel's Sabbath observance is described as participation in the heavenly observance of Sabbath by angels ("with us", 2:21-22). In Jubilees, the angels are often paralleled to Israel with their circumcision (15:27), observance of Sabbath (2:18), and celebration of *Shebuot* (6:18). The angels are also said to function as the heavenly parallel to Israel's earthly priesthood (30:18).[112] Jub 2:30 indicates that Israel's Sabbath observance represents the earthly accomplishment of what has happened in the heaven.

The second feature of Israel's sonship in Jubilees is that the status of the sons surpasses that of the angels. Jubilees ch. 5 describes the account of the angels' sin of mating with human beings. Here there are two interesting modifications of the biblical account by the author of Jubilees. First, the rebellious angels are not called "the sons of God" as in the Genesis text. Second, the divine proclamation of the shortened life span, which Gen. 6:3 attests, is applied only to the offspring of the sinful angels.[113] These modifications are congruent with the clear contrast in God's response to the sinful

---

[111] We can observe a similar link between the creation and Israel's sonship in the Old Testament. The first place where this link appears is Gen. 5:1-3 where the first genealogy of the OT begins. Here God creates Adam in his image and likeness, and Adam fathers Seth in his own image of likeness, implying a connection between creating and begetting. In Deut 31:6, God is described as the Father who "made" Israel. The prophet Isaiah calls to God for the restoration of Israel from the oppression of their enemies by appealing to the fact that God is the Father and the potter: "all of us are the work of Thy hand" (Isa 64:8).

[112] A. Y. Reed well recognizes that a maor role of angels in Jubilees is as foils for Israel's exaltation. Annette Yoshiko Reed, "Enochic and Mosaic Traditions in Jubilees: The Evidence of Angelology and Demonology," in *Enoch and the Mosaic Torah: The Evidence of Jubilees* (Grand Rapids ; Cambridge: Eerdmans, 2009), 356.

[113] For the same understanding of Jubilees modification, see Segal, *The Book of Jubilees*, 120.

angels and sinful Israelites. The rebellious angels were "bound in the depths of the earth forever, until the day of great judgment in order for judgment to be executed upon all of those who corrupted their ways and their deeds before the Lord" (Jub 5:10). This passage highlights that there was no exception to this strict judgment (v.11). Meanwhile, the following passage demonstrates God's great mercy toward Israel by mentioning the Day of Atonement when "He will have mercy on all who return from all their error, one each year" (5:18) even as he exercises his justice. The text presents God's merciful partiality towards Noah in the midst of his solemn judgment through the Flood (v.19). Jubilees, furthermore, illuminates the fact that the angels are standing outside the special relationship between God and Israel (Jub 15:32).

Jubilees describes the eternal covenant established in the creation based on the filial relationship between God and his firstborn, Israel. The author points out that Israel's special status as God's firstborn son coexists with the requirement of their moral and cultic purity, and envisions that, with the new creation, the filial relationship between God and Israel is eternally secured. God will cut off the foreskin of Israel's heart, and create a holy spirit for them so that they will obey all God's commandments, so that the covenant will be eternally ensured: "And they will all be called 'sons of the living God.' And every angel and spirit will know and acknowledge that they are my sons and I am their father in uprightness and righteousness" (1:25).

2.4.4 Summary

Jubilees envisages that the promised land will be given to the chosen people as their eschatological inheritance. Through the narrative framework that reflects Exodus 24–31, Jubilees places its readers and the wilderness generation in tandem, while spotlighting on the fact that, after the present time of "the wilderness," the chosen people will finally achieve the promised land that the previous generations of Israel could not keep. Being placed at the foot of Mount Sinai, readers are also reminded that the covenant based on the filial relationship with God, which Israel has had from the creation, cannot be thwarted by Israel's rebellion.

Along with the connection between the historical inheritance of Israel and the eternal inheritance, the author of Jubilees envisions an *Urzeit-Endzeit* eschatology. This eschatology is observed in five points in Jubilees. First, Eden is located in the land of Canaan, thus the chosen people's eschatological possession of the land means the restoration of Eden. Second, while Eden is clearly described as a sanctuary, Jubilees defines the "new creation" at the eschaton with the establishment of the temple on Mount Zion. Third, the present time of purification, which is compared to the forty years of wilderness wandering of the first generation, is paralleled with the time of purification before Adam entered the first sanctuary, Eden. Fourth, Israel is described as priests who succeed the priesthood of Adam. They are called "a holy nation to the Lord" and "a nation of priests" (Jub 33:20) and introduced as the descendants of Adam who is presented as a priest. Enoch's entering into the Garden of Eden for "greatness and honor" and his offering of incense to God foreshadows what will be restore in the temple on Mount Zion. Fifth, human lifespan which was shortened because of Adam's sin will be restored to the original length of 1000 years and more. The eternal inheritance, which Adam forfeited, and previous generations of Israel could not keep, is finally achieved by the last generation at the designated time of Jubilees: after the present time of purification, God will "descend and dwell" with the people (Jub 1:26), and in the eschatological temple on Mount Zion, which will restore the first sanctuary, Eden, Israel will enjoy the primordial bliss and serve God as the first priest, Adam, did.

2.5 Liber Antiquitatum Biblicarum

Liber Antiquitatum Biblicarum, which is falsely ascribed to Philo and thus often called Pseudo-Philo, was almost certainly composed in the first century CE. Some elements in the text such as the attitude toward the Temple and sacrifice, the negative view on Jewish rulers not chosen by God (possibly an anti-Herodian polemic), and the free attitude toward the biblical text suggest the date before 70.[114] We shall continue to investigate how Pseudo-Philo formulates the eschatological vision in his biblical exegesis. A good starting point for a study of Pseudo-Philo's eschatology is its presentation of Israel's eschatological inheritance, the eternal dwelling place.

2.5.1 The Connection Between the Historical and Eschatological Inheritances

In ch. 19, God says to Moses concerning the promised land: "To you ... I will show the land (*terra*) before you die, but you will not enter it *in this age (hoc saeculum)*" (19:7).[115] He continues with a promise:

> Now I will take you from here and glorify you with your fathers, ... you are to be buried until I visit the world. And I will raise up you and your fathers from the land of Egypt in which you sleep and you will come together and dwell in the immortal dwelling place that is not subject to time ... I will hurry to raise up you who are sleeping in order that all who can live may dwell in the place of sanctification I showed you.
>
> 19:12-13[116]

God's proclamation that Moses would not enter the land "in this age," which is placed in tandem with the promise of his eternal dwelling place in the coming age, suggests some continuity between two entities, the promised land and the eternal dwelling place. Furthermore, the place where Moses and his fathers sleep and from which

---

[114] Charlesworth, *The Old Testament Pseudepigrapha*, vol.2, 299. For more discussions of its dates, see Daniel J. Harrington et al., *Pseudo-Philon: Les antiquités bibliques*, Sources chrétiennes 229, 230 (Paris: Éditions du Cerf, 1976), vol. 2, 10–78; Nickelsburg, *Jewish Literature Between the Bible and the Misnah*, 265–68; Emil Schürer et al., *The History of the Jewish People in the Age of Jesus Christ, Vol. 3, Part 1*, New English version (Edinburgh: T & T Clark, 1986), 325–31.

[115] Howard Jacobson, *Commentary on Pseudo-Philo's "Liber Antiquitatum Biblicarum", with Latin Text and English Translation*, Arbeiten zur Geschichte des antiken Judentums und des Urchristentums 31 (Leiden: Brill, 1996), 121.

[116] Ibid., 122–23.

God will raise them up is called "the land of Egypt." This implies that Pseudo-Philo understands the identity of the "immortal dwelling place," to which the sleeping people in "the land of Egypt" will be brought up, with the idea of the promised land. Another passage which supports this connection is 3:10. In this account of the Flood in Gen. 6–9, the author presents the eschatological vision of the new heaven and earth. The passage shows that "an everlasting dwelling place," the new heaven and earth, is the ultimate fulfillment of God's postdiluvian promise to give people their inhabitancy.[117]

In God's promise to Abraham, there is another indication of the connection between the eschatological dwelling place and the land of Canaan. Pseudo-Philo emphasizes Israel's eternal possession of the land of Canaan. The author states that God's eye "has looked from of old" on the land of Canaan, and thus he has preserved it even from "the water of the flood" adding a promise as follows: "For there I will have my servant Abram dwell and will establish my covenant with him and will bless his seed and be lord for him as God *forever*" (7:4).[118] God promises to give the land of Canaan to Abraham's "everlasting seed" (8:3). In fact, Pseudo-Philo proclaims that Israel will rebel against God, and therefore, even while physically located in the promised land, Israel will enjoy bliss only intermittently, being repeatedly re-subjected to their enemies as a result of their continued sinning (e.g. 12:4; 19:7; 21:1). Meanwhile, Pseudo-Philo highlights God's faithfulness in keeping his promise with Israel's patriarchs will ultimately be fulfilled at the end of the age (13:10; 26:13; 28:2; 30:7; 32:17). Pseudo-Philo plausibly understands the new heaven and earth which will be established at the eschaton is the consummation of the promised land. Israel's bliss in the promised land, which was a temporary fulfillment of God's covenantal promise, will be ultimately completed in the eschatological inheritance. This concept is additionally supported in the following discussions.

2.5.2 The Connection Among Eden, the Promised Land, and Paradise

In Pseudo-Philo, the link between the historical inheritance (the promised land) and the eschatological inheritances is further connected to the Garden of Eden. Clear examples of the link of three entities are observed in 13:8-10 and 19:10-13. The passage 13:8-10 states that God showed the people of Noah "the place of creation" which had been granted to Adam as an eternal inheritance but was forfeited through his sin. Now through Moses, God shows Israel "the ways of paradise (*paradysus*)" which both Adam and the people of Noah failed to keep and encourages the Israelites to follow God's commandments in the promised land so that they continuously enjoy the provision of the land. This seamless rhetoric from the Patriarchs' loss of Eden, i.e. the paradise, to Israel's possession of the promised land indicates that Israel's possession of the land has

---

[117] Moffitt aptly suggests an integrated understanding of the two passages, 19:7-13 and 3:10 in light of certain parallels between them: first, 19:12 mentions God's promise witnessed in 3:10; second, both texts state that the light will cease; third, the promise of resurrection occurs in both texts; fourth, both mention the eternal dwelling place; fifth, both texts speak of the pure state of the inheritance (Moffitt, *Atonement and the Logic of Resurrection in the Epistle to the Hebrews*, 107).

[118] Emphasis added.

a close link to what Adam and the forefathers lost. Noticeably, in 19:10-13, "the place of sanctification" that God showed Moses as his immortal dwelling place (v. 13) most likely refers to the paradise (*paradysus*) in the vision showed to Moses (v. 10).[119] This understanding is undergirded by the description of paradise in 19:10 as one of the places that "are prohibited for the human race because they have sinned against me" which is congruent with the feature of the eschatological inheritance as "the place of sanctification" in 19:13.

Pseudo-Philo presents two stimulating features of the promised land that demonstrate its relation to Eden and to the eschatological paradise: fertility and light. The promised land is described as a fertile land: "the land will quickly yield its fruit, and there will be rains for their advantage, and it will not be barren" (13:10). The eschatological place is described in terms of the most intensive concept of fertility. It is the land of perfect progeny: "the earth will not be without progeny or sterile for those inhabiting it" (3:10). Intriguingly, in Pseudo-Philo, Eden is depicted as the source of the rain. One of the places that God showed Moses in 19:10 is "the place from which the clouds draw up water to water the whole earth" which is reminiscent of the depiction of Eden in Gen. 2:10-14 as the source of the four rivers which flow over the whole earth.[120] As Jacobson points out, there is no explicit indication in the present context to support this understanding.[121] *LAB* 26:8, however, demonstrates that the place from which a cloud takes dew is paradise, and it suggests that the source from which clouds draw up water for the whole earth in 19:10 refers to paradise as well. Additionally, in *LAB* 11:15, the short narrative that a branch of the tree of life changes the water of bitterness to sweet water implicitly indicates the position of Eden as the origin of life/ source of life-giving water. In sum, the description of the fertility of the promised land implies the relationship among Eden, the promised land and the eschatological inheritance: 1) The eschatological blessings for Israel are the restoration of what Adam originally enjoyed in Eden but lost as a consequence of his sin (cf. "thorns and thistles" brought forth by the sin of Adam in *LAB* 37:3); 2) this restoration was granted temporally in the promised land and will be consummated in a perfect form in the eschatological inheritance.

Another element to show the relationship among Eden, the promised land and the eschatological inheritance is light. In Pseudo-Philo, light refers to God's statutes.[122] A close relationship between the light and God's commandments is observed in 11:1. In 9:8, where God proclaims the divine favor on Moses, an eternal light is most likely identified with God's Law. The dwelling place in the promised land, where the Israelites will live according to God's Law is described as the place of light that will "shine more brilliantly than the splendor of lightning" (18:12). The eschatological world is described

---

[119] Jacobson, *Commentary on Pseudo-Philo's "Liber Antiquitatum Biblicarum,"* vol. 2, 645. Markus Bockmuehl and Guy G. Stroumsa, *Paradise in Antiquity: Jewish and Christian Views* (Cambridge: Cambridge University Press, 2010), 52.

[120] Harrington et al., *Pseudo-Philon: Les antiquités bibliques*, vol. 2, 229–30.

[121] Jacobson, *Commentary on Pseudo-Philo's "Liber Antiquitatum Biblicarum,"* vol. 1, 634.

[122] Frederick J. Murphy, *Pseudo-Philo: Rewriting the Bible* (Oxford: Oxford University Press, 1993), 193; Harrington et al., *Pseudo-Philon: Les antiquités bibliques*, vols. 2, 30.

with the image of ultimate and perfect light: It is the place where the darkness will fade away (3:10).[123]

Related to this theme of light, the account of the precious stones in chs. 25–26 is noticeable. The text mentions light coming from the precious stones. These shining stones that are originally taken from the land of Havilah were deprived from Adam because of his sin (26:6). They would be restored to Solomon's people temporarily but taken away due to their sins and enemies' invasion. Finally at the coming age, they will be ultimately given to the righteous, and the people "will not lack the brilliance of the sun or the moon, for the light of those most precious stones will be their light" (26:13).[124] The Torah, which was given to Israel on Sinai is stated as being prepared "from the creation of the world" (32:7). In the same vein, the account of the holy stones illuminates on Pseudo-Philo's understanding of *Urzeit-Endzeit* in terms of the divine light, God's Law. The light originally granted to Adam was temporarily restored to the people in the promised land, and at the eschaton, they will enjoy its ultimate restoration.

2.5.3 Other Elements of *Urzeit-Endzeit* Eschatology

The eschatology of *Urzeit-Endzeit* which we have observed in Pseudo-Philo's description of Israel's eternal inheritance also appears in its presentation of the following two ideas: 1) Israel's Adamic identity; 2) death as the result of Adam's sin and resurrection in the *eschaton*. Concerning the first idea, Israel's Adamic identity, Pseudo-Philo's demonstration of Exodus in a relationship with the creation is very suggestive. In the account of the Red Sea (10:5), the author highlights God's direct intervention in the division of the Red Sea, with expressions such as "God rebuked the sea" and "by the fearful din of God and by the breath of the anger of the Lord."[125] Concerning Pseudo-Philo's intention behind this emphasis, another passage portraying the division of the Red Sea, 15:6, presents a thought-provoking factor, i.e., connection to the creation. Here God's commandment over the Red Sea is described with the image of the division of waters which appears in the creation account of Gen. 1:9 (15:6): "And there was never anything like this event since the day I said, 'Let the waters under the heaven be gathered together into one place,' until this day."

These images of God's rebuking the sea arguably reflect a background of the OT which understands the Exodus as the new creation. In Psalms 74 and 89, Israel's redemption from Egypt and possession of the promised land are linked to the motif of creation by the association of the creative power of God with God's redemptive power

---

[123] The phrase "the light will cease" in the present passage most likely refers to the ceasing of the light of sun and moon which mentioned in the previous verse (cf. 12:1; 26:13).

[124] The precious stones in the present account aptly have multiple roles. We will discuss their role related to priesthood later.

[125] This has aroused scholars' attention (In later rabbinic texts, *Pes. K.* 19.6 Yehiel E. Poupko, *Pesikta Derab Kahana*, 2nd ed. (Philadephia: The Jewish Publication Society, 2002), 440. Among modern scholars, Jacobson, *Commentary on Pseudo-Philo's "Liber Antiquitatum Biblicarum,"* vol. 1, 547). For example, D. Boyarin asks, "If Moses had been empowered to split the sea with his hand, as implied by God's command to him in the previous [sic] verse. . ., then why does God intervene directly and perform the splitting Himself?" Daniel Boyarin, *Intertextuality and the Reading of Midrash*, Indiana Studies in Biblical Literature (Bloomington: Indiana University Press, 1990), 96.

in the Exodus. These texts particularly portray the deliverance of Israel in terms of God's smiting of the sea monster. Other ANE writings frequently reflect a deity's conflict with a sea monster as a necessary task in the work of creation.[126] In light of this OT background, i.e., association between the motif of defeating a sea monster and the work of creation, the use of this motif in *LAB* 10 and 14, especially in describing God's Exodus deliverance of Israel, suggests this: the Exodus is another divine act of creation. In 16:3, Pseudo-Philo states that the camp of the Egyptians was destroyed by "the water of the flood." The Flood is understood in the same ANE background above with the picture of the chaotic power which had been placed under control in the creation but unleashed at the moment. The author's adoption of the language of the flood supports the existence of a given tradition which understands Exodus as the new creation behind Pseudo-Philo's depiction.[127]

Another intriguing passage relevant to the idea of Israel's Adamic identity is to be found in ch. 32 where the author mentions that on Mount Sinai, God provided Israel with "the foundation of understanding that he had prepared from the creation of the world" (32:7). The reference is not made explicitly, but there can be no question that what is described is the giving of the Torah on Mount Sinai.[128] In addition to the fact that the law is said to have been prepared from the creation, the establishment of the covenant between God and Israel is depicted as having cosmological impact (earthquake, flood, and movements of abyss and waves) and as attracting all of creation (gathering together of all creatures). These factors imply Israel's special status in creation, which is comparable with the status of Adam who had influence and authority over the whole creation as an obedient steward of the creator God. The text further states that "paradise gave off the scent of its fruit" on this occasion of the establishment of the Mosaic covenant (v. 8). This understanding of the present vision, which is that the Torah was originally given to Adam and eventually inherited by Israel, is consistent with the portrayal of the succession of the task to follow God's commandment from Adam to Noah and finally to Israel in ch. 13 as we have observed in the discussions above.

Israel's identity as the new Adam is developed in Pseudo-Philo through the fact that Israel is descended from Adam. In ch. 32, this fact is presented with a vivid picture of

---

[126] Genesis does not portray a battle or chaotic forces, but there is a clear notion of establishment of order from disorder, which is described in Gen. 1:2, as "formless and empty." J. Walton rightly points out that the concept of subduing chaos, which is often characterized as the raging sea and darkness, is canonically observed in Revelation: no sea (21:1), no night (22:5), no death (21:4). John H. Walton, *Genesis*, The NIV Application Commentary (Grand Rapids: Zondervan, 2001), 72. In the Canaanite Ugaritic Baal Epic, Baal is enthroned after his defeat of the prince of the Sea, Yamm (Mark S. Smith and Simon B. Parker, eds., *Ugaritic Narrative Poetry*, Writings from the Ancient World / Society of Biblical Literature 9 (Atlanta: Scholars Press, 1997), 89, 160). Similarly in the Babylonian *Enuma Elish*, Marduk defeats Tiamat, becomes the king of the gods and makes a resting place for all the gods (Niels-Erik A. Andreasen, *The Old Testament Sabbath: A Tradition-Historical Investigation*, Dissertation Series 7 (Missoula: Society of Biblical Literature, 1972), 174–82; Stephanie Dalley, ed., *Myths from Mesopotamia: Creation, the Flood, Gilgamesh, and Others*, Rev. ed., Oxford World's Classics (Oxford: Oxford University Press, 2000), 227–77).

[127] In the present context, the Torah which was given on Mount Sinai is interestingly called "laws for creation" (15:6).

[128] Jacobson, *Commentary on Pseudo-Philo's "Liber Antiquitatum Biblicarum,"* vol. 2, 874.

Israel's birth from the rib of Adam: "Rejoice, earth, over those dwelling in you, because the knowledge of the Lord that builds a tower among you is present. Not unjustly did God take from you the rib of the first-formed, knowing that from his rib Israel would be born" (32:15).[129] The text highlights the fact that the chosen people born from Adam are God's "firstborn" (32:17). Along with this positive stance that Adam is the ultimate ancestor of Israel, Pseudo-Philo shows that the Adamic task of increasing and multiplying upon the earth (Gen. 1:28) is given to and accomplished by Noah (*LAB* 3:8, 11), Shem (4:10), Abraham (17:5), and sons of Israel (9:1).

A noteworthy point to make at this stage of the discussion is that the concept of Israel's Adamic identity correlates with Pseudo-Philo's depiction of Adam's priestly character. In ch. 26, angels take away the seven stones profaned by the Asher's idols and the Israelites are provided with twelve new stones from the same origin, Havilah. The place Havilah is mentioned for the first time in Gen. 2:10-12 which states that Pishon, one of the four rivers, flowed out from the Garden of Eden and surrounded the land of Havilah. In addition to this hint that the stones had their origin in Eden, the text makes a direct connection to Adam. After the failed attempt to destroy the seven stones and "the books," Kenaz praises God as follows:[130]

> Blessed be God, who has done so many mighty deeds for the sons of men, and he made Adam as the first created one and showed him everything so that when Adam sinned thereby, then he might refuse him all these things (for if he showed them to the whole human race, they might have mastery over them).
>
> *LAB* 26:6

The books and precious stones originally belonged to Adam but were taken away from him as a consequence of his sins. The text indicates the cultic role of the precious stones, more specifically as a core element of priestly garments: They are placed on the breastplate of the high priest (*LAB* 26:4).[131] Adam's priestly status does not appear explicitly in Pseudo-Philo, however, the exclusive role of the stones, which originally belonged to Adam allows a reasonable inference that Adam was a priest.[132]

---

[129] Targum Neofiti contains an interesting parallel idea: "Behold, the First Man whom I have created is unique in the world as I am Unique in highest heaven. From him are destined to arise many nations; and from him shall arise one nation which shall know how to distinguish between good and evil. If he had observed the commandments of the Law and had fulfilled its ordinances, then he would have lived and endured like the Tree of Life" (Targum Neofiti of Gen. 3.22). For the translation of the text, see Michael L. Klein, ed., *The Fragment Targums of the Pentateuch According to Their Extant Sources*, Analecta Biblica 76 (Rome: Biblical Institute Press, 1980), vol.1, 46, 127.) This Targum text indicates the understanding that Israel is the descendant of Adam and shares the task of observance of the Law which was originally given to Adam.

[130] The reference of the books is not clear in the text.

[131] Interestingly, in rabbinic tradition as well, Pishon is considered to supply the precious stones for the high priest's garments (Targum *Pseudo-Jonathan* of Exodus 35:27; *T.B. Yoma* 75a; *Shemoth Rabbah* 33:8). The text of Targum *Pseudo-Jonathan* of Exodus 35:28 states that the oils, spices, and incense for the tabernacle were brought by the clouds of heaven from the Garden of Eden.

[132] Verse 26 presents the reason why the stones had to be removed from human beings: "they might have mastery over them." It indicates that Adam was not a mere beneficiary of the supernatural power of the stones but a person who mastered the sacred stone for a certain purpose.

The text's highlight on Israel's identity as the Adamic people who were directly born from Adam's rib suggests Israel's priestly identity succeeding Adam. Restoration of the precious stone to Israel (26:13) most likely means the restoration of Adam's priesthood. At the eschaton, the precious stone will not be limited to shed light for the priests in the solomonic temple (26:12; cf. 25:12), rather will shine on the new creation, upon the whole priestly people of Israel. The light of the precious stones will be the light of the righteous (26:13) at the eschaton. *LAB* 19:13 further supports the priestly identity of the righteous by indicating that their dwelling place is called "the place of sanctification."

Regarding the priesthood of Israel, the regulations for the righteous in ch. 13 are intriguing. Before the link between Adam, Noah, and the people of Moses (*LAB* 13:8-10, see section 2.6.2), the first seven verses of ch. 13 focus on Israel's cult. The chapter begins with God commanding Moses to prepare the Tent of Meeting, vessels and sacred things, priestly garments, and the sacred oil. After two specific laws (animals for sacrifice and ordinances about leprosy), finally the annual feasts are listed. God then proclaims to Moses:

> And I will remember the whole earth with rain, and the measure of the seasons will be established, and I will fix the stars and command the clouds, and the winds will resound, and lightning bolts will rush about, and there will be a thunderstorm. And this will be an everlasting sign; and the nights will yield dew, as I said after the flooding of the earth.
>
> *LAB* 13:7[133]

C.T.R. Hayward reasonably argues that the context of the passage suggests the interpretation that cultic practices such as the inauguration of the Tent, preparations of its appurtenances and sacrifices and observance of festivals makes the Noahic covenant effective and firm.[134] The context extends its scope to Adam: the following verses indicate that God wanted the people of Noah to restore what Adam ("the first man") forfeited through his transgression and now, he expects Moses' people to enjoy the fulfillment instead of the failed people of Noah (*LAB* 13:8-10). God will grant obedient Israel the ways to Paradise (v.9) and reverse Adam's curse, i.e., give fertility (v.10), instead of thistles and thorns. This text implies that the cult and temple/tabernacle service that Moses establishes according to God's commandments is a substantial element of the covenants which God made with Noah and with Adam. This fact strongly supports the priestly identity of Adam and his descendants Israel. In Pseudo-Philo, there is no explicit statement of the priesthood of Adam or Israel. Yet, specifically in its presentation of Israel's succession to Adam's inheritance and task, we can still observe hints of the idea.

---

[133] James H. Charlesworth, ed., *The Old Testament Pseudepigrapha*, Anchor Bible Reference Library (New York: Doubleday, 1983), vol. 2, 321.

[134] Robert Hayward, *Targums and the Transmission of Scripture into Judaism and Christianity*, Studies in the Aramaic Interpretation of Scripture, v. 10 (Leiden ; Boston, Mass: Brill, 2010), 56. Concerning the possibility that 13:7 is only related to the Feast of Tabernacles (the well-known association of the festival with the provision of rain cf. Zech, 14, 16-17; *M. Succ.* 4, 9-10), Hayward rightly points out that the mention of the ordering of seasons, stars, clouds, winds, lightning, thunder and dew are more likely related to the whole temple service.

The second element in which Pseudo-Philo's *Urzeit-Endzeit* worldview is to be observed is its presentation of death and resurrection. The relevant texts follow the biblical account of Adam's sin and the consequence, stating that death was introduced into the world as the result of Adam's sin:

> And when the first-formed was condemned to death, the earth was condemned to bring forth thorns and thistles.
>
> 37:3

> But the man transgressed my ways and was persuaded by his wife; and she was deceived by the serpent. And then death was ordained for the generations of men.
>
> 13:8[135]

In 3:10, Pseudo-Philo states that at the *eschaton*, the two curses caused by Adam's sin, that is, death and the barrenness of the earth, will be reversed:

> But when the years appointed for the world have been fulfilled, ... I will bring the dead to life and raise up those who are sleeping from the earth ... And the world will cease, and death will be abolished, and hell will shut its mouth. And the earth will not be without progeny or sterile for those inhabiting it ... And there will be another earth another heaven, and everlasting dwelling place.

The readers cannot find an explicit statement that resurrection is the eschatological restoration of what Adam evoked through his sin. Nevertheless, the clear envisioning of death as the result of Adam's sin and resurrection as the key element of the eschatological restoration allows the readers to connect the two and thus support the understanding of the *Urzeit-Endzeit* eschatology of Pseudo-Philo.

2.5.4 Summary

Pseudo-Philo shows an *Urzeit-Endzeit* eschatology in five points. First, *LAB* envisions the renewal of the creation when the earth will be transformed and will be given to the righteous as their eternal dwelling place (3:10). Second, *LAB* indicates that paradise that Adam and the previous generations of Israel forfeited in their sins will be given to the righteous as their eschatological dwelling place. Third, *LAB* states that the fertility and light (i.e. God's words) which Adam enjoyed in Eden and which Israel possessed temporarily will be perfected in the eschatological world. Fourth, *LAB* describes Israel as the firstborn who were created in Exodus and succeed to Adam's task of filling the earth and to his priesthood. Fifth, *LAB* envisions the resurrection at the eschaton when death that was caused by Adam's sin will be abolished. Additionally, it is to be

---

[135] This sentence is missing in the π tradition. Yet, as H. Jacobson properly points out, this fact can be understood in different ways. The sentence could be a Christian interpolation or it could have been removed from the text by Jews who did not hold this view and considered it too Christian. Jacobson, *Commentary on Pseudo-Philo's " Liber Antiquitatum Biblicarum,"* vol.1, 521.

highlighted that Pseudo-Philo sees a connection between the eschatological inheritance and the historical inheritances of the Patriarchs. The author sees parallelism between the renewed creation after the Flood and the new heaven and earth and that between the promised land and the immortal dwelling place promised to Moses. Pseudo-Philo describes how the bliss of fertility and God's words (i.e. light), which Adam possessed in Eden, was granted to Israel in the promised land, albeit temporarily, and how it will be completely obtained by the chosen people at the eschaton.

2.6 Summary of Chapter 2

The pre-70 Jewish texts observed above, i.e. Book of Watchers, Book of Parables, some Qumran texts, Jubilees, and Pseudo-Philo, all attest similar *Urzeit-Endzeit* eschatologies. For them, a key element of the eschatological inheritance for the chosen people is the restoration of the first sanctuary, Eden, through the eschatological temple. This eschatological vision appears along with the identity of the chosen people as the priests who succeed to Adam's priesthood (CD 3:21-4:4; 4Q418 F 81 1-5; Jub 33:20; *LAB* 26:13) or the vision of their eternal dwelling in the sanctuary (1 En 61:12; cf. 1 En 25:6; 4QpPs37 3.8-12; *LAB* 19:13). They envision that, at the eschaton, the chosen people will serve God in the eschatological temple, restoring Adam's priesthood in the first sanctuary, Eden. The chosen people's identity as God's firstborn son is also highlighted, in some cases along with their superiority over angels (Jub 5:10; cf. 5:18; 15:32). These texts show agreement in the understanding that this eschatological restoration was temporarily accomplished in the promised land so that Israel could enjoy the primordial blessings with the existence of the temple among them. The eschatological generation of Israel will finally complete the possession of the eternal inheritance that the previous generations of Israel forfeited through their continuous disobedience. The eschatological restoration includes the reversal of the consequences of Adam's sin: fertility and longevity will be restored; evil, sin, defilement will be removed; and Adam's glory will be regained. The eschatological inheritance encompasses not only the temple or the promised land but also the whole renewed creation (1 En 10:20-11:2; CD 2:11-12; 4Q423 F1-2 1-4; Jub 1:29; *LAB* 32:17).

3

Urzeit-Endzeit Eschatology in Post-70 Second Temple Literature

3.1 Introduction

Prior to the destruction of Jerusalem in 70 CE, the national and religious life of many Palestinian Jews revolved around the cultic system of the Temple despite many political changes.[1] The catastrophe of 70 CE caused the omnipotence of God and the certainty of Israel's election to be called into question. Jewish and early Christian writings in the second half of the first century C.E. reflect the chaotic situation of the devastation of Judea and destruction of the Temple. In this context, on the one hand, they began to conceive of the revelation of the heavenly world as their eternal inheritance instead of focusing only on the promised land and the temple in it. On the other hand, these texts maintain the tradition of the renewed creation and the restoration of Eden with the bliss that Adam enjoyed in it, the *Urzeit-Endzeit* eschatology observed in some apocalyptic texts in previous times. As a result, the post-70 texts contain the idea of some kind of union between heaven and earth. In this chapter, I shall particularly look into the eschatology of 4 Ezra, 2 Baruch, and the Book of Revelation.

3.2 4 Ezra and 2 Baruch

4 Ezra and 2 Baruch reflect on the destruction of 70 by looking back to events connected with 587 BCE and the Babylonian exile.[2] Through the voices of the pseudonymous authors, Ezra and Baruch, these two texts offer answers to questions raised about divine

---

[1] According to Philo, even the Jews of the diaspora who were geographically remote from Jerusalem, continued to "hold the Holy City where stands the sacred Temple of the most high God to be their mother city." Philo, *Flacc.* 7.46 (LCL 9. 327-29) For the religious and social context of the first century Jews, see F. Strange, *Archaeology, the Rabbis, and Early Christianity* (Nashville: Abingdon, 1981), 142–47.

[2] The consensus position places the two texts between the end of the first century CE and the Bar Kokhba revolt of 132–35. On the issue of dating 4 Ezra and 2 Baruch, see James H. Charlesworth, P. Dykers, and M. J. H. Charlesworth, *The Pseudepigrapha and Modern Research with a Supplement*, Septuagint and Cognate Studies Series, no. 7S (Chico, CA: Scholars Press, 1981), 112; Nickelsburg, *Jewish Literature Between the Bible and the Misnah*, 287, 305 nn.12–13.

justice and faithfulness in the wake of the traumatic situation of 70.[3] In the present section, I compare the eschatological hopes presented in the two texts.

3.2.1 4 Ezra[4]

3.2.1.1. Hopeless Humanity and the Eschatological Hope

The author of 4 Ezra had a particular issue to deal with, namely the uncertainty of the covenantal relationship between God and Israel caused by the destruction of the Temple in Jerusalem. More precisely, the covenantal crisis that the author of 4 Ezra faces can be epitomized in two points: 1) human nature is so corrupt that only a few will be saved from divine judgment (3:20-22; 4:24; 7:17-18; 8:31; 9:14); 2) the chosen people of Israel were delivered to the Gentile nations (3:2; 4:23; 5:28-30; 8:15-16).[5] 4 Ezra addresses these problems by revealing information about the eschatological hope, specifically of the two worlds and the messianic era.

First, the vision of the two worlds offers a solution to Ezra's question about why only a few can be saved from humanity's evil inclination. 4 Ezra states that God created two worlds instead of one (7:50). The author finds no hope in the present world. With the absence of divine intervention (3:8), unrighteousness in the world has been increased

---

[3] Most scholars agree that there is an intimate relationship between 4 Ezra and 2 Baruch. Not only are they responding to the same historical situation, the two texts show similarities in their terminology, concepts, and the seven-fold structure. (Michael E. Stone and Frank Moore Cross, *Fourth Ezra: A Commentary on the Book of Fourth Ezra*, Hermeneia-a Critical and Historical Commentary on the Bible (Minneapolis: Fortress Press, 1990), 39.). Nevertheless, the precise nature of their relationship, e.g., the priority of either, remains difficult to ascertain. B. Violet argued that 4 Ezra served as a source for 2 Baruch (Bruno Violet, *Die Apokalypsen des Esra und des Baruch in deutscher Gestalt* (Leipzig: Hinrichs, 1924), 4. So also Russell, Hilgenfeld, Dillmann, Box, Gunkel, Schreiner, Lagrange). P. Bogaert reached the opposite conclusion. (Bogaert, *Apocalypse de Baruch*, 144–45. So also Bissell, Thomson, Kabisch, Klausner, Clemen, Wellhausen).

[4] The first critical issue to be discussed about 4 Ezra is the inconclusiveness of the dialogues (episodes 1–3) and the different emphases in the visions and epilogue (episodes 4–7). For over a century, some utilized source criticism to conclude that 4 Ezra is a relatively careless redaction of prior texts (Richard Kabisch, *Das vierte Buch Esra auf seine Quellen Untersucht* (Göttingen: Vandenhoeck & Ruprecht, 1889); E. P. Sanders, *Paul and Palestinian Judaism: A Comparison of Patterns of Religion* (London: SCM Press, 1977), 417–18). Careful studies of the structure of 4 Ezra, however, have challenged this older view (e.g. Breech's highlight on the finely designed structure of 4 Ezra. Earl Breech, "These Fragments I Have Shored against My Ruins: The Form and Function of 4 Ezra," *Journal of Biblical Literature*, no. 2 (1973): 267–74.). Recently, some have sought to harmonize 4 Ezra's seemingly conflicting views from a fresh perspective based on authorial intentions reflected in its narrative frame and flow (Alexander E. Stewart, "Narrative World, Rhetorical Logic, and the Voice of the Author in 4 Ezra," *JBL* 132 no. 2 (2013): 373–91; Lydia Gore-Jones, "The Unity and Coherence of 4 Ezra: Crisis, Response, and Authorial Intention," *JSJ* 47, no. 2 (2016): 212–35). The author of 4 Ezra attempts to provide answers to these issues by narrating the process in which Ezra's understanding—which was not erroneous but still had a myopic and pessimistic focus – is broadened and refocused through the conversations with Uriel the angel and divine visions. This keen attention to authorial intention opens the way to read 4 Ezra in its coherence and unity. For a detailed discussion on different approaches to this issue, see Lydia Gore-Jones, "The Unity and Coherence of 4 Ezra: Crisis, Response, and Authorial Intention," *JSJ* 47, no. 2 (2016): 212–35.

[5] Alden Lloyd Thompson, *Responsibility for Evil in the Theodicy of IV Ezra: A Study Illustrating the Significance of Form and Structure for the Meaning of the Book*, Dissertation Series – Society of Biblical Literature, no. 29 (Missoula, MT: Scholars Press, 1977), 288–90.

(3:12; 4:32; 5:2). The forefathers could not avoid recapitulating Adam's failure (3:8, 27), and the present world bears people who "are smaller in stature than those who were before" (5:54). Ezra cries out, "[F]or in truth there is no one among those who have been born who has not acted wickedly, and among those who have existed there is no one who has not transgressed" (8:35). Even Ezra himself cannot ensure his own salvation (8:49).

His fundamental pessimism about this world originates from his anthropology. In ch. 7, Uriel mentions that "when Adam transgressed my statutes, what had been made was judged. And so the entrances of this world were made narrow and sorrowful and toilsome" (7:12). 4 Ezra identifies Adam's transgression as the reason for the curse on the land and the consequent toil of people to overcome the evil root within them.[6] 4 Ezra further shows a deeper pessimism about humanity in the present world by pointing out that the evil seed was initially sown in Adam's heart (4:30).[7] Right before this verse, the text states:

> For the evil about which you ask me has been sown, but the harvest of it has not yet come. If therefore that which has been sown is not reaped, and if the place where the evil has been sown does not pass away, the field where the good has been sown will not come.
>
> 4:28-29

The text implies that until the evil seed is removed from the human heart, the good fruits cannot be produced. 4 Ezra does not say that Adam and his descendants had no chance to bear good fruits and keep the Law. Yet the author implies that the present world has the meaning of the time of testing (i.e. struggling to bear a good fruit even with the evil seed) and that the fruit of immortality can be born only in the coming age when the evil root will be removed from human hearts, bringing restoration to the land (7:13). In the vision of the two worlds, 4 Ezra answers the question of many/few. This hopeless world is given to many but the world to come will be given only to the few who have passed the test of the present time (8:1-2). These few are likened to mining gold which produces a lot of material, but "only a little dust from which gold comes" (8:2; cf. 7:58).

---

[6] The image of the "evil root" in the hearts of Adam's descendants in 3:22 is very interesting compared to a single "grain of evil seed" sown in Adam's heart. In light of other passages concerning the consequence of Adam's sin, the statement that "the disease became permanent" in Adam's descendants likely refers not only to the duration of the evil heart throughout the following generations but also to its incurability in comparison with the evil heart in "the first Adam" which could be overcome (3:21). A detailed discussion on the cursed land/human heart in ch. 7 will follow below.

[7] The concept of evil heart in 4 Ezra shows similarity to the rabbinic concept of the evil inclination. In rabbinic texts, the term יצר "intention" is used almost interchangeable with לבב "heart." For the rabbinic concept of יצר, see Efraim Elimelech Urbach, *The Sages, Their Concepts and Beliefs*, Publications of the Perry Foundation in the Hebrew University of Jerusalem (Jerusalem: Magnes Press, Hebrew University, 1975), 471–83; J. Schofer, "The Redaction of Desire : Structure and Editing of Rabbinic Teachings Concerning Yeser ('Inclination')," *JJTP* 12, no. 1 (2003): 19–53. The difference between 4 Ezra and rabbinic concepts of evil heart is that while Ezra avoids directly attributing the creation of the evil inclination to God, rabbis make it clear that the evil inclination is created by God. Urbach, *The Sages, Their Concepts and Beliefs*, 480.

Second, the eschatological vision of the two worlds also provides an answer to the question of why the chosen people of Israel were delivered to the Gentile nations. Ezra disputes with God over why the nations who oppose God have trodden on those who believe in God's covenants (5:29). God responds that "you cannot discover...the goal of the love that I have promised my people" (5:40). This implies that the city of Jerusalem and the land around it, at least in their present form, were not what God had really promised his people. In the account of Abrahamic covenant of 3:14-15, the text states that God showed Abraham "the end of the times." 4 Ezra believes that the everlasting covenant that God established with Abraham included the eternal inheritance in the coming world. The text of 7:129 also points out that Moses' exhortation to the wilderness generation to choose life (Deut 30:19) refers to the contest of "self-control," which is necessary not only for the wilderness generation but for all people to obtain the eternal paradise (7:119, 121, 123). From the forefathers to the contemporary readers of 4 Ezra, what has been promised by God is the coming, greater world.

Third, the messianic era provides another answer to the problem of Israel's deliverance into their enemies' hand. The Messiah, the son of God, will come to Mount Zion (13:32-36). The heavenly Jerusalem will come down and the Messiah will reprove the nations and destroy them by the Law, thereby vindicating Israel (13:37-38). The remnants of Israel in exile will return to the holy land through a new Exodus (13:44). They will enjoy the Messiah's rule and glory until the last times (13:46). The injustice of Israel's captivity and of the destruction of the holy city and temple will be made right during this messianic era.

3.2.1.2 *The* Urzeit-Endzeit *Eschatology*

The coming world shows clear elements of continuity with the first world. First, the new world begins with resurrection. This resurrection, which is described as the reunion of the bodies sleeping in the earth and the souls committed to the heavenly treasuries, suggest some level of "material continuity" between two worlds (7:31-32).[8] Second, the text plainly presents God as the creator (e.g. 3:4; 5:42-45; 6:1-6), and highlights God's ongoing love for his creation (8:47). This corresponds with the emphasis on God's sovereignty, i.e. what God planned in the beginning is ultimately accomplished at the end (4:43; 6:6). Despite 4 Ezra's recognition of the increasing evil and decay in the world in its present condition, the author does not embrace an anti-creational stance but envisions creation's renewal. This renewal appears with the image of the shaking earth. In 6:14-16, Ezra is warned not to be afraid if the earth shakes:

> If the place where you are standing is greatly shaken while the voice is speaking, do not be terrified; because the word concerns the end, and the foundations of the earth will understand that the speech concerns them. They will tremble and be shaken, for they know that their end must be *changed*.

---

[8] Concerning this verse, Stone comments "There is no suggestion that in the renewal of creation the body or the earth will have lost its material qualities." Stone and Cross, *Fourth Ezra*, 219-20; Edward Adams, *The Stars Will Fall from Heaven: Cosmic Catastrophe in the New Testament and Its World*, Library of New Testament Studies 347 (London; New York: T & T Clark, 2007), 80.

Stone and Cross conclude that "the context being evoked is quite unmistakable. It is cosmic creation/re-creation, with all that this implies."[9] The text clarifies that the shaking of the earth is connected to its change or renewal. The prediction of this passage is prefigured in 6:29: "While he spoke to me, behold, little by little the place where I was standing began to rock to and fro." The shaking of the ground underneath Ezra in 6:29 seems to foreshadow the ultimate cosmic change to come. This idea is strongly supported by the use of the language of the "renewal of creation" (*creaturam renovare*) in 7:75 to describe the eschatological cosmic transformation.[10]

Regarding the concept of renewal of creation, 4 Ezra's description of the end of the messianic era is noticeable. After the time of 400 years, the Messiah and all human beings will die, and the world shall be "turned back to primeval silence for seven days" (7:29-30). In light of the creation account in 6:38-54 in which "darkness and silence embraced everything" and "the sound of man's voice was not yet there" at the beginning of the world, the text above most likely refers to an eschatological reversion to the chaos that existed before the creation.[11] The mention of a period of seven days for creation in 6:38-54 also suggests that the new world being roused after the seven days at the end of the messianic era means the renewal of the first creation.

The link between the first world in the beginning and the new world at the eschaton forms a dominant feature of the eschatology of 4 Ezra: what has been made wretched by Adam's sin will be reversed in the eschaton. The first place to observe this is 6:27-28. Here the author provides a clear vision that the two consequences of Adam's sin, i.e., evil root and death, will be removed from humanity.[12] At the eschaton, "the heart of the earth's inhabitants shall be changed and converted to a different spirit" because "evil shall be blotted out" (6:27-28). Along with this, death will also be overcome (6:27-28, cf. empty storehouses in v.22). A similar *Urzeit-Endzeit* connection is observed in ch. 7. 4 Ezra 7:10-11 mentions that, due to Adam's sin, "what had been made was judged," and thus, the ways of this world were made "narrow, sorrowful and toilsome." This passage strongly alludes to the curse on the land and the consequence upon Adam himself that resulted from his transgression in Gen. 3: the land, which was cursed due to Adam's sin, will produce thorns and thistles, and accordingly humans need to toil to get good products from it. In some places in 4 Ezra, the language of infertile land is linked to the human heart: "the land shall be *barren of faith*. And unrighteousness shall be increased beyond what you yourself see, and beyond what you heard of formerly" (5:1-2). 4 Ezra thinks that the seed of the Law was sown in people's hearts. Thus, they are supposed to toil to produce the fruit that no longer grows naturally due to the infertility of their heart, i.e. because of the existence of the evil root. The eschatological vision in 7:10-11 envisages a situation in

---

[9] Stone and Cross, *Fourth Ezra*, 167.
[10] Concerning the shaking of "the foundation of the earth," a biblical tradition of Isa 24:18 is noticeable. The text describes the occasion of the shaking of the foundation of the earth, i.e., God's visit on Mount Zion (24:23), his judgment (24:21), and the eschatological feast (25:6).
[11] Stone and Cross, *Fourth Ezra*, 217; Adams, *The Stars Will Fall from Heaven*, 79-80. The concept of a primordial silence is attested in other Jewish texts as well (e.g. *LAB* 60:2; 2 Bar 3:7).
[12] As I have discussed above (2.7.1.1), 4 Ezra thinks that the evil seed was sown in Adam's heart from the beginning, but Adam's sin made "the disease" permanent, in other words, Adam caused the evil root deeply engrained.

which the current barren world and heart will be transformed at the eschaton. In the eschatological world, "the fruit of immortality" will be yielded without hardships (7:14, 18) since the evil root in the people's heart will be removed (6:26). The curse on the human heart which Adam's sin brought forth is reversed in the eschatological era, and at the same time, death will be removed: they will obey God without any toil and will enjoy the reward of it, i.e. immortality in the new world.

In addition to this vision of the reversal of Adam's curse, 4 Ezra describes that the righteous will inherit the paradise as their eschatological dwelling place. In some places of 4 Ezra, Paradise, which is mentioned as the dwelling place of the righteous (8:52-55), is placed in tandem with hell/Gehenna. Particularly in 4:7-8, the parallelism between vv. 7 and 8 suggests the location of Paradise in heaven.[13] The people of God will enjoy rest, wisdom, and immortality in the heavenly realm, paradise, where "the tree of life" is planted (8:52-55). Similarly, in 7:123, the author presents the paradise whose fruit "remains unspoiled and in which are abundance and healing."[14] The current context indicates that paradise equates to "an everlasting hope" and "safe and healthful habitations" reserved for the people of God (v.121). Clearly the vision of the end in those texts is determined by the Genesis account of the beginning. The righteous will inherit the paradise that Adam forfeited in his sin.

In light of the *Urzeit-Endzeit* concept in 4 Ezra, Israel's identity and status compared to Adam's is interesting. In 6:59, Ezra appeals to God regarding why Israel cannot now possess the world that has been created for them. For this argument, he draws on the creation account. He discusses the creation which was completed in six days and then highlights that "over these," God placed Adam "as ruler over all the works" that he had made (6:54). Then, he asks why God does not allow Israel to rule over the world. Uriel begins to answer Ezra with a portrayal of the eschatological inheritance for the people of God and the present toilsome way to obtain it. Here Uriel draws an analogy between the narrow entrance of a city that has been "given to a man for an inheritance" (7:6-9) and the entry into the coming world. In this conversation, both Ezra and the angel presuppose that Israel will inherit what was originally given to Adam; the creation is "our (Israel's) inheritance" (6:59). One more thing to notice here is that Israel's identity as God's "firstborn" is highlighted in this context of Adam's inheritance.

As observed above, 4 Ezra envisions the renewal of creation, and at the same time, it conceives of a heavenly inheritance as well. Concerning how these two locations of

---

[13] In v. 7, some questions about cosmic geography, "exits of hell" and "the entrances of Paradise" forms a parallelism with the places such as "deep," "hell," and "heaven."

[14] P. B. Smit interestingly points out that a connection between *Urzeit* and *Endzeit* appears in 4 Ezra in terms of the image of fruit. In 6:44, an abundance of fruits is presented in a description of the creation: "On the third day...fruit came forth in endless abundance and of varied appeal to the taste." In 7:123, the paradise that will be revealed at the eschaton is portrayed as follows: "a paradise shall be revealed, whose fruit remains unspoiled and in which are abundance and healing." Smit points out first that the fruit of righteousness in 4 Ezra is associated with the redeemed and the renewed world to come (3:20; 6:28). He then suggests that the three combined concepts of "paradise, its abundance, and its connection with the world to come" in 7:123 conceptualize the world to come as a "return to paradise." P. B. Smit, "Reaching for the Tree of Life: The Role of Eating, Drinking, Fasting, and Symbolic Foodstuffs in 4 Ezra," *JSJ* 45, no. 3 (2014): 379.

the eschaton, the renewed earth and the heavenly dwelling place, can be harmonized, the scene of the Messiah' coming is quite suggestive. When the Messiah comes, the mountain "carved out without hands" and Zion "will come and be made manifest to all people" (13:35-36). 4 Ezra envisions that, at the messianic era, the heavenly Zion will be revealed, i.e. come down to the earth, and establish the messianic Zion, from which the Messiah will rule over the earth.[15] In the same way, 4 Ezra envisages that the heavenly paradise will come down from heaven and unite with the renewed earth in order to form the coming world. In ch.7, the author points out that the new world is "not yet awake" and "shall be roused" at the eschaton (7:31), even though he envisions the renewal of the creation that the people have. The specific element of the new world, i.e. the heavenly realm, might cause the author to state that the new world is not yet here ("not yet awake," 7:31) at the present time.

3.2.1.3 *Summary*

4 Ezra envisions the eschatological world in terms that draw on the Genesis account of the beginning. This *Urzeit-Endzeit* eschatology appears in five points. First, the eschatological world is described as the renewal of creation in an explicit mention of it (7:75) and in a depiction of the primeval silence at the beginning of the new world (7:30). Second, the eschaton is envisioned as the completion of what God planned at the beginning (4:42; 6:6). Third, in the eschatological world, the consequence of Adam's sin, the evil root and death, will be reversed. People will bear the fruit of immortality in their pure heart without the evil root. Fourth, the heavenly paradise with the tree of life will be given to the righteous as their eschatological dwelling place. Fifth, in the new world, people will fulfill the Adamic vocation detailed in Genesis; they will rule over all creation as originally intended for Adam. The author argues that the eschatological world consists of the renewal of the earth and coming of the heavenly world and that this is what has been promised by God as the eternal inheritance from the forefathers to the contemporary readers of 4 Ezra. In this eschatological vision, 4 Ezra encourages the readers to toil to bear good fruits even with the evil root within, hoping that they will be ultimately born in the coming world.

3.2.2 2 Baruch

In their responses to the catastrophic context, 2 Baruch and 4 Ezra share a similar rhetorical structure. As 4 Ezra's theology develops in the forms of Ezra's conversations with Uriel the angel, so in 2 Baruch, Baruch's dialogues with God functions as the main structure that presents Baruch's gradual acceptance of the current catastrophe and the divine plan for the redemption of Israel. The author encourages readers to remain

---

[15] In some NT texts, the concept of a sanctuary made with human hands appears as the contrast with the heavenly sanctuary (e.g. Acts 7:48; 17:24; 2 Cor 5:1; Heb. 9:11; 24; cf. 1 Kg 8:27; 2 Ch 6:18; Isa 66:1).

faithful to the Law and covenant in the hope of eschatological salvation.[16] As in 4 Ezra, eschatological salvation in 2 Baruch consists of two stages, a messianic era and the new world, which is promised to the righteous. 2 Baruch, however, presents a different view from 4 Ezra concerning the role of the messianic era.

3.2.2.1 The Promised Inheritance

In 21:19, Baruch questions how long corruption and the wickedness of this world will continue. He points out that the world, created for the sake of the patriarchs, is dying now (v.22). He then asks God to make good on what he has "promised" (v.25). Before a discussion on eschatology in ch. 21, the reference to the object of God's promise needs to be clarified. 2 Baruch indicates that the coming world is what has been promised by God, and the righteous hope for (14:13; 44:15; 51:3; 83:4, 6 cf. *T. Mos* 1:12; 4 Ezra 6:55). Chapter 57 transforms the account of the Abrahamic covenant by replacing the promise of descendants and the land with the promise of life in the coming world.[17] 2 Bar 4:4 shows a similar interpretation of the Abrahamic covenant by presenting the account of Gen. 15 as God's promise of the city, which is not in the midst of the people (not "in your midst now").[18] Chapter 4 also contains 2 Baruch's distinctive interpretation of Isa 49:16, which clarifies that the city "carved on the palms" of God's hands is not Jerusalem on earth but the heavenly city/sanctuary.[19] In these texts, 2 Baruch appears to conclude that God's ultimate promise to Israel is the coming world, not the promised land per se.

In ch. 21, God answers Baruch's appeal to fulfill his promise by assuring Baruch that he will surely accomplish what he has begun. In this response, the text develops four analogies: destination of a journey, harvest of what was sown, the fruit from a vineyard, and fulfillment of the promise of a gift.[20] These analogies resonate with Baruch's descriptions of the heavenly world in chapters 4 and 51. Chapter 4 claims that the heavenly world promised to Abraham and his descendants was originally shown to Adam. At first glance, the language of "showing" this world to Adam suggests the idea of a momentary revelation to him. Yet, the text states that, due to his transgression, the heavenly world and "paradise" were taken away from Adam, indicating that the heavenly world was intended to be given to Adam. In ch. 51, which describes the

---

[16] A number of scholars suggest that the obedience to the Law and the covenantal faithfulness are the main messages of 2 Baruch. E.g. Charles, *The Apocalypse of Baruch*, 26; Albertus Frederik Johannes Klijn, "Recent Developments in the Study of the Syriac Apocalypse of Baruch," *JSP* 4 (1989): 7; Martin Leuenberger, "Ort und Funktion der Wolkenvision und ihrer Deutung in der syrischen Baruchapokalypse: eine These zu deren thematischer Entfaltung," *JSJ* 36, no. 2 (2005): 226–31.

[17] Gwendolyn B. Sayler, *Have the Promises Failed?: A Literary Analysis of 2 Baruch*, Dissertation Series / Society of Biblical Literature 72 (Chico, CA: Scholars Press, 1984), 70.

[18] 4 Ezra 3:14-15 shows a similar shift of focus from on the earthly inheritance of the promised land to the other world in its rewriting of Gen. 15.

[19] Charles, *The Apocalypse of Baruch*, 6; Bogaert, *Apocalypse de Baruch*, 85–92; Liv Ingeborg Lied, *The Other Lands of Israel: Imaginations of the Land in 2 Baruch*, Supplements to the Journal for the Study of Judaism 129 (Leiden; Boston: Brill, 2008), 296.

[20] The reference of the analogies is not explicitly mentioned, but the context of Baruch's asking for what God has promised makes it clear (cf. 15:7-8; 43:2-3; 44:9-15).

heavenly world and the glory that the righteous will possess, paradise is described as "spread out for them" (51:11). Paradise, which was withdrawn from Adam after his transgression (4:3), will be given to the righteous at the eschaton. A comprehensive reading of the two texts in light of the analogies in ch. 21, suggests a link between *Urzeit* and *Endzeit*: As the vine will bear the fruit that was expected, the divine inheritance intended for Adam in the primordial time and promised to Abraham's descendants will be ultimately possessed by the righteous at the eschaton.

3.2.2.2 *The Messianic Kingdom for the Restoration of Eden on Earth and Israel's Vindication*

The heavenly world is not the only inheritance that 2 Baruch envisions for the people of God to obtain at the eschaton. The text hopes for the renewal of the creation as well. 2 Baruch notices that the consequence of Adam's transgression influenced the destiny of the creation. In the present world, "everything is in a state of dying," and the angels of death and the realm of death are at work (21:22-23). Yet, 2 Baruch does not think that this corrupted creation will be merely nullified and invalidated at the end. Baruch's visions of the messianic era on earth show that, when the Messiah comes, the earth will be restored to be the place that will provide the remnants the primordial bliss of the Garden of Eden. Additionally, 2 Baruch presents that Israel who have been scattered from the promised land and suffered at the hands of their enemies will be vindicated under the Messiah's rule on Zion.

The apocalypse of the cloud (chs. 55–74) epitomizes Israel's history with the vision of the twelve sets of bright and black waters. Chapter 73 presents the messianic reign after the tribulation on earth, which is described as the last black water. Interestingly, the messianic kingdom is portrayed as the restoration of what Adam forfeited for human beings. The consequence of the transgression of Adam appears in the description of the first black water:

> For when he transgressed, untimely death came into being, mourning was mentioned, affliction was prepared, illness was created, labor accomplished, pride began to come into existence, the realm of death began to ask to be renewed with blood, the conception of children came about, the passion of the parents was produced, the loftiness of men was humiliated, and goodness vanished.
>
> 56:6

The account of the eschaton of ch. 73 envisages the reversal of the consequence of Adam's sin: untimely death, lamentation, tribulation, and illness will disappear; blood and passions will "go into condemnation." This text also describes the reversal of the curse on Adam and Eve after their sin (Gen. 3:16-19): "women will no longer have pain when they bear, . . . it will happen in those days that the reapers will not become tired, and the farmers will not wear themselves out, because the products of themselves will shoot out speedily, during the time that they work on them in full tranquility" (73:7–74:1). Furthermore, wild beasts' service to men and serpents' subjection to children (73:6) are clearly reminiscence of Isaiah's vision of the new creation, which itself uses images of Eden (Isa 65:25). The vision of the messianic era envisages the restoration of the pre-fall state of Adam and Eve in the Garden of Eden.

Chapter 29 demonstrates a similar portrayal of the messianic era. Here the messianic era is introduced with a cornucopia of food stuffs for the righteous remnant. Noticeably, in some contemporary Jewish texts, images used in 2 Bar 29, are also linked to the Garden of Eden. Thus, the language of "fragrance of aromatic fruits," described in 2 Bar 29 among the food for the remnant, appears in some contemporary texts to describe the fruit bearing trees of the Garden. *LAB* 32:8, for example, states that the Garden gives off "the scent of its fruit." 1 En 25:4 depicts the fragrance of the tree of life, which allows the righteous long life by penetrating their bones. Concerning the image of dew in 2 Bar 29, Jub 2:7 mentions that dew was created on the third day of creation along with the fruit bearing trees and the Garden of Eden. This provides an interesting context to understand the combination of fruit and dew images in 2 Baruch. Related to "manna" in 2 Bar 29, L. I. Lied also notes that the *Jerusalem Targum* includes manna in the ten things which were created on the Sabbath's eve of the creation week.[21] *Jerusalem Targum to Exod* 16:4 and 15 states that manna was hidden since the creation to descend again in the messianic era.[22] In addition to all these parallel usages of given images, 2 Bar 29 describes the two monsters that were created on the fifth day of creation and have kept until the eschatological feast. The depictions of food and the sources of that sustenance during the messianic era indicate that the righteous in the messianic era will be nurtured by the goods of the Garden of Eden or what has been prepared from the primordial time. The chosen people of God will enjoy the primordial food in the messianic era.

The time of the messianic era has significance for Israel's vindication as well. Clearly, the author of 2 Baruch claims that the coming world is Israel's inheritance, but, at the same time, he does not ignore Israel's unfolded history, which has been revolving around the promised land and Zion. The text envisages Israel's vindication that will be accomplished through the Messiah's rule over the earth on Zion. The author provides a comprehensive portrayal of the messianic era in relation to the holy land in 40:3-4: "And after these things he (the Anointed One) will kill him (the last wicked ruler) and protect the rest of my people who will be found in the place that I have chosen. And his dominion will last forever until the world of corruption has ended." In 40:1-2, Mount Zion is identified as the locus of the judgment. The current context of chs. 39–40, which combines the judgment of the wicked ruler of the world on Mount Zion, the protection of the remnant in the promised land, and the dominion of the Anointed One, suggests a strong possibility that the messianic community is located in Zion. In the dying world after Adam's sin, the land of Canaan was functioning as a separated place for the righteous to live within the covenant and to enjoy the divine blessings, even though the land itself was not the promised inheritance, i.e. the coming world. In the messianic kingdom on earth, Israel will enjoy peace and abundance in the promised land and see their vindication by the Messiah's judgment over their enemies.

---

[21] Lied, *The Other Lands of Israel*, 218.
[22] Bruce J. Malina, *The Palestinian Manna Tradition: The Manna Tradition in the Palestinian Targums and Its Relationship to the New Testament Writings* (Leiden: Brill, 1968), 57–58.

3.2.2.3 *The Messianic Era as a Bridge Between the Two Worlds*

Concerning the two-worlds concept in 2 Baruch, F. J. Murphy concludes: "the author of 2 B places great emphasis upon the radical discontinuity between this world and the future one."[23] Before him, Bultmann also emphasized the incommensurability between this world and the coming age observed in 2 Baruch and other apocalyptic literature:[24]

> The end is not the completion of history but its breaking off, it is, so to speak, the death of the world due to its age. The old world will be replaced by a new creation, and there is no continuity between the two aeons. The very memory of the past will disappear, and, with that, history vanishes.

It is true that in 2 Baruch differences between the two worlds are highlighted. Whereas this world is corruptible, sinful, and transitory, the coming world is incorruptible, glorious, and eternal.[25] Nevertheless, 2 Baruch presents their continuity through the liminal period of the messianic era. 2 Bar 74:2 defines the messianic era as follows: "For that time is the end of that which is corruptible and the beginning of that which is incorruptible." This statement obviously indicates that the messianic era is a transitional period. Arguably, however, it also implies that the messianic era substantially connects the two worlds insofar as it contains features of both worlds. In other words, the messianic era functions as the culmination of this earthly world and at the same time, overlaps with the everlasting, incorruptible world. This overlapping of the two eschatological stages well corresponds with some of the contradicting features of the messianic era. On the one hand, the messianic kingdom is said to be established in Zion on the corruptible earth. On the other hand, Baruch says that the era extends into eternity.[26] 32:4 presents the Zion that will be renewed in glory through the Messiah's coming and states "[I]t (the renewed Zion) will be perfected into *eternity*." In 40:3, a similar tension appears. Here the dominion of Messiah is said to "last forever until the world of corruption has ended and until the times which have been mentioned before

---

[23] Frederick James Murphy, *The Structure and Meaning of Second Baruch*, Dissertation Series / Society of Biblical Literature, no. 78 (Atlanta: Scholars Press, 1985), 67. For a similar view on 2 Baruch's eschatology, see Dietrich Rössler, *Gesetz und Geschichte: Untersuchungen zur Theologie der jüdischen Apokalyptik und der pharisäischen Orthodoxie* (Kreis Moers: Neukirchener Verlag, 1962), 60–61; Bogaert, *Apocalypse de Baruch*, 144–45.

[24] Rudolf Bultmann, *The Presence of Eternity: History and Eschatology* (New York: Harper and Brothers, 1957), 30. Bultmann neglects unique characteristics of 2 Baruch as he presents the text as an example of the common eschatology of the first century CE.

[25] Murphy, *The Structure and Meaning of Second Baruch*, 1985, 52–55.

[26] Concerning the end of the messianic era, 2 Baruch differs from 4 Ezra. In 4 Ezra, a fixed time is set for the messianic reign (see my discussion in section 2.7.1.2 above). According to the Arabic manuscript (1) and Latin manuscripts, it will last four hundred years. The Syriac manuscripts state thirty years, and the Arabic manuscript (2) says a thousand years. For the textual variations above, see B. M. Metzger, "The Fourth Book of Ezra: A New Translation and Introduction," in *The Old Testament Pseudepigrapha*, vol. 1 (Garden City, NY: Doubleday, 1983), 537. Furthermore, 4 Ezra clearly indicates the end of the Messianic era, which is the death of the Messiah and the return to a seven days primal silence (7:28-29). Lied, *The Other Lands of Israel*, 196.

have been fulfilled." Some scholars claim that this text indicates an everlasting kingdom rather than a temporal era of Messiah.[27] This view, however, does not explain the mention of the limit of the given time, which is "until the world of corruption had ended." The text is better explained by the understanding that Messiah's dominion will last until the corruptible world is ended, but the eschatological era which has already begun in the messianic era will continue forever.

With regard to this understanding of the messianic era, Baruch's description of the messianic era in chs. 36–37 is intriguing. The Messiah is portrayed as a vine that rises over against a forest that occupies the plain. The vine uproots the entire forest, and finally the vine proclaims the judgment over the last cedar. When the Messiah comes to the world, the wicked kingdoms are uprooted and the ruler of the fourth kingdom (the cedar, cf. 39:3-6) will be judged. Chapter 37 describes the scene that after all these judgments, the plain around the vine becomes "a valley full of unfading flowers." L. I. Lied suggests a link with Job 14:1: "A mortal, born of woman, few of days and full of trouble, comes up like a flower and withers, flees like a shadow and does not last" (cf. Ps. 103:15-16; Wis 2:7-8; Matt 6:28-30). The most common usage of the metaphor of fading flowers is the short and transitory life of human beings.[28] On the other hand, the image of everlasting flowers is often used in Greek and Roman texts to refer to paradisiacal spaces or immortal life (*Jos. Asen.* 16:16; Eusebius, *HE* 5.1.36; Minucius, *Octavius* 38). 1 Enoch also describes the people of God in their eternal life with the image of the everlasting plant (10:16 and 84:6). In contrast to the uprooted forests and cedar, the image of the unfading flowers aptly implies the idea of immortal life for the followers of the Messiah. The messianic era spreads over the earth, and the new earth, which was occupied by the vine, the messiah, and its fountain, is portrayed as a land of unfading flowers, the everlasting world for the righteous.

This messianic restoration of Eden on earth continuing to the eschaton raises a question how it is harmonized with the vision of the heavenly world/paradise. Chapters 50–51 suggest ways to understand 2 Baruch's eschatology. Two features are to be highlighted. Here, 2 Baruch envisages the future resurrection and the beginning of the incorruptible world. First, the text envisions some kind of change of what the people already have. 2 Baruch 51:1 states that "the glory" of the righteous will be changed. It is said about the righteous that "the root of wisdom" has been planted in their hearts. At the time of eschaton, "*their* splendor" and "*their* beauty," which the righteous have already retained (49:2), will be magnified and glorified (51:3). In other words, the eschatological form of existence of the righteous is not totally new. Rather, they will possess a glorified version of what they already had, like a fully-grown flower or a plant whose beauty and glory have already been present in its root or seed. The text says that

---

[27] Paul Volz, *Die Eschatologie der jüdischen Gemeinde im neutestamentlichen Zeitalter* (Repr. Hildesheim: Georg Olms, 1966), 73; Hans-Alwin Wilcke, *Das Problem eines messianischen Zwischenreichs bei Paulus* (Zürich: Zwingli Verlag, 1967), 43.

[28] Lied, *The Other Lands of Israel*, 280. For the biblical metaphors of grass and flowers for perishable human beings, see T. Stordalen, *Echoes of Eden: Genesis 2–3 and Symbolism of the Eden Garden in Biblical Hebrew Literature*, Contributions to Biblical Exegesis and Theology 25 (Leuven, Belgium: Peeters, 2000), 87–88.

thus, the glorified people will be recognized by the evil people in their sorrow and jealousy (51:5-6). Second, the heavenly reality will come to the righteous rather than them having to be transferred to the heavenly reality. The heavenly reality appears to the righteous: "miracles, however, will *appear* at their own time to those who are saved" (51:7). The text highlights that the righteous now can see what has been hidden and invisible: "they shall see that world which is now invisible to them, and they will see a time which is now hidden to them" (51:8). The next phrase describes the change of the existing time: "And time will *no longer* make them older" (51:9). Thus, the text does not envision God's people's going off to Paradise. Rather Paradise comes to them. Paradise is spread in front of them, and the beauty of the heavenly place and the beings who dwell there are "shown" to them. Hobbins rightly notices that the concept of resurrection in chs. 50–51 is presented in terms of a "consistent-with-history" transformation. Indeed in 2 Baruch, "eternity will be the continuation of identity, the perfection of history" for God's people.[29]

3.2.2.4 Summary

2 Baruch envisages the accomplishment of the coming world in two stages, the transformation of the creation and the coming of the heavenly realm. 2 Baruch presents an *Urzeit-Endzeit* eschatology by describing the coming world in terms of the beginning of the creation. Three points are in order. First, in the messianic era on earth, the curse that was caused by Adam's sin will be reversed. Pain (esp. the pain of birth and toil to gain products from the earth) and death will no longer exist in the eschaton. Wild beasts will serve humans, and serpents will be subject to children in the coming world. Second, at the time of the Messiah's rule, the people will be nurtured by goods of Eden or what has been prepared from the beginning. Third, paradise and the heavenly world which were forfeited through Adam's sin will be restored to the people of God. In this new world formed with the union of the heaven and earth, the chosen people will enjoy the eternal inheritance that Adam lost by his sins in the beginning.

3.2.3 Summary of the Section on 4 Ezra and 2 Baruch

In light of the catastrophic events of their historical context, 4 Ezra and 2 Baruch both place their ultimate hope in the world to come. They claim that what God has promised to his people, from the patriarchs to their contemporary readers, is not simply the promised land on earth, but the immortal coming world. Concerning this coming world, they share the view that, in the eschatological world, the chosen people will obtain what Adam enjoyed in Eden, i.e. an *Urzeit-Endzeit* eschatology. On the one hand, the creation will be renewed to return to Eden. The curses caused by Adam's sin will be reversed, and the people will enjoy the Edenic abundance and rest. On the other hand, the heavenly realm, Paradise, which was taken away after Adam's

---

[29] John F. Hobbins, "The Summing up of History in 2 Baruch," *JQR* 1/2 (1998): 76.

sin, will be restored to the people. As a result, the two texts imply some kind of union between heaven and earth in the coming world. The eschatological world consists of two elements, the renewal of the earth/creation and the revelation of the heavenly world.

A dominant difference between the eschatological visions of 4 Ezra and 2 Baruch is the role of the messianic era. 4 Ezra states that the messianic era when Israel will enjoy the bliss in the promised land and the vindication under the reign of the messiah will be finished after 400 years, while it envisions the renewal of creation afterward (through seven days of primeval silence). 2 Baruch describes now the restoration in the messianic era will continue merging into the eschaton. The creation is described as renewed during the time of the Messiah's rule; one essential part of the coming world is accomplished in the messianic era. The limited role of the messianic era in 4 Ezra can be understood in light of the author's keen interest in the issue of the evil seed in the human heart. The author of 4 Ezra thinks that this fundamental problem of all following issues will be totally resolved in the coming world. Therefore, until then, the renewal of creation cannot be accomplished in the present world even at the messianic era.

3.3 Revelation

The majority of scholars place the composition of Revelation toward the end or immediately after the reign of Nero (54–68 CE) or the reign of Domitian (81–96 CE).[30] The author, identified as John, wrote the book for Christians in seven churches in Asia Minor, who were suffering persecution and temptation on a number of fronts, in order to assure them that their oppressors would be judged and the people of God would be vindicated in the end.[31] After the prologues and short letters for the seven churches, the main section of the author's vision (chs. 4–22) is set between scenes that project a cosmic vision of God's eschatological salvation. At one end, chs. 4–5 present hymnic acclamations to the creator God, which are coupled with acclamations of the Lamb and his redemptive work for the new creation. At the other end, the text of 21:1–22:5 concludes the author's vision with a comprehensive portrayal of the new creation. Through an examination of these two passages, I shall discuss how in Revelation the author understands the eschatological world.

---

[30] Robert H. Mounce, *The Book of Revelation*, Rev. ed, The New International Commentary on the New Testament (Grand Rapids: Eerdmans, 1997), 15; G. K. Beale, *The Book of Revelation: A Commentary on the Greek Text*, The New International Greek Testament Commentary (Grand Rapids : Carlisle: Eerdmans ; Paternoster Press, 1999), 3.

[31] Richard Bauckham, *The Theology of the Book of Revelation*, New Testament Theology (Cambridge ; New York, NY: Cambridge University Press, 1993), 15; Beale, *The Book of Revelation*, 30–31; Grant R. Osborne, *Revelation*, Baker Exegetical Commentary on the New Testament (Grand Rapids: Baker Academic, 2002), 7. Bauckham does not mention the pressure from the Jewish world, but some verses such as 2:9 and 3:9 indicate the persecution by the Jews.

3.3.1 Christ's Redemption and the New Creation (chs. 4–5)

As scholars have noted, the vision of the heavenly court in chs. 4–5 functions as a major turning point providing the theological fulcrum for the entire book.[32] The heavenly liturgy in chs. 4–5 has a triadic structure:[33]

1. Two hymns to God (Rev 4:8 [A], 11 [B])
2. Two hymns to the Lamb (Rev 5:9b-10 [C], 12 [D])
3. The hymn of all creation to God and the Lamb (Rev 5:13 [E]).

The last hymn dedicated to both God and the Lamb forms the climax of the whole worship scene. The communities in heaven and on earth together offer their praise. Before this concluding hymn, a noticeable parallelism of hymns B and D appears:

> Worthy are You, our Lord and our God, to receive glory (δόξαν) and honor (τιμήν) and power (δύναμιν); for You created all things, and because of Your will they existed, and were created.
>
> Rev 4:11 NASB

> Worthy is the Lamb that was slain to receive power (δύναμιν) and riches and wisdom and might and honor (τιμήν) and glory (δόξαν) and blessing.
>
> Rev 5:12 NASB1995

They both highlight the worthiness of God and the Lamb to receive praises and the basis of that worthiness. Hymn B contains a special emphasis on God's act of creation that is the reason for praise, and hymn D praises Christ for the salvation he brought to the people of all nations through his death and resurrection.[34]

In connection with the parallelism between the hymns for God and Christ, G. K. Beale aptly argues that the "new song" in 5:9 dedicated to Christ for his redemptive work must include a reference to the new creation. He provides the following evidence

---

[32] George R. Beasley-Murray, ed., *The Book of Revelation*, Century Bible (London: Oliphants, 1974), 108; L. W. Hurtado, "Revelation 4–5 in the Light of Jewish Apocalyptic Analogies," *JSNT* 25 (1985): 110; Bauckham, *The Theology of the Book of Revelation*, 40. J. Roloff posits that chs. 4–5 function as both the point of departure and the point of reference. The actions of the seals, trumpets and bowls begin in the chapters, and these chapters contain numerous allusions that recur throughout the book. Jürgen Roloff and John E. Alsup, *The Revelation of John: A Continental Commentary*, 1st Fortress Press ed, A Continental Commentary (Minneapolis: Fortress Press, 1993), 68.

[33] Gottfried Schimanowski, "Connecting Heaven and Earth," in *Heavenly Realms and Earthly Realities in Late Antique Religions* (Cambridge ; New York: Cambridge University Press, 2004), 79.

[34] In fact, hymn D (along with C) does not explicitly mention Christ's resurrection, whereas the text speaks of Christ's blood by which he "purchased" the people. The inclusion of resurrection in the means of salvation can, however, be inferred. In the present passage, the Lamb is described as the one who has "overcome" (5:5), and the concept of overcoming clearly refers to Christ's resurrection and his sitting on the throne in the previous chapters (1:5; 3:21). In 5:6, the Lamb is standing in heaven and receives the book indicating that his resurrection from the dead. In chs. 1–3, moreover, the author highlights the significance of the resurrection of Christ, "the first-born of the dead," (1:5) for the sake of believers.

for this claim:[35] 1) The rhetorical flow of the passage suggests that the mention of God's work of creation in 4:11 relates to Christ's work, which means that Christ's work must have something to do with creation; 2) the hymn in 5:12-13 shows parallelism with the hymn in 4:11 about God's work of creation; 3) in six other occurrences of the term "new" in Revelation, the concept refers to the coming renewed creation (21:1-2, 5), to some elements of the new cosmos (3:12; 2:17 in the light of 3:12), and to the new song (14:3); 4) in some OT texts, the phrase "new song" is related to God's work of creation in connection with Israel's salvation (Ps. 33:1-22; 96:1-13; 149:1-9; Isa 42:5-13); 5) in later Jewish texts, there are some examples of the language of a "new song" being related to the coming new creation (*Num.Rab.* 15:11; *Midr. Tanh. Gen.* 1.32; *b. Árak.* 13b). In addition, the concept of new creation is already foreshadowed in 4:3. The three stones in this verse are an anticipation of the fuller list of precious stones in ch. 21, where God's glory is revealed throughout the new creation. The image of the rainbow encircling around God's throne alludes to the Noahic covenant (Gen. 9:12-17) and is a reminder of the idea of the renewed creation after the Flood.[36]

The "new song" in 5:9 clarifies what Christ's death and resurrection accomplished: Christ made people from all the nations into "a kingdom and priests." A natural question arises at this point. In what sense is this redemptive work related to the new creation? We can find hints in the first three chapters of Revelation. The letters for the seven churches describe how Christ leads believers to life and glory as the firstborn of the dead and faithful witness of the resurrection (1:5).[37] Christ gives them eternal life (2:7, 10, 11, 3:5) and makes them rulers over the earth (1:6; 2:26; 3:21) and priests of God (1:6). This bliss of life and glory is expressed in different terms in each letter for the seven churches. In the letter for the church in Ephesus, believers are promised "the tree of life which is in the Paradise of God" (2:7). Notably, the eschatological life for the

---

[35] G. K. Beale, *A New Testament Biblical Theology: The Unfolding of the Old Testament in the New* (Grand Rapids: Baker Academic, 2011), 347–48.

[36] Bauckham, *The Theology of the Book of Revelation*, 51; Heinz Giesen, *Die Offenbarung Des Johannes*, Regensburger Neues Testament (Regensburg: F. Pustet, 1997), 149; Osborne, *Revelation*, 227; Ian Boxall, *The Revelation of Saint John*, Black's New Testament Commentaries 18 (Peabody, MA; London ; New York: Hendrickson Publishers ; Continuum, 2006), 84.

[37] Concerning the question of how Jesus might be viewed as a faithful witness, some scholars focus on a particular part of Jesus' ministry. For example, D. Aune argues that the reference is to "the exalted Jesus who guarantees the truth of the revelation transmitted through John" (David Edward Aune, *Revelation 1–5*, Word Biblical Commentary, v. 52 (Dallas: Word Books, 1997), 255.). M. G. Reddish insists that three epithets in 1:5—"a faithful witness, the firstborn of the dead, and the ruler of the kings of the earth"—refer to a chronological depiction of Jesus' history. According to him, Jesus' role as witness refers to his role as "the bearer of God's revelation during his earthly ministry" (M. G. Reddish, "Followers of the Lamb : Role Models in the Book of Revelation," *PRSt* 40, no. 1 (2013): 67.). Yet, a close look at the context of the OT background of the present verse leads one to a different conclusion. Commentators see Ps. 88 (89): 27, 37 as the background of the three titles of Christ in Rev 1:5. The Psalm presents David as an "anointed" king whose seed will be established on his throne forever. In this context, God's faithfulness is manifested in what God has done for David, i.e., making him the king by defeating all his enemies. And this faithfulness of God to David plays a role as an assurance of his faithfulness to David's descendants. In light of this context, Christ's role as a witness most likely refers to Christ's resurrection from death and exaltation to the throne, which assure future believers that they too will be raised and glorified.

righteous after the resurrection is presented as the restoration of Adam and Eve's privilege in Eden. In the letter for the church in Philadelphia, we can observe a further link of this *Urzeit-Endzeit* idea to the sanctuary. Here, believers are promised that they will have "an open door" (3:8) and become "a pillar in the temple of God" so that "they will not go out from it anymore" (3:12). The idea that believers will be made pillars in the temple of God conveys the concept of "stability and permanence."[38] The author's concept of the life after resurrection is that of the righteous dwelling in God's temple. In ch. 22, a clear link appears between this dwelling of the righteous in God's temple and their vocation as high priests. Only the high priest, who wore God's name on his forehead, could enter the holy of holies once a year. Revelation describes that all people of God will be standing in God's presence like high priests with God's name "on their foreheads" (Rev 22:4).

In sum, the author envisions that believers, who will become priests of God and rulers of the earth, will stay in God's Temple and enjoy the tree of life. Such notions strongly imply the restoration of Adam's state and privileges as the priestly king in the first sanctuary, Eden.[39] Further, these ideas fill out the connection of Christ's redemption of believers with those of the new creation.

Revelation does not explicitly blame Adam as the person who brought death to humanity by means of his sin. The close link of eternal life with the tree of life and the notion that one is never expelled from God's presence, however, imply the idea. In 22:14-19, the author highlights the privilege of the righteous, that is, entering the holy city and participating in the fruit of the tree of life (22:14). On the other hand, he proclaims that the unrighteous, who will experience the second death (20:6), will be "outside" the holy city (22:15). The author links the second death with the images of expulsion from the holy city and exclusion from the right to eat from the tree of life. This alludes to the first death that Adam experienced after his expulsion from Eden and prohibition from approaching the tree of life. Accordingly, the portrayal of the eschatological redemption in chs. 2–5 implies the notion that the curse of Adam will be reversed at the end.

3.3.2 The New Jerusalem (21:1–22:5)

The passage 21:1–22:5 is the *locus classicus* of the idea of new creation in Revelation. The text contains the same *Urzeit-Endzeit* eschatology as in chs. 2–5 in terms of the restoration of the first sanctuary, Eden, in the New Jerusalem. In this section, I investigate the geographical relationship between the first and second worlds.

---

[38] Mounce, *The Book of Revelation*, 103. S. Smalley aptly points out a possible background to the use of the imagery of pillars in the temple. In Isa 22:23, Eliakim is informed that he will become "like a peg in a secure place ... a throne of honour to his ancestral house." While the prediction in the Isaiah text is that , in the end, the peg will give way, and the house will fall, the believers in the Philadelphia church are promised that they will become not pegs, but firm pillars in God's Temple. Stephen S. Smalley, *The Revelation to John: A Commentary on the Greek Text of the Apocalypse* (Downers Grove, IL: InterVarsity Press, 2005), 94.

[39] For the discussion of Eden as a sanctuary, see section 2.8.2.

In 21:1, the author sees "a new heaven and a new earth; for the first heaven and the first earth passed away, and there is no longer any sea."[40] A close look at Revelation's concept of the new heaven and earth provides keys to the fate of the first heaven and earth. The author envisions the new heaven and earth in 21:1, and from v. 2 he begins to describe the New Jerusalem. In v.1, there is no explicit explanation how the new heaven and earth appears, while the next verse describes the New Jerusalem as "coming down" (v. 2). Yet, the γάρ clause in v. 1bc provides some hints about the context of the new world's appearance: 1) the "first heaven and the first earth passed away"; 2) the sea was no more. In other words, the text indicates the idea that the new heaven and earth is nothing else than the destiny of the cosmos after passing away of the first world that contains the sea. The detailed structure of 21:1-5 implies the reference of the sea in the present passage.[41] The text is composed with a chiastic framework:[42]

A new (καινόν) heaven and earth v.1a
  B first heaven and earth have passed away (ἀπῆλθαν) v. 1b
    C the sea is no more (οὐκ ἔστιν ἔτι) v. 1c
      D the New Jerusalem descends v. 2
      D' God dwells among his people v. 3
    C' tear, death, mourning, crying or pain shall be no more (οὐκ ἔσται ἔτι) v. 4b
  B' first things have passed away (ἀπῆλθαν) v. 4c
A' God is making all things new (καινά) v. 5b

---

[40] On the one hand, some scholars argue that the verbs "passing" and "fleeing" are to be construed in a visionary sense: they state that heaven and earth have "left the scene" of John's vision (S. W. Pattemore, "How Green Is Your Bible? Ecology and the End of the World in Translation," *BT* 58, no. 2 (2007): 81; Gale Heide, "What Is New about the New Heaven and the New Earth? A Theology of Creation from Revelation 21 and 2 Peter 3," *JETS* 40, no. 1 (1997): 43). M. B. Stephens rightly points out that the verb "fleeing" in 20:11 is used with the epexegetical phrase, "no place was found for them (καὶ τόπος οὐχ εὑρέθη αὐτοῖς)." This particular phrase refers to the end of something in intertextual and intratextual parallels (Dan 2:35; Rev 12:8). It is highly unlikely that John is speaking merely of the disappearance of the heaven and earth from his vision. (Mark B. Stephens, *Annihilation or Renewal?: The Meaning and Function of New Creation in the Book of Revelation*, Wissenschaftliche Untersuchungen zum Neuen Testament. 2. Reihe 307 (Tübingen: Mohr Siebeck, 2011), 229. On the other hand, some scholars claim that 20:11 and 21:1 demonstrate cosmic annihilation (Martin Kiddle, *The Revelation of St. John*, 4th reprint of 1st edition published 1940, The Moffatt New Testament Commentary (London: Hodder and Stoughton, 1947), 401, 411; C. Deutsch, "Transformation of Symbols : The New Jerusalem in Rev 21:1-22:5," *ZNW* 78, no. 1 (1987): 115–16; Charles Homer Giblin, *The Book of Revelation: The Open Book of Prophecy* (Collegeville: Michael Glazier Inc, 1991), 192; Roloff and Alsup, *The Revelation of John*, 235; Osborne, *Revelation*, 729. Yet, as we have observed above (5:13), the emphasis on God the creator and the eschatological worship of all creatures implies some kind of continuation between the old and new worlds. And this undermines the validity of this notion of the annihilation of the first creation.

[41] In Revelation, the sea appears with various identifications: 1) a part of the old creation together with the earth (5:13; 7:1-3; 10:2); 2) the place of the dead (20:13); 3) the origin of evil (13:1; 15:2).

[42] J. van Ruiten, "The Intertextual Relationship between Isaiah 65,17-20 and Revelation 21,1-5b," *EstBíb* 51, no. 4 (1993): 475–77; David Edward Aune, *Revelation 17–22*, Word Biblical Commentary, v. 52C (Nashville: T. Nelson, 1998), 1114; Felise Tavo, *Woman, Mother, and Bride: An Exegetical Investigation into the "Ecclesial" Notions of the Apocalypse*, Biblical Tools and Studies, v. 3 (Leuven; Dudley: Peeters, 2007), 310.

In this structure, we can see that v. 1bc and v. 4bc are linked. The disappearance of the first heaven and earth with the sea most likely refers to the vanishing of pain, mourning, and death. The first heaven and earth will be freed from its bondage to chaos and evil that permeated the first world.[43] In accordance with the eschatological vision of the earlier chapters observed above, ch. 21 implies the transformation of the first world into something resembling the pre-fall creation that does not contain the curses caused by Adam's sin. After the description of the transformation of the first world, Revelation envisions the coming of the New Jerusalem in which God dwells with his people (D and D′, vv. 2-3).

Revelation 21:2 describes "the holy city, New Jerusalem, coming down out of heaven from God, made ready as a bride adorned for her husband" (cf. 21:9, "the bride, the wife of the Lamb"). In 19:7, the author calls the saints "the bride" of the Lamb who was adorned with fine linen, which refers to their "righteous acts." A link between the two passages, 19:7 and 21:2, 9 is substantiated by two bits of evidence. First, the marital imagery of the Lamb appears only in these two texts in the Book of Revelation.[44] Second, the author's addition of γυνή to νύμφη in 21:9 plausibly indicates his intention to connect this verse to γυνή of 19:7.[45] The verb ἑτοιμάζω that appears in both 19:7 and 21:2 supports the intended connection.[46] The relationship between the New Jerusalem and the Church is observed in some places in Revelation. The author indicates that the believers will become part of the heavenly city.[47] Revelation 3:12 states that the believers become permanent pillars in the temple. The vision of ch. 21 arguably presents a similar idea. There is no physical temple in the heavenly Jerusalem but "the Lord God almighty

---

[43] Tavo, *Woman, Mother, and Bride*, 307; M. Eugene Boring, *Revelation*, Interpretation, a Bible Commentary for Teaching and Preaching (Louisville: John Knox Press, 1989), 216–17; Beale, *The Book of Revelation*, 1041.

[44] Among nineteen occurrences of the noun γυνή, only in 19:7 and 21:9, is the noun used to refer to the bride of the Lamb. The mention of γυνή in 22:17 inevitably recalls 21:2. Tavo, *Woman, Mother, and Bride*, 317.

[45] Alfred Firmin Loisy and Friedrich Hügel, *L'Apocalypse de Jean* (Paris: Nourry, 1923), 372. Some scholars argue that the seemingly redundant noun γυνή was a later scribal addition (Wilhelm Bousset and Heinrich August Wilhelm Meyer, *Die Offenbarung Johannis*, 5. Auflage, Kritisch-Exegetischer Kommentar über das Neue Testament, Abt. 16 (Göttingen: Vandenhoeck und Ruprecht, 1896), 446; Robert Henry Charles, *A Critical and Exegetical Commentary on the Revelation of St. John: With Introduction, Notes, and Indices: Also the Greek Text and English Translation*, The International Critical Commentary (Edinburgh: T&T Clark, 1920), vol. 2, 156). Nevertheless, the phrase τὴν νύμφην τὴν γυναῖκα τοῦ ἀρνίου is supported by א, A, 025, 1006, 1611, 2030, 2377, et al. This seems to be the original. There are some different forms such as "the bride of the Lamb, the wife" (051), and "the wife, the bride of the Lamb" (94Byz), but not without the noun "wife." For more discussions, see Smalley, *The Revelation to John*, 529.

[46] Here, a possible interpretation of the link between the Church and the New Jerusalem is understanding the New Jerusalem as a symbol of a spiritually perfected Church (see Kiddle, *The Revelation of St. John*, 410–11; Philip Edgcumbe Hughes, *The Book of the Revelation: A Commentary* (Leicester: Grand Rapids: Inter-Varsity Press; Eerdmans, 1990), 222–23; J. Ramsey Michaels, *Revelation* (InterVarsity Press, 1997), 235; Mounce, *The Book of Revelation*, 382. Revelation, however, clearly describes the New Jerusalem as an entity distinct from the saints. It is the inheritance for the saints to "enter" (21:23-26).

[47] P. E. Hughes correctly states that "the saints are the vibrant components of the new Jerusalem in the same way as they are the living stones that form the spiritual temple of which the incarnate Son is himself the chief cornerstone (1 Pet 2:4ff). Hughes, *The Book of the Revelation*, 222–23.

is its temple and the Lamb" (21:22; cf. 7:15-17), which indicates the fulfillment of the prophecy in Ezek 37:25-27 that God's dwelling place would be with the people. The "twelve gates" of the wall upon which are inscribed "the twelve names of the twelve tribes of the sons of Israel" and the "twelve foundations" of the wall upon which were the "twelve names of the twelve apostles of the Lamb" refer not to a physical wall but to the people (21:12-14).[48]

A question is raised here: what exactly does it mean that the Church (the redeemed) comes down from the heaven as part of the heavenly temple? To answer this question, I will explore first the idea that the redeemed are spiritually in the heavenly Temple; second, the feature of the New Jerusalem as the restoration of the first sanctuary Eden; and, third, the issue of the equivalence of the New Jerusalem and the new heaven and earth. Some texts in Revelation indicate that the redeemed, who live on earth, are spiritually in the heavenly city. In 13:6, the author portrays the persecution of the redeemed by mentioning that the beast blasphemes God's name and "his dwelling, that is, those who dwell in heaven" for forty-two months.[49] Revelation 11:1-2 envisions that, for forty-two months, "the holy city" is trod under foot by the nations. In Revelation, the term, "the holy city," only appears referring to the heavenly Jerusalem (21:2, 10; 22:19).[50] The idea of the heavenly Jerusalem trodden by the nations plausibly reflects the unique stance of the redeemed who are in the heavenly city while they are living on earth. During the given period, the church will be persecuted by their enemies. Chapter 12 presents an interesting idea that this period of persecution is the time in the wilderness for God's people.[51] God's people, who are portrayed as a woman, flee from the dragon into the wilderness after giving birth to a son, and they are nourished there for one thousand two hundred and sixty days (12:6, 14). The text of 12:6 defines the wilderness where the woman fled into as "a place (τόπος) prepared (ἑτοιμάζω) by God." In Rev 2:5, the term τόπος refers to the place of the unrepentant believers, from which in the heavenly temple their lampstand is removed. The combination of ἑτοιμάζω and τόπος appears in the author 14:2-3 mentioning the place for the disciples in "the Father's house." In light of the parallel passages that present the same period of three and half years, such as 11:1-2 and 13:6, "the place" in 12:6 most likely refers to the

---

[48] Tavo, *Woman, Mother, and Bride*, 324; Beale, *The Book of Revelation*, 1070.
[49] J. C. Thomas, and F. D. Macchia points out that the phrase "those who dwell in heaven" in Rev 13:6 reflects the "continuity between these who dwell in heaven and the believing community in heaven and, by extension, the believing community upon the earth." John Christopher Thomas and Frank D. Macchia, *Revelation (THNTC)* (Grand Rapids: Eerdmans, 2016), 234.
[50] Beale, *The Book of Revelation*, 562. Beale helpfully highlights that "11:2 must refer to the initial form of the heavenly city, part of which is identified with believers living on earth" (p. 568).
[51] The period of forty-two months in 11:2 implies a connection to the time of Israel's wilderness wandering. Num 33:5-49 indicates that Israel's wilderness wandering includes forty-two encampments (Leon Morris, *Revelation: An Introduction and Commentary*, The Tyndale New Testament Commentaries 20 (Downers Grove, IL: IVP, 2007), 147). Their wilderness wandering might have been recognized as forty-two years, since two years passed before Israel received the punishment of remaining in the wilderness for forty years (Austin Farrer, *The Revelation of St. John the Divine: Commentary on The English Text* (Oxford: Clarendon Press, 1964), 132). The temporal designation of 42 months is also presented as 1260 days (11:3; 12:6) and "a time, times and half a time" (12:14), referring to the time for the triumph of evil before the end of the age and discipline for the believers under divine protection. Mounce, *The Book of Revelation*, 215.

heavenly Temple.[52] In sum, the author of Revelation envisions the redeemed as protected and nourished in the heavenly Temple, even though, until the end comes, they are still in danger of persecutions from Satan and the world where they live. And this particular status of the redeemed is compared with that of Israel who was in the wilderness.

Related to the meaning of the heavenly city coming down with its key part, the Church, G. K. Beale properly points out that the author of Revelation "seems to equate the 'new heaven and new earth' with the following description of the city and the temple."[53] Revelation describes the city which has "no need of the sun or the moon" and the procession of nations and kings in the city (21:23-24). The punishment of the unrighteous is described as their existence outside the city, whereas the reward for the righteous is their right to "enter by the gates into the city" (22:14-15). These passages indicate that the city is coextensive with the new world itself.

Regarding this equivalence of the New Jerusalem and the new world interpretation, two features of the New Jerusalem are worth investigating. First, Rev 21:9-27 describes the New Jerusalem as a cube overlaid with gold. Some scholars note that this specific feature recalls the holy of holies in the Solomonic temple which was cubic in shape and covered with gold (1 Kgs 6:20; 2 Chr 3:8-9).[54] Verse 22 strongly buttresses this connection: "And I saw no temple in it, for the Lord God, the Almighty, and the Lamb, are its temple." The portrayal of the New Jerusalem shows God's presence that fills the space and implies the identity of the eschatological city as the holy of holies. Secondly, in ch. 22, the New Jerusalem is described with some clear Edenic features. It contains the tree of life (Gen. 2:9; cf. Rev 2:7) and the river of the water of life (Gen. 2:10; cf. Ezek 47:1-12; Zech 14:8).[55] The statement that "there shall no longer be any curse" in v. 3 is inspiring as well. Although there is no further indication, in the present context of Edenic motifs, it is quite plausible that this statement echoes Gen. 3.[56] The fertility, healing and life that the tree of life brings forth in the eschatological city are, indeed, a reversal of the curse in Gen. 3 (i.e., infertility, pain, and death). In sum, New Jerusalem is presented as the holy of holies which has Edenic features. This portrayal of the eschatological city in chs. 21–22 well resonates with the salvation of believers observed in chs. 2–5. The New Jerusalem is the holy of holies where believers who are made priests and kings enter and enjoy the tree of life. Considering the perspective that this

---

[52] Beale, *The Book of Revelation*, 648. Beale provides some LXX, NT, and rabbinic texts that use the term τόπος referring to the Temple or sanctuary.

[53] Beale, *A New Testament Biblical Theology*, 616.

[54] Boring, *Revelation*, 215; Giblin, *The Book of Revelation*, 205; Smalley, *The Revelation to John*, 532; Stephens, *Annihilation or Renewal?*, 244; Beale, *A New Testament Biblical Theology*, 640.

[55] The definite article in v. 2 supports the connection of the tree with the tree of life in Eden. Aune, *Revelation 17–22*, 1178. For the discussion about whether John is depicting one tree or many trees in this text, see Beasley-Murray, *The Book of Revelation*, 331; Aune, *Revelation 17–22*, 1177; Osborne, *Revelation*, 770–71. M. B. Stephens aptly says that the expanded number of trees would be understood in light of "the escalated fulfillment" of Eden. Stephens, *Annihilation or Renewal?*, 251, n. 377.

[56] Pilchan Lee, "The New Jerusalem in the Book of Revelation: A Study of Revelation 21–22 in the Light of Its Background in Jewish Tradition" (1999), 292; Tze-Ming Quek, "The New Jerusalem as God's Palace-Temple: An Exegetical Study of the Eden-Temple and Escalation Motifs in Revelation 21:1-22:5" (Regent College, 2004), 193–96.

eschatological bliss is seen as the new creation, the New Jerusalem is nothing other than the restoration of Eden, the first sanctuary.

This identity of the New Jerusalem explains its encompassment of the new heaven and earth in relation to some Old Testament traditions.[57] Several scholars have noted that some OT texts considered Eden as a sanctuary.[58] Major observations are as follows. First, the Hebrew words indicating Adam's two tasks in the garden (עבד and שמר) are translated "cultivate" and "keep" but in other places, they are usually translated "serve" and "guard" and used to refer to priestly service in the temple (Num 3:7-8; 8:25-26; 18:5-6; 1 Chr 23:32; Ezek 44:14). Second, the Hebrew word for God's "walking back and forth" in the garden (Gen. 3:8) is used to describes God's presence in the tabernacle (Lev 26:12; Deut 23:14 (23:15 MT); 2 Sam 7:6-7; Ezek 28:14). Third, the temple of Israel contains Edenic images (the lampstand with the image of the "tree of life"; carved images of trees and flowers, in 1 Kg 6:18-35; 7:18-20). Fourth, several OT texts employ the description of sacred waters originating in and flowing from the temple in an allusion to Edenic rivers (Joel 3:18; Ezek 47:1-12).

It is noteworthy that Adam's priestly task in the first sanctuary, Eden, was not only to keep the sanctuary but also to expand the sanctuary over the whole world. This can be seen in God's commands to Adam in Gen. 1:28—namely the commands to multiply ("be fruitful," "multiply," and "fill the earth") and to subdue the earth ("subdue" the creation). These commands are passed on to Adam's descendants, whose identity and vocation are defined in terms of the creation mandate first given to Adam.[59] These commands are repeated in God's promise to Abraham and reaffirmed to the subsequent patriarchs. A number of scholars note the parallel between Abraham and Adam.[60] For example, N. T. Wright helpfully points out that what God promises to do for Abraham and the other patriarchs (i.e., the promises and blessings expressed to them on various occasions) echoes what God intended Adam to do (as reflected in God's commands to Adam). This is shown by the observation that at key moments of the patriarchs' narrative (e.g. Gen. 1:28; 12:2; 17:2; 22:16; 26:3; 26:24; 28:3; 35:11f; 47:27; 48:3f), the Genesis account makes the point that Abraham and his descendants inherit the role of Adam.[61] These

---

[57] All scholars agree that no other book of the NT is as "permeated by the OT" as is Revelation although they differ about the exact number of allusions or echoes. (Beale, *The Book of Revelation*, 75; Osborne, *Revelation*, 25.) This fact supports the exegetical approaches that understand the book of Revelation in light of OT backgrounds.

[58] Margaret Barker, *The Gate of Heaven: The History and Symbolism of the Temple in Jerusalem* (London: SPCK, 1991), 68; Donald W. Parry, *Temples of the Ancient World: Ritual and Symbolism* (Salt Lake City, UT: Deseret Book Company, 1994), 129–33; G. K. Beale, *The Temple and the Church's Mission: A Biblical Theology of the Dwelling Place of God*, New Studies in Biblical Theology 17 (Downers Grove, IL: InterVarsity Press, 2004), 66–75. For an overview of further works, see Richard M. Davidson, *Flame of Yahweh: Sexuality in the Old Testament* (Peabody, MA: Baker Academic, 2007), 47–48.

[59] W. J. Dumbrell insightfully states that "Gen. 12:1-3 is the rejoinder to the consequences of the fall and aims at the restoration of the purposes of God for the world to which Gen. 1–2 directed our attention." William J. Dumbrell, *Covenant and Creation: An Old Testament Covenantal Theology* (Exeter: Paternoster, 1993), 66.

[60] Beale, *A New Testament Biblical Theology*, 46–48; Stephen G. Dempster, *Dominion and Dynasty: A Biblical Theology of the Hebrew Bible*, New Studies in Biblical Theology 15 (Downers Grove, IL: InterVarsity Press, 2003), 55–92.

promises, given to the patriarchs, reach their initial but partial fulfillment in Exodus 1:7 according to which Israel became "fruitful" (פרה), "multiplied" (רבה), and "filled" (מלא) the land.[62] Some prophetic texts which contain the image of the expansion of the temple are of interest in connection with this Adamic vocation to fill the earth. They proclaim that the temple was to extend over all of Jerusalem (Isa 4:5-6; Jer 3:16-17; Zech 1:16–2:13), over all of the land of Israel (Ezek 37:26-28; Lev 26:10-13), and over the whole earth (Dan 2:34-35, 44-45).[63]

If Revelation retains the idea of the expansion of the first sanctuary Eden and Adam's task of achieving this, roots of which can be found in some OT traditions, its identification of the new heaven and earth with the New Jerusalem makes good sense. Eden, which was intended to be expanded by Adam the priest and his descendants, will have the fulfillment of its designed goal at the eschaton. The redeemed who comprise the heavenly city will come with the heavenly Jerusalem and fill the world accomplishing the task given to Adam (Gen. 1:27-28). The holy of holies will be expanded to the whole world as Eden was destined to be in the beginning.[64] If the new heaven and earth is considered as the culmination of Eden, then, we can understand the fate of the first heaven and earth in terms of transformation rather than annihilation. The transformed heaven and earth, from which evil, sin and death are removed, will unite with the coming heavenly Jerusalem. The evil permeating the old world is no longer to be found: "the first heaven and the first earth passed away" (21:1b). It is, indeed, "a new heaven and earth" (21:1a).

3.3.3 Summary

Revelation envisages the eschatological world in terms of the beginning of the world in Genesis. Its *Urzeit-Endzeit* eschatology appears in five points. First, Revelation 2–5 presents Christ's redemptive work as the renewal of creation that reverses the curses of Adam's sin, i.e. expulsion from Eden (no access to the tree of life) and death. Believers will enjoy eternal life as dwelling in God's temple/the Paradise of God. Second, the people of God will restore Adam's state and privileges as the priestly king in the first sanctuary. They will rule over the earth as a kingdom (1:6; 2:26) and will stand in God's presence as high priests (22:4). Third, Revelation 21 envisions the new heaven and earth that refers to the renewed first heaven and earth, from which the Adamic curses (i.e. pain and death) are banished. Fourth, the New Jerusalem reflects the first sanctuary

---

[61] N. T. Wright, *The Climax of the Covenant: Christ and the Law in Pauline Theology* (Edinburgh: T&T Clark, 1991), 21–22.
[62] P. Enns insists that creation language not only appears in this opening verse of Exodus but pervades the subsequent narratives: the story of Moses' birth (Exod 2:1-10; cf. Gen. 1 and Gen. 6–9); the parting of the Red Sea (Exod 14; cf. Gen. 1:9); and the tabernacle as a microcosm of creation. P. Enns, 'Exodus,' in *New Dictionary of Biblical Theology* (Leicester: IVP, 2000), 147-48.
[63] Beale, *A New Testament Biblical Theology*, 642.
[64] In this regard, it is an intriguing fact that the size of the New Jerusalem (i.e. covering an area of some 1500 square miles) was the approximate size of the known Hellenistic world at that time. Dieter Georgi, "Die Visionen vom Himmlischen Jerusalem in Apk 21 U 22," in *Kirche: Festschrift für Günther Bornkamm zum 75 Geburstag* (Tübingen, Germany: J C B Mohr, 1980), 367.

Eden with its features of Eden and the holy of holies. Fifth, through the coming of the New Jerusalem and its key component, the Church, and through its encompassing and uniting with the renewed earth, the redeemed will fulfill the Adamic vocation to expand the sanctuary of Eden.

3.4 Summary of Chapter 3

The three post-70 texts, 4 Ezra, 2 Baruch, and Revelation, begin to envision the coming of the heavenly world and hope for its union with the renewed creation. Despite this new perspective, the basic framework of the *Urzeit-Endzeit* eschatology, observed in some pre-70 texts, continues in those post-70 texts. It is true that the given post-70 texts do not claim, as pre-70 texts do, that Israel's historical inheritance, i.e. the promise land, is equated with the eschatological inheritance of the chosen people. 4 Ezra and 2 Baruch, however, envision the restoration of the promised land to Israel at the Messianic era, and 2 Baruch, in particular, indicates the concept of continuity of the messianic restoration during the eschatological world. The eternal inheritance that God promised to the Patriarchs will be finally obtained by the chosen people of God at the eschaton, and this refers to the restoration of what Adam lost due to his sin. Furthermore, all three texts, 4 Ezra, 2 Baruch, and Revelation, contain the idea of the renewal of creation at the eschaton.

In 4 Ezra and 2 Baruch, with their attention to the revelation of the heavenly realm, the emphasis on priesthood and the temple, which is observed in some pre-70 texts, is lessened. Revelation, however, shows keen interest in those while conceptualizing Eden and the eschatological inheritance as the sanctuary. Additionally, the particular themes, such as firstborn, Adam's glory, and superiority over angels that are observed in pre-70 *Urzeit-Endzeit* eschatology, appear in the three post-70 texts as well. In 4 Ezra, Israel's status as God's "firstborn" appears in Ezra's appeal to God asking why God's firstborn, Israel, do not possess the world, which God created for them, as their inheritance (4 Ezra 6:58). God replies that, after "the entrances of this world," which was made narrow for Adam's transgression, God's firstborn will possess the greater world as their inheritance. 4 Ezra also states about the "glory" of the chosen people since "Paradise is opened, and tree of life is planted" (4 Ezra 8:51-52). 2 Baruch, in ch. 51, describes how the righteous will be "exalted" and "glorified" when Paradise will be granted to them. In the current context, their glory and status is compared to that of the angels: "the excellence of the righteous will then be greater than that of the angels" (2 Bar 51:12). 2 Baruch mentions the discipline from God the father "who created me, who loved us from the beginning" (78:3-4) although there is no explicit mention of the concept of firstborn. In the next chapter, I highlight the two common elements of the eschatologies in the apocalyptic texts observed in chs. 2-3 and categorize the texts by their understandings of the venue of the element, God's presence. Through this process, I examine the way in which Hebrews' discussion aligns with variations that respective texts contain along with the common patterns of an *Urzeit-Endzeit* eschatology that they share.

4

A Comparison of the Eschatological Visions

4.1 Introduction

The eschatological visions of the apocalyptic texts, observed in the two previous chapters, reveal a common belief in God's faithfulness and sovereignty: God ultimately accomplishes his will toward the creation and the chosen people. They all either emphasize or imply that, at the eschaton, God will grant his people the eternal inheritance that he promised to their patriarchs, and that this eternal inheritance was or is akin to what God originally intended for Adam in Eden. In other words, the eschatology of *Urzeit-Endzeit* is observed to one degree or another in all these texts: what was intended for Adam in the beginning will ultimately be restored at the end. The texts that present this *Urzeit-Endzeit* eschatology attest two universal elements of the eschatological inheritance that restore the primordial bliss. The first element is the renewal of creation. The curses of Gen. 3 upon the creation will be revoked. At the eschaton, pain, illness, labor, death, and evil will disappear from the earth, and people will enjoy rest, fertility, and either a great expansion of their life span or immortality. Second, the presence of God among the people will be restored. As regards how this second element existed in Eden and how it will be restored in the eschaton, the apocalyptic texts are generally categorized into two groups divided by the time of the calamity of 70 CE. The pre-70 texts, such as the Book of the Watchers, Qumran texts, Jubilees, and *LAB*, assume that the Jerusalem Temple is the venue of God's presence among the people. Accordingly, they hope for the eternal inheritance on earth with a focus on the Jerusalem temple. Meanwhile, the post-70 texts, such as 4 Ezra, 2 Baruch, and Revelation, begin to regard the revealed heavenly realm as the way in which God dwells among the people. They envision the coming world as consisting of the union of the revealed heaven and the renewed earth. In the *Urzeit-Endzeit* eschatology of the two groups, each text's description of the eternal inheritance is closely linked to the respective understanding of the status of Eden and the bliss that Adam enjoyed in it, and also the concepts of Eden and the eternal inheritance influence their understanding of Israel's possession of the promised land.

4.2 The Pre-70 Eschatological Visions

Pre-70 texts, the Book of Watchers, Qumran texts, Jubilees, and *LAB* envision the earthly inheritance with the Jerusalem temple as the venue where a major aspect of the eschatological restoration, i.e. God's presence among the people, will be granted. They are divided into two sub-groups (Jubilees vs. the rest of the texts) according to how they portray the phase of the eschatological change.

4.2.1 Gradual Transformation of the Earth (Jubilees)

The expectation of a gradual transformation of the earth is uniquely observed in Jubilees among the apocalyptic texts mentioned above. Jubilees emphasizes that history follows divinely designed cycles of time that are not going to be altered by human or angelic sin. Adam's fall, in fact, brought forth consequences: the human lifespan became shorter; the earth was corrupted and deteriorated physically (e.g. infertility, diseases, and plagues). Yet, Jubilees presents the belief that, at the appointed time, the creation will gradually be renewed through Israel's golden age in the promised land.[1]

Jubilees makes a direct connection between Eden and the promised land by specifying the geographical location of Eden in the land of Canaan. In other words, Israel's possession of the land itself means the restoration of Eden (10:33; cf. 8:21). A deeper reasoning of this connection between Eden and the promised land appears in the status of Eden as God's sanctuary.[2] Jubilees indicates that Eden was the first sanctuary (3:8-14; 8:19) and defines the eschaton as the time when the eternal temple will be established on Mount Zion (1:29, see section 2.4.2). The eschatological temple of Jerusalem where God will dwell among the righteous and will rule the earth (1.17-18, 26-29) reflects the holy sanctuary of Eden on earth. As the descendants of the first priest Adam,[3] Israel will be privileged to enjoy God's presence and communion with the heavenly temple through their observation of the services and feasts in the eschatological temple. They will also lead the peaceful and abundant life that will be restored to the original length of 1000 years or more (Jub 23:27). In this Edenic life of Israel in the promised land, the whole earth will be sanctified from all sin and pollution throughout eternal generations; the creation will be gradually renewed (4:26). Thus, Israel will ultimately restore the full status and privilege of the priest Adam in the first sanctuary Eden.

Jubilees ch. 50 places the eschatological generation in parallel with the wilderness generation: after the last Jubilee of the divinely appointed time cycle, i.e. the present time of purification, the people of God will possess the promised inheritance just as Israel's first generation entered the promised land after the time in the wilderness. The

---

[1] D. S. Russell, *The Method & Message of Jewish Apocalyptic, 200 BC–AD 100* (London: SCM Press, 1964), 292; Gene L. Davenport, *The Eschatology of the Book of Jubilees*, Studia Post-Biblica, v. 20 (Leiden: Brill, 1971), 45, 78. Cf. Michel Testuz, *Les Idées Réligieuses Du Livre Des Jubilés* (Genève: Droz, 1960), 171–72.

[2] For a detailed discussion on this concept of Eden as the temple in Jubilees, see section 2.4.2. This concept is well recognized by scholars. Ruiten, *Primaeval History Interpreted*, 2000, 85–86. Cf. Baumgarten, "Purification after Childbirth and the Sacred Garden in 4Q265 and Jubilees."; Ego, "Heilige Zeit—heiliger Raum—heiliger Mensch," 211–15; C. T. R. Hayward, "The Figure of Adam in Pseudo-Philo's Biblical Antiquities," *JSJ* 23 (1992): 1–20.

[3] For Adam's identity as a priest and Israel's identity as "the nation of priests," see section 2.4.2.

parallelism can be reasonably understood in light of the concepts of Eden as a sanctuary and its restoration through the eschatological temple. In keeping with these concepts, Jubilees places the chosen people's eschatological inheritance in tandem with Israel's initial possession of the land—the fertility and peace of the land and God's presence in the temple of Jerusalem. The eschatological generation is the culmination of what the first generation could not properly maintain because of their transgressions.

4.2.2 The New Creation at the Day of Judgment (The Book of Watchers, Qumran Texts, and *LAB*)

Unlike Jubilees, the Book of Watchers, various Qumran texts, and *LAB* attest visions of divine intervention in the day of judgment, which marks a drastic division between the present world and the eschatological world.[4] 1 Enoch 1:3-9 vividly describes cataclysmic disasters and the following judgment when God will come to the earth in the day of judgment. During this time, the sinners and the rebellious angels will be thrown into eternal punishment (10:13-15), and injustice, defilement, and all sin will be removed from the earth (10:20). Certain Qumran texts (CD 1:6; 1QS 2:9; 4Q418 F69 ii; 1QH^a 11.10-12) and *LAB* (see *LAB* 3:10) similarly envision the sudden coming of the renewal of the creation at the day of judgment. Instead of Jubilees' extreme optimism and confidence about Judaism and the nation of Israel, the three texts above recognize sin and the consequent corruption of the creation as fundamental problems that cannot be completely dealt with by cultic sacrifices in the temple and learning the Torah, without supernatural intervention of God.

Nevertheless, the Book of Watchers, some Qumran texts, and *LAB*, basically share with Jubilees the same vision that God's presence, i.e. a core element of Eden, will be restored in the Jerusalem temple. The immediate connection between the Jerusalem temple and Eden that Jubilees makes through locating Eden in the land of Canaan does not appear in the other three pre-70 texts. The connection, however, appears in various ways in the three texts. The Book of Watchers indicates a transformation of the temple into an Edenic place by the transplanting of the Tree of Life in the eschatological Temple.[5] In this temple, the chosen people will regain God's presence. It will be as it was in Eden. The Damascus document states that the chosen community, who are now living the sanctified life that protects the temple from defilement, will ultimately serve God as the sons of Zadok and priests in the eschatological temple (CD 3:12–4:4; 6:11-14, see section 2.3.1). The text noticeably connects their priesthood in the temple with Adam's glory (3:20). 4QpPs37 envisions that the chosen community will possess

---

[4] For a similar understanding, see Marinus de Jonge, *Jewish Eschatology, Early Christian Christology and the Testaments of the Twelve Patriarchs: Collected Essays* (Brill, 1990), 28–47; Michael E. Fuller, *The Restoration of Israel: Israel's Re-Gathering and the Fate of the Nations in Early Jewish Literature and Luke-Acts* (Berlin; New York: W. de Gruyter, 2006), 148–62.

[5] Lee correctly points out that "the blessings and function" of Eden are transferred into the eschatological temple by the relocation of the tree of life from the Garden of Eden. Pilchan Lee, "The New Jerusalem in the Book of Revelation: A Study of Revelation 21-22 in the Light of Its Background in Jewish Tradition" (University of St. Andrews, 1999), 60.

"Adam's inheritance," which refers to "the high mountain of Israel," i.e. the temple on Zion (3.8-12, see section 2.3.2).[6]

In Pseudo-Philo, the temple's role as the location where God's presence of Eden is restored is not explicit but reasonably inferred. *LAB* states that "the place of sanctuary," which was originally granted to Adam and the previous generations of Israel, will be obtained by the chosen people at the eschaton (13:8-10; 19:10-13). In ch. 13, the account of paradise that Adam forfeited by his sin appears in the midst of the two sections of Israel's obedience, especially of the laws about the tabernacle, priests, and services in the sanctuary (13:1-7), and the consequent blessing on the earth (13:10). Along with Adam's status as the priest (ch.25-26), ch.13 suggests Adam's task in Eden is comparable to the ministries in the sanctuary, and this implies the parallelism between Israel's sanctuary and Eden (see section 2.5.3). God's presence in Eden, where Adam served God with the precious stones, will be restored to the chosen people in the eschatological temple.[7]

The concern for God's presence in the sanctuary led the authors to think that this restoration had occurred in Israel's temporal possession of the promised land. The Book of Watchers compares the eschatological bliss with the life that their "fathers lived in their days" (1 En 25:6). The eschatological bliss presented in 1 En 10:16–11:2, consisting of light, joy, peace, inheritance of the earth, wisdom, absence of plagues, extension of their lifespan, reflects what Israel could have enjoyed in the promised land (e.g. Deut 28, see section 2.2.1.2). *LAB* 3 and 19 parallel the restored creation after the Flood (ch. 3) and the promised land (ch. 19) with the eschatological dwelling place, which suggests that the author understands the eschatological world to be the completion of what Israel enjoyed in the promised land (see section 2.5.1). In 1QS 8, the sectarian author believes that the community, "the everlasting planting," is now in exile and will be brought back to their "homeland" at the appointed time. At that time, they will repossess the land forever. 4Q 171 F 1-2 I interprets Ps. 37 and applies it to the present community. The promised land will be returned to "the poor" who are enduring the time of "the wilderness" (F1-2 ii 5-8, see section 2.3.2). For these Qumran texts and *LAB*, which envision immortality at the eschaton, the full restoration will be possible only after the resurrection. The Book of Watchers requires the transplanting of the Tree of Life for the complete temple at the eschaton. These texts affirm, however, that other elements of Eden, God's presence in the temple and the following bliss (i.e. rest and

---

[6] There are some scholars who notice that the community of the Dead Sea Scrolls equates Eden with the temple. G. Martínez links 4Q265 to Jubilees 3 since both combine the Eden narrative with the laws of childbearing written in Lev 12:2-5 (Florentino García Martínez, "Man and Woman: Halakhah Based upon Eden in the Dead Sea Scrolls," in *Paradise Interpreted: Representations of Biblical Paradise in Judaism and Christianity* (Leiden ; Boston ; Köln: Brill, 1999), 109–14. G. Brooke also argues that 4Q265 and 4Q421 link together Eden and the Jerusalem temple (George J. Brooke, "Miqdash Adam, Eden and the Qumran Community," in *Gemeinde ohne Tempel / Community without Temple: zur Substituierung und Transformation des Jerusalemer Tempels und seines Kults im Alten Testament, antiken Judentum und frühen Christentum* (Tubingen: Mohr, 1999), 294–97).

[7] P. Church aptly points out that the story of the twelve stones indicates "continuity between the primeval sanctuary with its reference to Havilah, the source of the gold and precious stones of the Eden sanctuary (Gen. 2:11-12), the Ark of the Covenant and the temple, and the eschatological sanctuary that God will build." Philip Church, *Hebrews and the Temple: Attitudes to the Temple in Second Temple Judaism and in Hebrews* (Leiden: Brill, 2017), 240.

abundance) were indeed experienced by Israel in the promised land even if only to a limited extent. Thus, these texts present the notion that God's chosen people will ultimately obtain and permanently possess the eternal inheritance that the previous generations of Israel forfeited.

4.2.3 Summary

Among the pre-70 texts above, there is disagreement concerning whether the transformation of the creation will be gradual or sudden, whether the chosen people will have eternal life through the resurrection or a long life that would be equivalent to what was claimed to be the original human lifespan, or whether the location of the eternal inheritance is identified with that of Eden. They all, however, envision the restoration of God's presence in the temple, described in the language that recalls Eden. In the eschatological temple that is reminiscent of Eden, the priestly nation will serve God with sacrifices and feasts, and they will enjoy the reversal of Adam's curse, i.e. fertility, rest, and absence of pain and death in the renewed creation. In light of this understanding of the eternal inheritance, one can conclude that these pre-70 texts believe that Israel's possession of the promised land did not merely foreshadow the coming inheritance, but was the actual restoration of Edenic elements that Israel could have enjoyed, had they obeyed and not broken the covenant with God. Their contemporary readers are described as being in the time of "the wilderness," expecting to regain the restoration eternally at this time of eschaton.

4.3 Post-70 Eschatological Visions

The post-70 texts, 4 Ezra, 2 Baruch, and Revelation, share similar *Urzeit-Endzeit* eschatological hope with pre-70 texts, but an important shift in emphasis is notable. They envision the eschatological restoration in terms that recall what God originally intended for Adam. Nonetheless, the calamity of the destruction of the temple led them to focus on the heavenly realms, which the gentile nations cannot destroy. Instead of the earthly temple, they look to the revelation of the heavenly realm on earth as the venue of God's presence.[8] At the same time, their focus on the heavenly realm was not at the expense of hope for the renewal of creation and the vindication of their righteousness in the fabric of history. They present that the eternal inheritance of the chosen people is the coming world, which consists of the union of the renewed earth

---

[8] F. Murphy correctly points out that "the author of 2 B wanted to direct the attention of Israel away from the destruction of the Temple and Zion as a cause for mourning [and] towards the real place of God's dwelling, heaven...." (Frederick James Murphy, *The Structure and Meaning of Second Baruch*, Dissertation Series / Society of Biblical Literature, no. 78 (Atlanta: Scholars Press, 1985), 114–15. Similarly J. Mueller contrasts this relativization of the temple in 2 Baruch to the expectation of the Apocalypse of Abraham (James R. Mueller, "The Apocalypse of Abraham and the Destruction of the Second Jewish Temple," *SBLSP* 21 (1982): 348–49.). See also Michael Knowles, *Jeremiah in Matthew's Gospel: The Rejected Prophet Motif in Matthean Redaction* (London: Bloomsbury Publishing, 2015), 276.

and the revealed heavenly realm. Meanwhile, Jewish texts, 4 Ezra and 2 Baruch, and a Christian text, Revelation, show different understandings of the time and meaning of the Messiah's coming. And Revelation reevaluates the significance of the temple which was comparatively underestimated in 4 Ezra and 2 Baruch in their spotlight on the revelation of the heavenly realm.

4.3.1 The Coming World in 4 Ezra and 2 Baruch

As regards one of the key elements of the Eden-like restoration, God's presence among the people, 4 Ezra and 2 Baruch envisage the revelation of the heavenly realm. They describe how the heavenly realm, which was originally revealed to Adam, was shown to Abraham and Moses and how it will be ultimately disclosed to the chosen people at the eschaton. They also indicate that Israel will be vindicated on earth only when Zion is perfected with the revealed heavenly Zion in the messianic era. Here, the different understandings of the temple in 4 Ezra and 2 Baruch result in their distinctive concepts of the messianic era.

4.3.1.1 The Revelation of the Heavenly Paradise

2 Baruch 4:1-3 describes how the city of Zion and paradise that belong to the heavenly realms were originally "shown" to Adam and how, after Adam's sin, they were "taken away." Adam's transgression caused the world to become defiled and wicked. The result of his deeds was the removal of the manifestation of the heights of heaven.[9] 4 Ezra does not explicitly refer to the withdrawal of paradise. Nevertheless, the notions that the world's corruption resulted from Adam's sin and that the eschatological hope of the disclosure of the heavenly paradise will mean the restoration of the tree of life (7:36, 123; 8:52)[10] strongly suggest an understanding similar to that of 2 Baruch: the heavenly paradise forfeited through Adam's sin will be restored to the chosen people at the eschaton. In both 4 Ezra and 2 Baruch, Eden is implied to be a place where the creation on earth is united with the revealed heavenly realm, paradise.

4 Ezra and 2 Baruch describe how God showed Abraham and Moses this forfeited heavenly realms in his promise to give it to them as their inheritance. 4 Ezra describes how God made an "eternal covenant" with Abraham by showing him the end of the times instead of the promised land (4 Ezra 3:14). 2 Baruch 4:4 states that, in the night of the covenant making recorded in Gen. 15, God "showed" Abraham the heavenly city and paradise which Adam forfeited. In the same vein, 4 Ezra and 2 Baruch present the event of Sinai as the occasion when God revealed the heavenly realms to Moses and Israel. 4 Ezra portrays the event as God "bent down the heavens" (4 Ezra 3:18). The same expression of "bent the heavens" with regard to the revelation on Mount Sinai also appears in *LAB* 15:6. In both texts, this revelation involves an earthquake along with other cosmic phenomena. Interestingly, in *LAB*, the revelation on Sinai is

---

[9] Lied, *The Other Lands of Israel*, 256.
[10] For a discussion on paradise's location in the heavenly realm in 4 Ezra, see the section 3.2.1.3.

described in relation to Israel's Adamic identity. The exodus is presented in parallel with the creation account in Genesis (*LAB* 15:6; cf. 10:5-6). The Torah given on that occasion is called "the laws for creation" (*LAB* 15:6). The event of Sinai includes the scent off paradise and its influence on the creatures (32:8). This parallel account of Mount Sinai in *LAB* suggests that the Sinai account of 4 Ezra contains a similar link to Eden. 2 Baruch ch. 4 explicitly indicates that the heavenly city and paradise revealed to Moses on Mount Sinai (2 Bar 59:4) was what Adam had lost. Interestingly, 2 Baruch indicates that Moses' entrance into the heavenly world caused severe shaking of the heaven (59:3).[11]

4 Ezra and 2 Baruch envision that paradise, which was promised to the Patriarchs, will ultimately be "revealed" to the chosen people as their eternal habitation (4 Ezra 7:121-123; 2 Bar 51:11; 52:7). The heavenly paradise was combined with the creation in Eden in its first revelation to Adam. After taking it up into heaven due to Adam's transgression, God showed it to the Patriarchs in his promise to restore it to his chosen people. In the two texts, this heavenly realm is called "hidden," "invisible" (2 Bar 51:8), and "not yet awake" (4 Ezra 7:31) in the present time. God's promise will finally be fulfilled at the eschaton when this hidden paradise is disclosed as the eternal inheritance of the righteous. The union between the creation and the revealed heavenly realm of Eden will be restored at the eschaton.

4.3.1.2 *The Revelation of the Heavenly Zion*

4 Ezra and 2 Baruch agree that the rule of the Messiah will be accomplished in the revealed heavenly Zion. 4 Ezra states that "the city which now is not seen" will appear (7:26). The vision of a weeping woman in 4 Ezra 9–10 describes the true Zion in heaven as a mother and the cities built in Jerusalem as her sons. The text teaches its readers not to mourn for the destruction of the city of Jerusalem by presenting the vision that the true Zion will be "revealed" on earth (10:54). 2 Baruch chs. 4–5 similarly indicate that Moses' tabernacle and the city of Zion in the promised land are built according to the likeness of the heavenly Zion. Although 2 Baruch does not explicitly mention the appearance of the heavenly Zion in the messianic era, the text points out that the city Zion will be not only rebuilt but also "perfected into eternity" in the messianic era (2 Bar 32:4). Chapter 44 also states that the city of Zion at the present time is "nothing" but it "will be very great" (2 Bar 44:8). The description of the heavenly Zion's coming in the parallel text, 4 Ezra, and the concept of the revelation of the heavenly paradise in 2 Baruch strongly suggest that 2 Baruch envisions the coming of the heavenly Zion in the messianic era as 4 Ezra does.

For 4 Ezra and 2 Baruch, the Jerusalem temple itself cannot be a true venue of God's presence until it has been perfected by being joined with the revealed heavenly Zion. This understanding is related to their traumatic experience of the destruction of the temple and their subsequent conceptualization of the revealed heavenly realm as the

---

[11] A detailed discussion on this shaking language will follow in the exegesis of Heb. 12:18-29.

venue of God's presence among the people, which is untouchable by their enemies.[12] 2 Baruch 5:3 proclaims that their "enemy shall not destroy Zion and burn Jerusalem." 4 Ezra 10 similarly emphasizes that the true Zion cannot be humiliated. Accordingly, Israel's possession of the promised land and the Jerusalem temple is considered as foreshadowing the eschatological inheritance.[13] The emphasis on the temple, sacrifices, and priesthood in the pre-70 texts is significantly lessened in 4 Ezra and 2 Baruch in comparison with earlier texts.

Meanwhile, the author of 2 Baruch still sees a link between the temple and the creation, even though he does not think of it as the place of God's dwelling among the people. In ch.3, Baruch asks God about the consequences of the destruction of Jerusalem: "[f]or if you destroy your city and deliver up your country to those who hate us, ... will the universe return to its nature and the world go back to its original silence?" (3:5-7). This text implies that the destruction of Zion means "the total reversal of creation."[14] Similarly, in 10:9-12, Baruch laments over ruined Zion asking for the cosmic order to be disturbed. He calls for the earth to stop producing food, the heaven to withhold dew and rain, and the sun and the moon to retain their light. He even begs the vine to stop giving wine since the offering of the first fruits is not being offered in Zion.[15]

The active role of the messianic era in 2 Baruch as the time for the renewal of creation can be understood accordingly. In light of the connection between Zion and the creation, Baruch links Zion's renewal in the messianic era to the renewal of the creation in ch. 32. The text states, "the building of Zion will be shaken in order that it will be rebuilt" (32:2).[16] The Temple will be "uprooted" for some time, but ultimately, "it will be renewed in glory" and "it will be perfected into eternity" (32:3-5).[17] The passage portrays this time of perfection as that "when the Mighty One will renew his creation"

---

[12] The separate concepts of heavenly paradise and heavenly Zion in 4 Ezra and 2 Baruch can probably be understood as their effort to avoid the pre-70 concept of Eden as the first sanctuary and its automatic connection to the sanctuaries of Israel's history, which could be destroyed by Gentiles. According to them, God granted Adam the heavenly Zion along with paradise. In the messianic era, the Heavenly Zion will appear on the earth for Israel's vindication in the perfected Zion, but the coming world is established with the revealed paradise.

[13] It is to be highlighted that the function of the temple, i.e. foreshadowing the eschatological inheritance, in 4 Ezra and 2 Baruch is different from the Platonic understanding of its function as a metaphor, which has no substantial connection to the transcendent realm. 4 Ezra and 2 Baruch envision that the temple will be transformed into the eternal inheritance at the eschaton.

[14] Lied, *The Other Lands of Israel*, 47.

[15] Murphy points out some parallel biblical ideas (F. J. Murphy, "The Temple in the Syriac Apocalypse of Baruch," *JBL* 106, no. 4 (1987): 680). Haggai 1 presents the idea that the land has withheld its produce and the sky has withheld its dew because the people failed to rebuild the Temple. Zechariah 14:17 contains the same link: "And if any of the families of the earth do not go up to Jerusalem to worship the king, the Lord of hosts, there will be no rain upon them." Isaiah 60:19 presents the idea that God's presence is said to be superior to the light of the sun and moon. Zion's destruction is considered to have a cosmic influence.

[16] Similarly, 4 Ezra uses the image of "shaking" for the renewal/change of creation (6:14-16, 6:29; 7:75) instead of its extinction. See section 2.7.1.3.

[17] F. J. Murphy argues that this passages refers to a third Temple the value of which "would be as relative as was that of the First and Second Temples," and which "was of no ultimate significance to him (Baruch)." Murphy, "The Temple in the Syriac Apocalypse of Baruch," 682. Yet, in light of the significance of Zion that influences on the creation and the connection between the rebuilding of Zion in the messianic era and the renewal of the creation, this argument is critically undermined.

(32:6). In 2 Baruch, the perfected Zion in its union with the revealed heavenly Zion not only marks Israel's vindication in the present world, as 4 Ezra thinks, but also has a role in the transformation of the creation into its Edenic status (e.g. the reversal of curses and the provision of Edenic food). One essential element of the coming world, the renewal of creation to the Eden-like status, is presented as being accomplished under the Messiah's reign on earth. Therefore, 2 Baruch claims that the messianic era will continue forever merging into the coming world (cf. the vine analogy in chs.36-37, see section 3.2.2.3).

4.3.2 The Coming World in the Book of Revelation

Revelation basically shares with 4 Ezra and 2 Baruch the hope of the coming world: at the eschaton, the coming of the heavenly world will unite with the renewed creation. Revelation first envisages the new heaven and earth after the first heaven and earth with the sea will "pass away" (Rev 21:1). Pain, lamentation, and death will no longer exist in the new heaven and earth (21:4). Then, the text describes how the new Jerusalem and its essential part, the righteous, will come from heaven. The text's seamless flow from the vision of the new world to the following descriptions of the new Jerusalem most likely implies the new Jerusalem's encompassment of the renewed creation. The revealed heaven will unite with the renewed earth.

In comparison with the eschatology of 4 Ezra and 2 Baruch, Revelation's eschatology shows different understandings of two factors, the Messiah and the temple. First, concerning the time of the Messiah's coming and his role on the earth, the early Christian text, Revelation, presents a different view from that of 4 Ezra and 2 Baruch. The latter expect that, at the end of the last days, the Messiah will come to gather Israel and to restore the kingdom in the land of Canaan for Israel's vindication. Early Christian writers, including the author of Revelation, present the Messiah as coming at the beginning of the last days, instead of at the end, and ascending back to heaven, instead of establishing Israel's kingdom in the earthly promised land. While the renewal of the creation is expected to be accomplished when Christ returns at the end of the present age, his followers will first pass through the time of testing during the last days.

Second, Revelation distinctively presents a clear connection of the heavenly realm that will be revealed at the eschaton to the temple and priesthood. This heavenly realm is called "the holy city, new Jerusalem" (Rev 21:2, 10), and its description reflects the vision of the eschatological temple in the prophecy of Ezekiel (Ezek 47–48). The new Jerusalem is described as a golden cube, which recalls the holy of holies in the Solomonic Temple (1 Kgs 6:20; 2 Chr 3:8-9). In the same vein, Revelation proclaims that the righteous whom Christ saved through his death and resurrection will stay in the eschatological temple as "a kingdom and priests" (Rev 5:10). In sum, Revelation portrays the heavenly realm that will appear at the eschaton as the temple. The new Jerusalem is described with some clear Edenic features: the tree of life (Gen. 2:9; cf. Rev 2:7), the river of the water of life (Gen. 2:10; cf. Ezek 47:1-12; Zech 14:8), and the statement that "there shall no longer be any curse" (Rev 22:3). The believers' vocation as "a kingdom and priests" in the new Jerusalem reflects Adam who was a priestly king in the sanctuary Eden (see section 3.3.2).

This identification of Eden and the heavenly realm which will eschatologically appear as temples is most likely based on some level of revaluation of the sanctuaries/temples in Israel's history, which has been comparatively less appreciated in some post-70 texts. The highlight on the heavenly realms in 4 Ezra and 2 Baruch, which they claim as the only venue of God's dwelling among his people, is based on their notion of God. The portrait of God in 4 Ezra and 2 Baruch is consistent. As R. Kirschner points out, in the two texts, "God is never implicated in human failure. He is beyond reproach; his realm is transcendent and unknowable."[18] Therefore, with the experience of the catastrophe of 70, they conclude that the destructible temple cannot reflect God's dwelling on earth. Meanwhile, early Christians experienced Jesus who came to earth with flesh and blood and took on himself the sins of his people on the cross. For them, God who dwells in the mortal sanctuary, the destiny of which depends on his people's obedience, cannot have been an alien concept. Another factor that motivated them to refocus on the temple and the services in it was probably Jesus' sacrifice of himself, which recapitulated the sacrifice in the earthly sanctuary. Against this background, Christian texts, including Revelation, possibly revaluated the historical location of God's presence among his people.[19] A human high priest could enter God's presence on earth, i.e., the revealed model of the heavenly realm, with the blood of sacrifice, albeit only once a year. The holy of holies was the revelation of the heavenly realm on earth, and Israel's observation of cultic services in their sanctuaries was an actual venue of God's presence among the people. This venue of God's presence was not untouchable, as some post-70 texts claim it to be, but sustainable depending on Israel's obedience to the covenant.[20]

The coming world in Revelation's eschatology, which combines not only the renewed earth but also the heavenly world, cannot be identified with the bliss that Israel enjoyed in the promised land. This feature proves one of the primary differences when compared to pre-70 eschatology. Nevertheless, Revelation's recognition of the unique meaning of the temple, especially the holy of holies, allows it to see the parallelism between Israel in the promised land and God's people in the eschatological inheritance. For Revelation, God's presence in the temple and Israel's peaceful and fertile life in the promised land are akin to the primordial bliss of Adam in Eden even though it can be called only a partial one, compared with the eternal inheritance containing the heavenly Temple. Revelation accordingly describes the present time of the last days as the time

---

[18] Robert Kirschner, "Apocalyptic and Rabbinic Responses to the Destruction of 70," *HTR* 78, no. 1–2 (January 1985): 38. Kirschner makes an interesting comparison between portraits of God in 4 Ezra and 2 Baruch, which describe God's distance from the catastrophe and the Rabbinic text, Lamentations Rabbah, which describes God's weeping at the catastrophe.

[19] Some scholars, especially in their analysis of the fourth Gospel, point out a Christian response to the destruction of the temple: transferring the meaning of the temple to a symbol of the person of Jesus and the Christian community (Mary L. Coloe, *God Dwells with Us: Temple Symbolism in the Fourth Gospel* (Collegeville, MN: Liturgical Press, 2001), 7; M. Eugene Boring and Fred B. Craddock, *The People's New Testament Commentary* (Louisville, KY: Westminster John Knox Press, 2010), 296. However, at the same time, Christian perspective possibly enabled them to understand the temple in Israel's history in a fresh view.

[20] This manner of God's presence in the temple, in fact, corresponds well with the relationship between God and Adam in the first sanctuary, i.e. being dependent on Adam's obedience.

in the wilderness (Rev 12:6, 14, cf. 11:1-2; 13:6, see section 3.3.2). The Israel who are expecting the promised land and the believers who are expecting the culminated, eschatological, inheritance are placed in tandem in Revelation.

4.3.3 Summary of Post-70 Eschatologies

After experiencing the destruction of the temple, post-70 Jewish and Christian texts began to envision the revelation of the heavenly realm itself as the venue of God's presence among the people. Eden was a sphere in which Adam experienced the union of the creation and the revealed heavenly paradise, and even after Adam forfeited it due to his sin, God has consistently promised the world to come, which draws heavily on Edenic images and ideas. The creation will be renewed as all sins and consequential curses will disappear. The heavenly paradise which was taken away will be restored and united with the renewed creation. Although they differ as to whether the messianic restoration of the earth will continue to eternity, 4 Ezra and 2 Baruch basically share the same vision of Israel's vindication under the Messiah's rule over the earth. Meanwhile, a Christian text, Revelation, understands that God's promise of Israel's vindication will be fulfilled in the eternal inheritance at the eschaton. Additionally, Revelation re-appreciates the temple/sanctuary in Israel's history as the venue of God's presence albeit partial, in which Israel could enjoy Eden-like bliss. This bliss will be consummated at the eschaton.

4.4 Summary of Chapter 4

In both the pre-70 and post-70 texts observed above, the Eden-like status that will be restored at the eschaton includes two key elements. First, the curses in Gen. 3 will be reversed, and thus, creation will be renewed: the righteous will have a long/eternal life instead of death, and they will enjoy rest and fertility instead of pain and toil for food. Second, God's presence among his people will be restored. The texts that have been observed above had different ideas concerning how this second element is accomplished. Their views can be categorized into three groups. First, all pre-70 texts, dealt with above, highlight the temple, cultic services, and priesthoods as the way in which God dwells among them. They envision that Adam's privilege (i.e. dwelling in God's presence as his priest in Eden) will be eschatologically restored to the priestly nation, Israel, in the perfected Jerusalem temple. In this view, Israel's possession of the promised land and the Jerusalem Temple indicates a temporal restoration of the kind of state that existed in Eden, which will be completed forever at the eschaton. Second, the two post-70 texts, 4 Ezra and 2 Baruch, consider the revelation of the heavenly realm as the venue of God's presence among them. They understand the union of the creation with the revealed heavenly realm that existed in Eden will be restored at the eschaton in a culminated form. In these texts, there is less emphasis on the temple, priesthood and sacrifices, and Israel's possession of the promised land. Third, Revelation shares with 4 Ezra and 2 Baruch the understanding of the revelation of the heavenly realm as the venue of God's presence. Yet it recognizes the temple as the way through which God dwells among his people. In Revelation, the coming world is described as the heavenly temple united with the renewed earth, in particular drawing heavily on concepts of Eden which appear in terms of the temple and priesthood (Rev 2:7; 3:12; 22:1-4; see section 3.3.1). Accordingly, Revelation places the eschatological inheritance in tandem with the promised land and the temple as it states that the believers are passing through the time in the wilderness.

In the coming two chapters, I examine the way in which the *Urzeit-Endzeit* eschatological framework of some apocalyptic texts, which show some variants according to their relative context, corresponds to Hebrews' discussions, and how this framework sheds fresh light on understanding of Hebrews' message. Specifically, in ch. 5, I highlight that the re-appreciation of the meaning of the temple, similar to what we observed in Revelation provides a valuable background against which Hebrews understands the continuity between Israel's rest in the promised land and the eschatological rest. In ch. 6, I examine how Hebrews envisions the unshakable kingdom that consists of the renewed creation and the revealed heavenly realm in a way that is similar to the eschatological visions of some post-70 apocalyptic texts.

5

God's Rest in Heb. 3:7–4:11

In the previous chapter, I highlighted two common elements of *Urzeit-Endzeit* eschatologies in some apocalyptic texts. I also categorized these texts into three groups according to their understandings of the venue of God's presence and highlighted Revelation's re-appreciation of the meaning of the temple along with its hope of the revelation of the heavenly realms. In the present chapter, I examine how these eschatological elements shed light on Hebrews' discussion of God's rest in 3:7–4:11. In this passage, the author of Hebrews exhorts his readers to enter God's rest, first by drawing on the idea of Israel's entrance into the promised land from Ps. 95:7b-11, and then by interpreting this act of entering the promised land, in light of Gen. 2:2, as the act of participating in God's own Sabbath rest after creation. Scholars propose various ways of understanding the author's rationale behind the connection of Ps. 95 and Gen. 2:2. My argument is that if we understand the author's association of Ps. 95 with Gen. 2:2 in light of the eschatological vision of the relevant apocalyptic tradition, we can identify allusions to the primordial rest of Adam in Eden that in turn help to clarify the author's logic underlying Heb. 3:7–4:11.

More specifically, by citing Ps. 95, the author of Hebrews argues that God's rest, which Israel was previously intended to obtain through entering the promised land, will be eschatologically obtained by his readers. The supposition that the author assumes an *Urzeit-Endzeit* eschatological framework provides a comprehensive explanation—which other scholarly views cannot—of how the author, who retains the hope of the coming heavenly realm, can argue for organic continuity between the historical inheritance of the promised land and the eschatological inheritance. As demonstrated in the previous chapters, the *Urzeit-Endzeit* framework commonly entails two core elements of restoration (i.e. God's presence and the renewal of creation), and some contemporary interpretations of each element (i.e. the re-appreciation of the temple in Revelation and an interpretation of the restoration of the land as the renewed heart in 4 Ezra) facilitate the author's vision of the substantial continuity between the two inheritances; God's rest which Israel could have enjoyed in God's presence in the temple and with their obedient heart will be consummated at the eschaton. Since, as argued above, this eschatological view often refers to the fulfillment of God's creational intention for Adam in the given eschatological framework, it is likely that the author of Hebrews cites Gen. 2:2 to make a similar point: the eschatological rest that Jesus has now made available for God's people is God's own Sabbath rest originally intended for Adam to enjoy as part of God's creational intentions. In other words, the author of Hebrews, like several of his Jewish contemporaries, envisions the eschatological future of God's people in protological terms, as the restoration of God's creational intentions for Adam. My argument in the present chapter develops in the two following parts. First, I investigate a plausible interpretation of the citation of Gen. 2:2. Second, I examine whether this interpretation properly explains how the author understands Ps. 95:7b-11 and applies it to his readers in the present passage.

5.1 God's Rest in Gen. 2:2

Concerning the author's connecting the rest of Ps. 95 that the wilderness people failed to enter with Gen. 2:2, one major interpretive tendency is to deny the protological orientation of Gen. 2:2 and understand Gen. 2:2 and Ps. 95 in terms of the contrast between the eternal heavenly reality and its earthly type. According to this view, the author of Hebrews uses Ps. 95 to derive a lesson from the history of Israel and cites Gen. 2:2 in order to emphasize the heavenly nature of the true rest attainable apart from earthly existence. For these interpreters, the author of Hebrews reflects on Ps. 95:11 together with Gen. 2:2 primarily on the basis of the shared word "rest" (κατά παυσις) that both verses use. The proponents of this interpretation commonly identify this connection of the two verses as an example of a rabbinic interpretive principle, *gĕzērâ šāwâ*, which many conceive as an *ad hoc* way to link two verses simply on the basis of the presence of the same terms.[1]

For example, Attridge comments that the citation of Gen. 2:2 reflects the author's Greco-Jewish understanding (similar to that of Philo) that God's own divine Sabbath is the eternal heavenly reality God's people will enter at the eschaton.[2] Lane thinks that the primordial rest of God in Gen. 2:2 is cited in order to emphasize the divine rest, which "precedes and stands outside human history."[3] Thompson claims that Gen. 2:2 emphasizes the transcendence of God's rest.[4] Ellingworth does not appeal to *gĕzērâ šāwâ* by understanding it as an *ad hoc* interpretive method like those commentators above, but similarly argues that the citation of Gen. 2:2 aims to highlight the divine origin (from the primordial time) of the transcendent rest discussed in Hebrews. He thinks that Gen. 2:2 is cited to show that the place of rest for God's people existed before as well as after the time of the exodus.[5] These scholars all argue that the author of Hebrews employs the divine rest of Gen. 2:2 because he envisions the eternal rest for God's people which exists completely outside time and space.

---

[1] The *Tosefta* lists seven hermeneutical principals (seven "*middôt*") for the appropriation of Scripture with the practice of Hillel (Sanh. 7.11). Douglas J. Moo, *The Old Testament in the Gospel Passion Narratives* (Sheffield: Almond, 1983), 28; Alexander Samely, *Forms of Rabbinic Literature and Thought: An Introduction* (Oxford: Oxford University Press, 2007), 67.
[2] Attridge, *The Epistle to the Hebrews*, 128–29.
[3] Lane, *Hebrews 1–8*, 99.
[4] Thompson, *Hebrews*, 94.
[5] Paul Ellingworth, *The Epistle to the Hebrews: A Commentary on the Greek Text*, The New International Greek Testament Commentary (Grand Rapids; Carlisle [England]: Eerdmans; Paternoster Press, 1993), 248.

This way of understanding the function of the citation of Gen. 2:2, as suggesting the transcendental and ahistorical nature of the rest results in a failure to explore adequately connections between Gen. 2:2 and Ps. 95 on the level of Israel's history as narrated in the OT and assumed by many Second Temple authors. Hence, those who adhere to this view tend to see no other connection between Gen. 2:2 and Ps. 95 than the conceptual resonance created by the shared use of the term "rest."[6] As I argue, however, if the author of Hebrews indeed operates with an eschatological vision based on the history of Israel – already evidenced in parts of the OT itself and further developed by many Second Temple authors – he has in view more thematic-historical connections between Gen. 2:2 and Ps. 95 than can be explained by an improvised connection simply based on the presence of the same term.

Instead, there are some interpretations of certain scholars that closely parallel the one which I am positing. These scholars argue that the link between the rest of Ps. 95 and God's rest in Gen. 2:2 is derived from the author's understanding of eschatology in light of protology.[7] According to these scholars, the rest that the wilderness generation failed to attain because of their unbelief, and that the author now claims is open to the readers of Hebrews, is the rest originally intended for Adam. These interpreters posit that Hebrews operates with the whole of the history of Israel in mind, a history framed by its primordial past and its eschatological future. For these scholars, the author of Hebrews cites Ps. 95 and Gen. 2:2 according to this historical framework with particular reference to the eschatological restoration of the protological arrangement, rather than citing these verses to de-historicize the history of Israel and re-present the future of God's people in transcendental terms. These interpreters, however, tend not to offer further adequate supporting evidence from extra-biblical texts other than canonical evidence. Often, they do not explore in a substantive way the larger question of the influence of such an eschatological vision on the argument at this point in Hebrews. In the following section, I argue that, on the supposition that the author of Hebrews

---

[6] In fact, the presupposition that *gĕzērâ šāwâ* is an *ad hoc* way of rabbinic interpretation has been questioned by a number of scholars who do not believe that midrashic interpretation was an eisegesis of scripture. Although it cannot be denied that rabbinic interpretations of scripture were influenced by the political and historical contexts in which they were formed, scholars have reached a fresh understanding of midrash as a biblical exegesis which is often found to be far from arbitrary. René S Bloch, "Methodological Note for the Study of Rabbinic Literature," in *Approaches to Ancient Judaism: Theory and Practice* (Missoula: Scholars Press, 1978), 51–75; Géza Vermès, *Scripture and Tradition in Judaism: Haggadic Studies*, 2nd ed, Studia Post-Biblica, v. 4 (Leiden: Brill, 1973); Alexander Samely, *Rabbinic Interpretation of Scripture in the Mishnah* (Oxford: Oxford University Press, 2002), 84–184. For the history of scholarly discussions on this issue, see Susan E. Docherty, *The Use of the Old Testament in Hebrews: A Case Study In Early Jewish Bible Interpretation*, Wissenschaftliche Untersuchungen zum Neuen Testament. 2. Reihe 260 (Tübingen: Mohr Siebeck, 2009), 83–120. I accept the possibility that the author of Hebrews adopts the interpretive method, *gĕzērâ šāwâ*, but do not agree with its concept as an *ad hoc* method which does not consider historical or contextual contexts.

[7] A. Lincoln and G. K. Beale argue for this view in their discussion of the meaning of Sabbath observance that they believe Hebrews deals with. Andrew Lincoln, "Sabbath, Rest, and Eschatology in the New Testament," in *From Sabbath to Lord's Day: A Biblical, Historical and Theological Investigation* (Grand Rapids: Zondervan, 1982), 205–9; Gerhard von Rad, *The Problem of the Hexateuch, and Other Essays* (London; Edinburgh: Oliver & Boyd, 1966), 99–102; Beale, *A New Testament Biblical Theology*, 786–88.

envisages a similar eschatological hope as those of the apocalyptic texts previously observed, his concept of God's rest developed in his interpretation of Ps. 95 can be explained more congruously than in any other scholarly views.

5.2 God's Rest in Ps. 95

In his quotation of Ps. 95, the author of Hebrews highlights the historical failure of the Israelites to obtain the rest in the promised land, Canaan. The author, then, points out the continuity between what the wilderness people forfeited and what his intended readers will obtain as he interprets Ps. 95. He presents that the message of Ps. 95 was given to the people in David's time, so that they could obtain the rest that their ancestors failed to enter (4:6-7). He insists that the "today" of the psalm is addressed to his readers by the Holy Spirit (3:13), indicating that the rest still "remains open" for them (4:1). With regard to this application of Ps. 95, a main issue to be dealt with is how he understands Israel's entrance into the promised land in relation to the eschatological rest for his readers. I argue that the author states that God's rest, which an earlier generation of Israel forfeited, "remains" open for his readers not based on the supposition that Israel's entrance into the promised land functions as a type to foreshadow (or a metaphor to symbolize) the eschatological rest—as most scholars assume—but in his understanding that the wilderness people had a genuine opportunity to obtain God's rest historically through entering the promised land. Hebrews' readers are reminded that, as Israel's descendants, they stand overlooking the substantially same rest that their ancestors forfeited, and that God has announced a new opportunity to enter.[8] This argument develops in three steps. First, I point out that the majority views, which consider Israel's entrance into the promised land as a type or a metaphor, cannot coherently explain the author's arguments related to his citation of Ps. 95 (section 5.2.1). Second, I examine how the author articulates the genuine opportunity for the wilderness people historically to obtain God's rest and their failure (section 5.2.2). Third, I explore the possibility of understanding Hebrews' concept of God's rest as parallel with the eschatological visions in relevant apocalyptic texts (section 5.2.3).

5.2.1 Limitations of Some Scholarly Views

Many scholars assume that God's rest in the present passage refers to the transcendent rest in the heavenly world.[9] J. Thompson argues that the wilderness generation's rest in

---

[8] Thompson, *Hebrews*, 95.
[9] There have been many scholars who attempted to understand the present passage with the spatial dualism found in Gnostic and Platonic sources. Ernst Käsemann, *Das wandernde Gottesvolk: Eine Untersuchung zum Hebräerbrief*, 3rd ed. (Göttingen: Vandenhoeck & Ruprecht, 1959); Gerd Theissen, *Untersuchungen zum Hebräerbrief* (Gütersloh: Mohn, 1969); Spicq, *L'Epître aux Hebreux* (Paris: Gabalda, 1977); George W. MacRae, "Heavenly Temple and Eschatology in the Letter to the Hebrews," *Semeia* 12 (1978): 179–99; Wilfried Eisele, *Ein unerschütterliches Reich: Die mittelplatonische Umformung des Parusiegedankens im Hebräerbrief* (BZNW 116; Berlin and New York: Walter de Gruyter, 2003), 135–368.

Canaan is used in both Ps. 95 and Hebrews as a metaphor for "the transcendent reality that awaits those who have a heavenly calling."[10] According to Thompson, by quoting Gen. 2:2 in 4:4 the author of Hebrews clarifies that his focus is on the transcendent rest which belongs to God and explains "how the church centuries later could participate in and complete the ancient story by entering into God's rest." Psalm 95 prepared the way for this interpretation with the reference to "my rest."[11] Similarly, H. W. Attridge claims that the author of Hebrews presents the hope of "an eternal, heavenly reality." He understands that 4:8 presents the identity of God's rest as the transcendent rest, saying that "the rest to which the psalm referred cannot have been the rest that Joshua provided in the promised land."[12] According to Attridge, this concept of heavenly rest is the key to understand how the author of Hebrews thinks the promise given to the previous generations remains open for his readers.[13] In his view, the failure of the desert generation is used as the "exodus typology" to show the way of God's people to obtain a divine goal.[14]

In the present passage, the author of Hebrews highlights Israel's historical failure to enter the rest in the promised land and also points out the continuity between this failed rest of Israel and the eschatological rest for the believers. In the view of the scholars who argue for the heavenly rest, Israel's entrance into the earthly entity cannot share any substantial continuity with the eschatological rest. Accordingly, they explain the logic of the present passage by dividing Israel's rest into two: the rest in the land of Canaan as a metaphor and the rest in the heavenly world as the reality. In their view, Israel's failure to enter the promised land symbolizes their failure to enter the eschatological rest, and the author exhorts his readers to enter the remained transcendent rest that Israel forfeited. The dichotomy between the earthly entity, Canaan, and the heavenly world functions as the basic assumption, through which they explain the author's logic to connect Israel's failure to enter the promised land with the opportunity for the eschatological rest that remained open for his readers.[15]

A critical weakness of this view is the fact that it is hard to find the dichotomy between entrance into Canaan and entrance into the heavenly rest in the logic of the present passage. Certainly, the author of Hebrews thinks that God's proclamation of Ps. 95 ("you shall not enter my rest") is applied to the Israelites who could not enter the promised land as recorded in Num 14. This understanding is naturally drawn from the quoted passage of Ps. 95, as most scholars recognize. The rhetorical emphasis of the present Hebrews passage, however, is on the people who could not enter God's rest even though they entered the promised land.[16] The author does not equate Israel's failure to enter Canaan with their failure to enter God's rest. The explanation of the

---

[10] Thompson, *Hebrews*, 84.
[11] Ibid., 95.
[12] Attridge, *Hebrews*, 130.
[13] Ibid., 123.
[14] Ibid., 114.
[15] Although many scholars argue for the transcendent rest in the heavenly world and typological function of Israel's historical failure in the present passage, the dichotomy between Canaan and the heavenly world is not always explicitly argued. See Johnson, *Hebrews*, 94; Lane, *Hebrews 1–8*, 90, 99.
[16] I will discuss in detail about this logic of the passage in the following section, 5.2.2.

continuity between what Israel failed and what the believers will obtain based on the metaphorical or typological function of Israel's historical failure does not coordinate with the passage's logic.

The mistake of considering Israel's history as a type is found also in Hofius's argument. In examining Käsemann and replying to Theissen, O. Hofius points out "a deep cleft" between the concept of rest in the gnostic or Philonic dualism and God's rest in Hebrews with a detailed comparison of the features of the two different worlds.[17] He also presents Hebrews' discussion of rest as aligning with some strands of apocalyptic literature which describe the vision of a resting place prepared for the righteous. Nevertheless, Hofius's argument shows some weaknesses. On the basis of the lexical study of the noun מנוחה, he suggests that Hebrews presents a typological application of Ps. 95. The wilderness people's entrance into the land (מנוחה) functions as a type for the heavenly temple (מנוחה) which the worshippers will enter at the end of the age.[18] As J. Laansma properly criticizes, although rest in the land and the temple are closely related in the OT tradition and Jewish literature, it is hard to find a usage of the noun referring simultaneously to the land for Israel's resting place and the temple building for God's resting place.[19] Like other scholars mentioned above, Hofius makes the same mistake of considering Israel's rest in Canaan merely as a type for the rest in the heavenly temple. He misses the possibility that, in the eschatological vision of the coalescence of heaven and earth observed in some apocalyptic texts including Hebrews and Revelation, the rest in Canaan is considered as a partial fulfillment of the eschatological rest.[20]

Cockerill acknowledges the essential significance of the continuity of God's people in the argument of Heb. 3:7–4:11. The wilderness generation is "an example for but not a 'type' of Christian believers," and a key element of the continuity of the two groups is "the same rest" they are expecting.[21] Cockerill emphasizes that the rest which the wilderness people could not enter refers to "God's eternal rest promised to modern believers." According to him, the author could connect the wilderness people's entering the promised land with the eternal rest of God because the distinction between temporal and eternal blessing does not exist in the OT text.[22] Cockerill aptly recognizes the author's rhetorical logic, in which Israel's entrance into the promised land, which cannot be considered as a metaphor or a type. He does not, however, provide any explanation for how the author adopts the OT hopes (i.e. the eschatological culmination of Israel's promised land and temple) and integrates it with his eschatological hope in the present passage. The idea alone that the author merely accepts the OT concept, i.e.

---

[17] Otfried Hofius, *Katapausis: Die Vorstellung vom endzeitlichen Ruheort im Hebräerbrief*, WUNT 11 (Tübingen: Morh, 1970), 100–101.

[18] Ibid., 35–41.

[19] Jon Laansma, *'I will Give You Rest': The 'Rest' Motif in the New Testament with Special Reference to Matthew 11 and Hebrews 3–4*, WUNT 98 (Tübingen: Morh, 1997), 39.

[20] In the next chapter I will discuss Hebrews' eschatological vision which consists of the revealed heaven and the renewed earth.

[21] Cockerill, *The Epistle to the Hebrews*, 154. He aptly says that this same "rest" and the same kind of faith and obedience to obtain it poses "the sternest warning to contemporary believers. On the basis of this continuity the pastor urges his hearers to separate themselves from their predecessors by persevering in faithful obedience."

[22] Ibid., 194.

no distinction between temporal and eternal blessing, cannot explain the comment that the people led by Joshua entered the promised land but could not enter God's rest.

5.2.2 The Wilderness Generation's Entrance into God's Rest in Heb. 3:7-19

I have mentioned that the majority views, understanding that the author uses Israel's entrance into the promised land as a type or a metaphor for the eschatological rest, do not provide a coherent or compelling explanation of Hebrews' rhetorical logic. In this section, I investigate the way in which the author discusses the wilderness people's genuine opportunity to obtain God's rest historically and their failure to do so. Two observations are made. First, the author of Hebrews shares with the Psalmist the idea that the older generation who did not enter the promised land failed to enter God's rest. Second, he argues that even the younger generation who entered the promised land could not enter God's rest because of their disobedience. The author particularly highlights the significance of obedience for entering into God's rest through his rhetorical emphasis on the failure of the younger generation.

5.2.2.1 Failure of the Israelites in Num 14

In 3:12-19, the author supplements the quotation of Ps. 95 with references from Num 14, which records the account of Kadesh-Barnea where the Israelites were denied entrance into Canaan because of their disobedience.[23] The author reminds his readers that the Israelites determined to "turn away" (ἀφίστημι) from the land and return to Egypt (Num 14:31; Heb. 3:12).[24] He also alludes to an "evil" (πονηρός) people (Num 14:27; Heb. 3:12), God's oath, "As I live" (Num 14:21, 28; Heb. 3:12), "bodies fell in the wilderness" (Num 14:32-33; Heb. 3:17), and the highlighted period of "forty years" (Num 14:33; Heb. 3:17). These extensive allusions interwoven in the author's presentation of Israel's failure to obtain God's rest suggest that the author connects the proclamation of Ps. 95:11, "they shall not enter My rest," to the proclamation of Num 14:30, "you shall not come into the (promised) land." In other words, the author considers the wilderness people's failure to enter the promised land as their failure to enter God's rest.

In his emphasis on the wilderness people's disobedience and unbelief as the reasons for their failure, the author of Hebrews arguably presupposes the genuineness of Israel's opportunity to obtain God's rest on the occasion of the entrance into the promised land. He makes a clear rhetorical point from the failure of the wilderness people: they could not enter God's rest because of nothing else but their disobedience and unbelief

---

[23] Ellingworth notes that the author viewed the quotation of Ps. 95 in the light of Num 14, his attention being "concentrated on the past historical situation. Ellingworth, *The Epistle to the Hebrews*, 237. See also George Wesley Buchanan, ed., *To the Hebrews*, 1st ed., The Anchor Bible 36 (Garden City, NY: Doubleday, 1972), 66.; Attridge, *The Epistle to the Hebrews*, 114; Allen, *Hebrews*, 256; Cockerill, *The Epistle to the Hebrews*, 153. LXX Ps. 94, which used generalized terms, "rebellion" and "testing" instead of the specific names of Massah and Meribah, allowed the representative rebellion of the wilderness people in Num 14 to be considered.

[24] Lane, *Hebrews 1–8*, 88.

(3:19; 4:6). This is more obviously manifested in a comparison with the argument of ch. 11, which contains a long list of the people who could not receive the promise despite the fact that they had been "attested through faith" (11:39).[25] The "perfection" of the faithful people of previous generations could not take place without "us." That is to say, what prevented them from receiving "the heavenly city" (11:16) was the divine plan. Meanwhile, pivotal to the exhortation in Heb. 3–4 is the idea that what had prevented people from entering the rest was their own disobedience (3:18; 4:11) and "lack of faith" (3:19), not God's will or the divine time schedule. The rationale of Heb. 3–4 suggests the author's understanding that the wilderness people had a genuine chance to obtain God's rest historically through entering the promised land. Yet, they could not enter the promised land through their disobedience (Num 14:30), and accordingly, they could not enter God's rest.

5.2.2.2 Failure of the Israelites in Num 20

We have discussed the possibility that the author's rhetoric presumes Israel's genuine opportunity to enter God's rest by entering the promised land. Concurrently, in Heb. 4:8, the author states that Joshua did not give the wilderness people God's rest, implying that even the Israelites who did not die in the wilderness but entered the promised land could not enter God's rest.[26] In this section, through close exegesis of Heb. 3:7-14 and Heb. 3:15-19, I investigate how the author develops his understanding that the younger

---

[25] Some scholars combine the discussion of ch. 11 with the present passage and come to the conclusion that God's rest which the wilderness people failed to enter cannot be the bliss in Canaan. Regardless of their response to God's words, the wilderness people would not able to enter the rest until the eschaton. Matthew Thiessen, "Hebrews and the End of the Exodus," *Novum Testamentum* 49 (2007): 355; Thompson, *Hebrews*, 99. This view, however, misses the author's idiosyncratic emphasis in the present passage placed on Israel's disobedience, which is distinguished from the focus of ch. 11 on the divine plan for the final fulfillment. The different rhetorical emphases of chs. 3–4 and 11 are well explained with the understanding of the substantial continuity between Israel's rest in Canaan as partial fulfillment and the eschatological rest as the complete fulfillment. For a comparison of different rhetorical focuses of chs. 3–4 and 11, see Herold Weiss, "Sabbatismos in the Epistle to the Hebrews," *CBQ* 1996, 681.

[26] Some use this verse to support the idea that the author deals with the transcendent rest of heavenly world in chs 3–4. In their view, the verse indicates that Israel's rest in Canaan cannot be God's rest. For example, Ellingworth argues, following Andriessen-Lenglet (P. Andriessen, *De Brief Aan de Hebreeën* (Roermond, Netherlands: J. J. Romen & Zonen., 1971), 75), that the wilderness generation could not participate in God's rest not only because of their disobedience (4:6), but also because of "the defectiveness of the Canaanite rest, a foreshadowing of the true rest (4:8)." Ellingworth, *The Epistle to the Hebrews*, 256. Attridge argues that 4:8 indicates that "the rest to which the psalm referred cannot have been the rest that Joshua provided in the promised land." Attridge, *Hebrews*, 130. Nevertheless, these scholars read their view into the text without considering the logical flow of the context. In Heb. 4:6-7, the author says that the good news was proclaimed in the day of David because "those who formerly received the good news failed to enter because of disobedience." The comment that Joshua could not give the people rest in 4:8 is an extension of the same logic: "a sabbath rest" which still remains for God's people (v.9) because the people with Joshua failed to enter it through their disobedience (v.8). Joshua's people are placed in the list of the people who forfeited the opportunity to enter God's rest due to their disobedience and thus handed it over to the next generations. The context points out that the focus of 4:8 is not on the transcendent nature of the rest.

generation of the wilderness people who had been exempted from the proclamation of Num 14:30 also failed to enter God's rest.

5.2.2.2.1 Hebrews 3:7-14

The author noticeably makes two modifications of the original text of Ps. 95 in order to shed light on his fresh understanding of God's proclamation. First, in Heb. 3:10, he attaches the phrase τεσσεράκοντα ἔτη to the previous sentence of v. 9 by adding διό: "where your fathers tried me by testing me and saw my works for forty years. *Therefore*, I was angry with this generation." The forty years are presented not as the time during which God's wrath continued but as the time of Israel's observance of God's works.[27] Some rightly note that, in Heb. 3:9-10, the author interprets the time of forty years as being a time to show his grace and blessing, not as a time of God's wrath.[28] Second, he changes τῇ γενεᾷ ἐκείνῃ to τῇ γενεᾷ ταύτῃ. This modification is congruous with the suggested purpose of the added διό.[29]

With the modifications, the author extends the object of the proclamation from the older generation of the Kadesh incident in Num 14 to include the younger generation of the incident of Num 20, i.e. the other Kadesh rebellion after forty years of wilderness wandering.[30] There are some indications in the passage that the author is reflecting on Num 20 together with Num 14. First, Num 20:10-11 calls the rebellious Israelites the

---

[27] Hebrews 3:17 seems to indicate that the author considers the forty years in the wilderness as the time of God's judgment since it mentions God being angry for forty years. Concerning the relationship between the seemingly contradictory understandings of the time of wilderness in 3:9-10 and 3:17, Vanhoye suggests that διό is added only to make the Psalm more "symmetrical" (Albert Vanhoye, *Structure and Message of the Epistle to the Hebrews* (Rome: Editrice Pontificio Istituto Biblico, 1989), 93–94.), and Ellingworth argues that the author is simply using two different LXX manuscripts in vv. 9-10 and 17 (Ellingworth, *The Epistle to the Hebrews*, 232.). However, R. Ounsworth correctly points out that 3:17 rather shows that the change of reference at 3:10 is deliberate (Richard Joseph Ounsworth, *Joshua Typology in the New Testament*, Wissenschaftliche Untersuchungen Zum Neuen Testament 328 (Tübingen: Mohr Siebeck, 2012), 57, n.5). Emphasis on a certain part of the citation by a slight addition (e.g. 1:12) or a division (e.g. 2:13) is typical of the author's style. See also Docherty, *The Use of the Old Testament in Hebrews*, 186; Gert J. Steyn, *A Quest for the Assumed LXX Vorlage of the Explicit Quotations in Hebrews*, Forschungen zur Religion und Literatur des Alten und NeuenTestaments, Bd. 235 (Göttingen: Vandenhoeck & Ruprecht, 2011), 182. The contradiction between vv. 9-10 and v. 17 can be understood congruently in the author's reasoning, a point that we shall discuss later.

[28] Friedrich Schröger, *Der Verfasser des Hebräerbriefes als Schriftausleger*, Biblische Untersuchungen 4 (Regensburg: F. Pustet, 1968), 102–3; Lane, *Hebrews 1-8*, 86; P. E. Enns, "Creation and Re-Creation : Psalm 95 and Its Interpretation in Hebrews 3:1–4:13," *WTJ* 55, no. 2 (1993): 273–74; Simon Kistemaker, *The Psalm Citations in the Epistle to the Hebrews* (Eugene, OR: Wipf & Stock Publishers, 2010), 35–36, 85; M. Thiessen, "Hebrews 12.5-13, the Wilderness Period, and Israel's Discipline," *NTS* 55, no. 3 (2009): 366–79.

[29] Some scholars think this difference from LXX is due to the different *vorlage* since they do not see "any particular purpose in Hebrews' application of the psalm." Attridge, *The Epistle to the Hebrews*, 115. I neither reject the possibility of a different *vorlage* nor argue that every change is theologically significant. There are, for instance, two possibly "stylistic" variations, namely more common verb forms εἶπον and εἶδον in Hebrews rather than Hellenistic form εἶπα in the LXX. In light of the author's logic in the passage, however, it is conceivably a deliberate change.

[30] The Kadesh-Barnea incident recorded in Num 14 happened two years after the Exodus. As a result of this rebellion, the Israelites were told that they could not enter the promised land and would wander in the wilderness.

disobedient (οἱ ἀπειθεῖς) and shows Moses' own disobedience, as Heb. 3:18 highlights God's oath that "those who were disobedient (τοῖς ἀπειθήσασιν)" shall not enter his rest. Second, Num 20:12 demonstrates the reason that Moses and Aaron could not bring the people into the promised land, i.e. they did not believe (πιστεύω) in God, just as Heb. 3:19 clarifies that the reason for the Israelites' failure to enter God's rest is their unbelief (ἀπιστία). It is true that the two terms, "disobedience" and "unbelief," appear in descriptions of the rebellious people of Num 14 as well (οὐ πιστεύουσίν μοι in Num 14:11; ἀπειθοῦντες κυρίῳ in Num 14:43). Nevertheless, Num 14 does not present these two in particular as the reason for the failure to enter the promised land as Heb. 3:18-19 does.[31] Numbers 20 records another prominent incident of Israel's rebellion that happened in the same place, Kadesh, after the wilderness wandering. When they met the lack of water in Kadesh, the second generation's response showed surprising similarity with their parents' forty years ago: "Would that we had died" (ὄφελον ἀπεθάνομεν, Num 14:2; 20:3); "why is the Lord bringing us to fall" (εἰσάγει ἡμᾶς εἰς τὴν γῆν ταύτην πεσεῖν, Num 14:3; ἀνηγάγετε τὴν συναγωγὴν κυρίου εἰς τὴν ἔρημον ταύτην ἀποκτεῖναι 20:4). Their response in Num 20 proved that the forty years of wilderness wandering did not change them: They were as disobedient as their parent generation.

It is quite intriguing that Deuteronomy also presents a conflation of the two incidents of Num 14 and 20:

> He was angry and took an oath, saying, "Not one of these men, this evil generation, shall see the good land which I swore to give your fathers except Caleb the son of Jephunneh ... The Lord was angry with me also *on your account*, saying, 'Not even you shall enter there.'"
>
> Deut 1:35-37

In this recollection of Israel's wilderness wandering, the author of Deuteronomy points out that not only Moses but also the whole congregation suffered the consequence of Num 20; Moses was punished as their representative while they all deserved the consequence (cf. Ps. 106:32). In the same vein, Num 14 and 20 are conflated in Deut 32:51 as well, where the place in Num 20 is called "the waters of Meribah-Kadesh."[32] The author of Hebrews most likely claims with Ps. 95 that God's anger and his proclamation in Num 14:30 was extended to the younger generation of the wilderness people. They "had seen" God's work for forty years but still put "him to the test." *Therefore*, God was angry not only with "that" older generation who rebelled forty years before, but also with "*this* generation," and proclaimed that they should not enter God's rest.

The author's emphasis on the wilderness period, during which the Israelites were to be disciplined so that they could respond differently from their parents, corresponds

---

[31] In God's oath in Num 14 that they shall not enter the promised land, complaining against God (γογγύζω, 14:27, 29), despising the land (ἀφίστημι, 14:31), and faithlessness (πορνεία, 14:33) are presented as the reasons why they shall not enter the land.

[32] Ellingworth sheds light on Sir 6:21, presenting the possibility that δοκιμάζω in Heb. 3:9 refers to Moses' striking of the rock recorded in Num 20. Ellingworth, *The Epistle to the Hebrews*, 218.

to his following exhortation in 3:12-14. The other passages in Hebrews that use the terms κατέχω ("hold firm") and ὑπόστασις ("assurance") suggest that the readers are exhorted to "hold firm" God's "promise" (10:23) that they "hope" to obtain (3:6; 11:1). During this time of waiting for God's promise, they are expected to encourage each other so that they may not fall away from God and harden their hearts through "the deceitfulness (ἀπάτη) of sin" (3:13). The term ἀπάτη is used in other biblical texts to refer to the desire for the world's riches or pleasure (e.g. Mt 13:22/Mk 4:19; Eph 4:22; 2 Pet 2:13).[33] In other words, the author warns his readers lest they harden their hearts and test God through worldly desire like the wilderness generation in Num 20 who rebelled against God on account of the lack of water.[34]

5.2.2.2.2 Hebrews 3:15-19

In Heb. 3:15-19, the author provides a further explanation of his quotation of Ps. 95. He continues to warn against unbelief and disobedience by highlighting God's proclamation given to the disobedient people including even the younger generation who could avoid the death in the wilderness. A noteworthy exegetical point of the present passage is that the author draws attention to the objects of the incident mentioned in Ps. 95 with the repeated use of "who" (τίς). The three questions are connected by the conjunction δέ. It is true that the term δέ can be translated as "and," indicating continuation or further development of an idea. Some Greek lexicons, however, point out that this particle basically implies an "adversative, distinctive, disjunctive" relation of the two ideas connected by it.[35] This implied meaning is clearly to be observed in Hebrews. Of the 71 instances in Hebrews, over two-thirds are translated by major English Bible translations as "but" with a clear notion of contrast. Other than these cases, in the NRSV version, it is translated as "now" or "on the other hand," denoting a shift of topic five times (7:9; 8:1; 11:1; 12:11; 13:20). In two places, it is used in an idiom with καί, meaning "and also" (7:2; 9:21). In 7 instances, the term is translated as "and," but, except for one case (9:27), it indicates a shift of topic rather than continuation.[36] Regarding the usage of δέ, the particular structure of "τίς δέ" in 3:16-19 requires another explanation than that it is simply a development of further features of

---

[33] According to the BDAG, the term ἀπάτη has the meaning of "seduction which comes from pleasure."
[34] In Heb. 12:16, the author brings the example of Esau who "sold his birthright for a single meal" when warning his readers about the possibility of apostasy for the pleasures of this world. I will discuss this in the coming chapter (section 6.2).
[35] Thayer's Greek Lexicon, δέ. See also Louw-Nida Lexicon, BDAG.
[36] In 6:11, it is used in the case of shift of topic from praise for the readers' good works that God remembers (vv. 9-10) to the exhortation of perseverance (vv. 11-12). The NIV omits "and" in this verse. The term in 10:15 indicates a shift of topic from the perfection of those who are sanctified to the witness of this by the Holy Spirit. The NIV omits "and" in this verse. In 10:33, the term is translated as "whilst" in the KJV and as "at other times" in the NIV. The term in 11:6 indicates a shift of topic from Enoch's case to the general principle and exhortation. The NET interprets it as "now." In 11:36, the term connects different examples of persecuted believers. The NIV and NRS version omits "and" for the first of its two occurrences in the verse. The term in 12:6 is from the quotation. The only place where the term possibly denotes continuation is 9:27. The KJV, however, understands it as "but."

the same group of Num 14.[37] The three questions of "who" in 3:16-19, connected with the conjunctive particle δέ, arguably reflect three distinctive groups.

In Heb. 3:16, by using the conjunction ἀλλά and a rhetorical question with a negative οὐ, the author places a strong stress on πάντες: "For who provoked Him when they had heard? *Indeed*, did not *all* those who came out of Egypt led by Moses?"[38] After emphasizing the fact that the whole wilderness people provoked God, he shifts his focus to another group: "But with whom (τίσιν δὲ) was he angry forty years? Was it not with those who sinned, whose bodies perished in the wilderness?" The author's fresh understanding, which applies God's proclamation even to the younger generation who were exempted from the judgment in Num 14, possibly raised questions from his readers. I argue that 3:17 is the author's response to the anticipated questions: yes, those whose bodies fell in the wilderness in God's anger were the first generation of the wilderness people, who were over twenty years old at the incident of Kadesh-Barnea in Num 14; although all the people who came out of Egypt provoked God (3:16), in his grace God initially judged only the older generation (3:17). In 3:18, the author shifts to another group: "But to whom (τίσιν δὲ) did God swear that they would not enter his rest, if not to those who were disobedient?"[39] He emphasizes that even the younger generation spared by God's grace were eventually unable to enter God's rest because of their disobedience and unbelief. In v. 18, with regard to the question "to whom did he swear (ὀμνύω) that they should not enter His rest?" the reader recalls God's oath in Heb. 3:9-10, and the disobedient people (τοῖς ἀπειθήσασιν) who rebelled after observing God's works for 40 years most likely reminds the reader of the second Kadesh incident in Num 20. Verses 18-19 claim that, as a result of unbelief and disobedience even after the forty years, not only the generation over 20 years old who died in the wilderness but the whole congregation could not enter God's rest.[40]

In the author's understanding of God's rest as manifested in his interpretation of Ps. 95, two points are observed. First, he considers the proclamation of Num 14:30 that they shall not enter the promised land as the proclamation of their failure to obtain God's rest. The people who could not enter the promised land could not enter God's rest. Second, the author draws attention to the fact that the younger generation who entered the promised land could not enter God's rest because of their disobedience and unbelief. These two points of observation allow a reasonable inference: entering the promised land and obedience are the core elements that cannot be omitted if the wilderness people are to obtain God's rest. In his using of the historical example of Israel, the author's focus is not on their entrance into Canaan. He talks about God's rest, for which Israel's entrance into Canaan was an essential element. The passage's logical flow observed above clarifies that the earthly entity, Canaan, is not used as a type or metaphor for the heavenly reality, the eschatological rest, as many scholars assume.

---

[37] Allen prefers the translation "and," claiming that 3:18-19 continue the grounds for the exhortation of 3:15 (Allen, *Hebrews*, 268). Lane also claims v. 18 continues to reflect Num 14. Lane, *Hebrews 1-8*, 89. See also Attridge, *The Epistle to the Hebrews*, 120.
[38] The NAS version of Heb. 3:16. Emphasis is added.
[39] My translation.
[40] It is interesting that the whole congregation identifies itself with the older generation who died in the wilderness: "if only we had perished when our brothers perished before the Lord" (Num 20:3).

The author highlights the genuine opportunity of the wilderness people to enter God's rest through entering the promised land as an obedient people of God. This, now, raises a significant question. In what sense could the author claim that God's rest, which Israel could have obtained through entering the promised land, is in continuity with the eschatological rest? Particularly, considering that the author of Hebrews envisions the heavenly realm that God's people will inherit at the eschaton (Heb. 11:16; 12:22), the given continuity requires a further explanation.

5.2.3 The Parallel Visions of the Eschaton in Some Apocalyptic Texts

In the discussion of Heb. 3:7–4:11, I have highlighted the two elements of God's rest that the wilderness people could have entered, i.e. entering the promised land and obedience. In the present section, I argue that the author considers these two elements of God's rest of the wilderness people as substantially connected to two elements of an *Urzeit-Endzeit* eschatological framework, i.e. the restoration of God's presence and the renewal of creation. More specifically, some contemporary apocalyptic texts, such as Revelation which re-appreciates the meaning of the temple as the venue of God's presence and 4 Ezra which interprets the change of heart as a major part of the renewed creation, provide plausible backgrounds against which the author of Hebrews could claim the continuity between Israel's rest in the promised land and the eschatological rest in the coming world. That is to say, in Hebrews' understanding, Israel's rest in the promised land is in substantial continuity with the eschatological rest in light of the fact that they share the two core elements.

My argument in the present section develops in the two stages. First, I investigate the two significant factors of God's rest implied in the author's discussion in the present passage and its immediate context (section 5.2.3.1). Second, I present some relevant apocalyptic interpretations, Revelation and 4 Ezra, as plausible frameworks in which Hebrews could see that these elements of Israel's rest in the promised land are substantially homogeneous with the elements of the eschatological inheritance (section 5.2.3.2).

5.2.3.1 *The Two Core Elements of God's Rest in the Present Passage*

Along with his emphasis on obedience in order to enter into God's rest, the author considers God's presence as another factor of God's rest that he envisions in 3:7–4:11. In both the initial discussion in 3:6 and the last verse of the section of Heb. 3:1–4:14,[41]

---

[41] Lane notes the *inclusio* in the section of 3:1–4:14:

3:1 Therefore,... consider *Jesus* the apostle and *high priest* of our *confession* (ὁμολογία)
4:14 Therefore,...we have a great *high priest...Jesus...* let us hold firmly the *confession* (ὁμολογία)

(Lane, *Hebrews 1–8*, 68). For other views on Hebrews' argument which begins in 3:1 and extends to 4:14, see A. Descamps, "La Structure de l'Épitre Aux Hébreux," *Revue Diocésaine de Tournai* 9 (1954): 256; A. Vanhoye, *La Structure Littéraire de l'Épitre Aux Hébreux.* (Paris: Desclée de Brouwer, 1976), 38–39.

the author places the exhortation for his readers to "hold firm" (κατέχω) their "confession of hope (τὴν ὁμολογίαν τῆς ἐλπίδος ἀκλινῆ)."[42] The author's exhortations to "hold firm hope" throughout the text (4:14-16; 6:9-20; 10:19-25) and another passage (7:19), which includes the term "hope," show a shared element.[43] While they are holding firm to hope, the readers are encouraged to draw near to (προσέρχομαι, 4:16 and 10:22; ἐγγίζω, 7:19) or enter (εἰσέρχομαι, 6:19; εἴσοδος, 10:19) the holy place in the heavenly sanctuary (4:16; 6:19; 7:19; 10:22). The author states that they can do this in the "confidence" (παρρησία) which is generated by the fact that their high priest, Jesus, entered it first (4:15-16; 10:19; cf. 10:35). In summary, the "hope" that Hebrews envisions is closely connected to entering the holy place of the sanctuary; through the help of the high priest, Jesus, the people of God will enter into God's presence in the heavenly sanctuary.[44]

It is true that Heb. 3:6, in which the author encourages his readers to hold firmly to their "confidence" and "hope," does not explicitly mention the high priest or drawing near to the holy place. The consistent vision throughout those passages that contain the combination of the two terms, "hold firm" and "hope," however, indicates that the statement, i.e. we are the house of God, in 3:6 most likely denotes the idea of the sanctuary where God dwells among his people. The exhortation to hold firm to the hope at the beginning and end of section 3:1–4:14 implies that this focus on God's presence continues throughout the whole discussion of God's rest in Heb. 3-4.[45] Two other verses support this understanding. Hebrews 4:4 presents the people of God participating in God's own sabbath rest. In 3:12, the danger of failure to enter the rest is described as the possibility of falling away "from the living God."

The author's focus on God's presence in Heb. 3:1–4:14 and features of God's presence elucidated through the relevant passages with the notion of "hope"—especially its connection to the temple/sanctuary—suggest a clearer meaning of Israel's entering into the promised land. When the author indicates that the Israelites who could not enter the promised land could not enter God's rest, he is apparently referring to their

---

[42] The author uses κατέχω in 3:6 (also in 3:14; 10:23) and κρατέω in 4:14 (also in 6:18). H. Kosmala argues that κρατέω with the genitive is distinguished from κατέχω with the accusative, and it means "grasp," exhorting non-Christians (Essenes) to receive Christian confession (Hans Kosmala, Hebräer—Essener—Christen: Studien zur Vorgeschichte der frühchristlichen Verkündigung, Studia Post-Biblica, v. 1 (Leiden: Brill, 1959), 7, 39 n.5). Nevertheless, as Attridge correctly points out, it is clear that κρατέω with the genitive can mean "to hold or maintain" (e.g., Polybius Hist. 18.11.8; Josephus Bell. 1.5.3 § 112; 1.9.1 § 183; Ant. 6.6.3 § 116), and it is synonymous with κατέχω with the accusative. Attridge, The Epistle to the Hebrews, 139. See also Erich Grässer, Der Glaube Im Hebräerbrief (Marburg: Elwert, 1965), 32 n. 108. Concerning the concept of "confession of hope," the author uses three expressions, confession of hope (10:23), confession (4:14), and hope (6:18; 7:19), interchangeably in his exhortation to "hold firm." He adds some nouns to "hope" in the cases of 3:6 (καύχημα, "boast" of hope) and 6:11 (πληροφορία, "assurance" of hope).

[43] Hebrews does not mention "hope" elsewhere, only in these four passages.

[44] One thing to be stressed is that the author does not equates the heavenly sanctuary itself as the eschatological inheritance. The final form of the eschatological inheritance, the "unshakable kingdom," which will involve the revelation of the heavenly sanctuary, will be discussed in ch. 6.

[45] Attridge points out that the discussion of 3:7–4:11 is "essentially a complex bit of paraenesis which develops the implications of the conditional clause in 3:6b." Harold W. Attridge, "'Let Us Strive to Enter That Rest' the Logic of Hebrews 4:1-11," HTR 73, no. 1/2 (1980): 280.

failure to obtain God's presence that is located in the temple of the promised land. The author regards God's presence in the temple and the obedient heart of the people, who have been disciplined through the wilderness time, as indispensable elements of God's rest for the wilderness people. In that sense, the author plausibly consider that Israel's rest in the promised land and the eschatological rest, which share the essential elements of God's rest, are in substantial continuity.

5.2.3.2 *Parallelism with the Eschatological Visions of Apocalyptic Texts*

In the apocalyptic texts examined in the previous chapters, two essential elements of the eschatological inheritance are commonly observed. First, they envision the restoration of God's presence among his people. God's presence, which Adam enjoyed in Eden will be restored to his people at the eschaton. Second, they present the hope of the renewal of creation, which was cursed through Adam's sin. In the present section, I compare Hebrews' concept of God's rest with the eschatology in some apocalyptic texts in terms of each of these two elements and discuss the way in which the author sees the continuity between Israel's rest in the promised land and the eschatological rest.

5.2.3.2.1 *The Continuity Between Israel's Rest in the Promised Land and the Eschatological Rest in Light of God's Presence*

Although the continuity between the Israelites' promised inheritance and the eschatological inheritance is generally observed in eschatological visions of some apocalyptic texts, their understandings of Israel's possession of the land of Canaan in particular are divided into two different groups categorized by the year 70 CE. This difference most likely stems from their concepts of the venue of God's presence. Revelation's re-appreciation of the significance of the temple provides a valuable key to deducing the background against which the author of Hebrews sees again the continuity between Israel's rest in the land of Canaan and the eschatological inheritance of God's people.

The pre-70 texts such as the Book of the Watchers, some Qumran texts, Jubilees, and *LAB*, regard the Jerusalem temple as the venue of God's presence among the people and the promised land as their eternal inheritance. Accordingly, they believe that their ancestors who had God's presence in the Jerusalem temple enjoyed the eternal inheritance. They forfeited their inheritance through the exile, but it will be restored at the end when Israel will return to the land (see section 4.2). They also highlight the identity of God's people as priests. They will succeed to Adam's priesthood (CD 3:21–4:4; 4Q418 F 81 1-5; Jub 33:20) and eternally dwell in the sanctuary (1 En 61:12; cf. 1 En 25:6). Meanwhile, post-70 texts, 4 Ezra and 2 Baruch, present the idea that what God promised to their patriarchs was not the land of Canaan, but the coming world. This notion was arguably derived from their understanding of the venue of God's presence, i.e. the revealed heavenly realm. God's dwelling among his people and corresponding eschatological inheritance can be accomplished only through the heavenly realm that will be revealed to them at the eschaton. Accordingly, the meaning of Israel's possession of the land of Canaan and the Jerusalem temple is diminished.

These foreshadow what God's people will obtain at the eschaton. In the same vein, interests in sanctuary or priesthood are minimized in these post-70 texts (see section 4.3).

Like 4 Ezra and 2 Baruch, Revelation also envisions the revelation of the heavenly realm in relation to God's presence. Unlike the other two, however, Revelation describes the identity of the revealed heavenly realm as the holy of holies (see section 3.3.2). The revealed heavenly realm, which has the shape of a cube overlaid with gold, recalls the holy of holies in the Solomonic temple (1 Kgs 6:20; 2 Chr 3:8-9). God's presence that fills the space without the need of the temple in 21:22 supports this understanding. Revelation 1:6 indicates that God makes his chosen people a kingdom and a priesthood. In its description of how Christ leads his people to life and glory, individual believers are promised that they will be "a pillar in the temple of God" (3:12). Revelation also describes all the people of God standing in God's presence as high priests with God's name "on their foreheads" (22:4, see section 3.3.1).[46] In Revelation, there is no explicit mention of the relationship between Israel's historical inheritance and the eschatological inheritance. Nevertheless, Revelation's re-appreciation of the significance of the temple provides valuable hints of the background against which Hebrews' notion of continuity developed between the promised land and the eschatological inheritance.

Revelation's description of the chosen people's dwelling in God's presence in terms of temple and priesthood shows a noticeable parallelism with Hebrews' eschatological vision of God's presence among his people linked to their entrance into the holy place of the heavenly sanctuary. The identification of the heavenly realm as the temple most likely reflects some level of re-evaluation of the temples and sanctuaries in Israel's history, which has been comparatively little appreciated in some post-70 texts. Although temporary and limited, the earthly temple was the actual venue for God's presence among the people. Through entering the promised land and the establishment of the temple in it, the wilderness people could obtain God's presence, which is a key element of God's rest. In other words, with the other element that they need to fulfill, which we will discuss next, they had a genuine opportunity to obtain God's rest when they entered the promised land. In the same vein, the author could consider the proclamation that they shall not enter the promised land in Num 14 as the same proclamation that they shall not enter God's rest. The author does not share the pre-70 apocalyptic concept that the promised land on earth *per se* is the eternal inheritance, but in terms of core elements of the eschatological inheritance commonly shared among apocalyptic texts, he can argue for continuity between the wilderness people's inheritance that they could have obtained through entering the promised land and the eschatological inheritance for his readers. Both inheritances are in substantial continuity as sharing core elements. Hebrews' connection of Israel's rest in the promised land and the eschatological inheritance that includes the heavenly realm is reasonably explained in the framework of apocalyptic eschatology.

---

[46] Steve Motyer aptly points out the interest in the sanctuary (temple or tabernacle) in both the book of Revelation and Hebrews. Steve Motyer, "The Temple in Hebrews: Is It There?," in *Heaven on Earth* (Carlisle: Paternoster Press, 2004), 177.

5.2.3.2.2 Change of Heart and the Renewal of Creation

4 Ezra's understanding of the renewal of creation provides a noticeable parallelism to Hebrews' view of the obedient heart. Like other apocalyptic texts, 4 Ezra hopes for the restoration of the creation. It considers the change of heart as the major element of this restoration by interpreting the hope of the restoration of the land to its original fertility as the change of the human heart into a good land without the evil root (see section 3.2.1.3). Through this restoration, the human heart will be able to produce abundantly from the seed of God's word. A feature that distinguishes 4 Ezra's hope from that of Hebrews is the process of this change. The author of 4 Ezra believes that the removal of the evil root from the human heart will happen supernaturally and immediately in the new world (4 Ezra 6:22; 7:13). The righteous, who practice "self-control" and strive to bear fruit from the seed of God's word even with the evil root (4 Ezra 7:125; 9:32), will enjoy a renewed heart in the coming world; they will reap the fruit of immortality from the good land.

Meanwhile, the author of Hebrews believes that the change of heart, occurs in the present world through the process of sanctification with the help of the Messiah.[47] Hebrews' extensive interest in the obedient heart or the renewal of the heart appears not only in the present passage but throughout the book. The author indicates that the new covenant prophesied by Jeremiah is fulfilled through Christ: "I will put my Laws into their minds, and I will write them upon their hearts" (Jer 31:33; Heb. 8:10). The role of Christ as "the mediator of a better covenant" (Heb. 8:6) contains provision for forgiveness of sin (9:15) and intercession for the people of God (7:25). Another noteworthy role of Jesus related to the change of heart is a presentation of the example of the obedient Son for his brothers (Jesus as the "pioneer" in Heb. 2:10 and 12:2). Hebrews 5 describes Jesus' suffering as the process of learning obedience.[48] The way to fulfill the new covenant requires learning obedience through enduring suffering with faith in God, following the example of the pioneer, Jesus. Chapter 12 makes it clear that this process of learning obedience is the core feature of sonship. The text states that discipline from one's father is the sign of the person's legitimate sonship (12:5-10) and that this privilege can be obtained through the son's proper response, i.e. "trained" by

---

[47] 2 Baruch similarly states that the renewal process, i.e. the restoration of Edenic features of the creation, under the reign of the Messiah over the present world, will continue up to the eternal new world (e.g. 2 Bar 73:1-7; 36:1-37:1, see section 3.2.2.4).

[48] The way in which Jesus learned obedience through suffering is illuminated in Heb. 5:7. The fact that Jesus prayed to "the one who was able to save him from death," which strongly implies Jesus' prayer for deliverance from death. The phrase, "loud cries and tears," is a common expression that appears in prayers for deliverance (Philo, *Worse* 92-93; 2 Macc 11:6; 3 Macc 1:16; 5:7, 25). As a mortal being, he experienced fear in the face of his coming death; the Son was vulnerable to testing, showing human weakness (4:15). The author calls the attitude of the Son in the crisis "reverent submission (εὐλαβείας)," which denotes the fearful respect of God's sovereignty on the basis of faith. Even though the death that he was facing seemed to be far from the promise of the eternal status of God's son, he retained faith in the Father's good will toward him. Instead of yielding to human weakness, he chose to confess his weakness before the Father ("with loud cries and tears") and ask the Father to save him from death ("to the one who was able to save him"). He completed his obedience to God on the cross. This reverence allows God's will be done for him: he was exalted as the eternal son through resurrection (being crowned with glory and honor through suffering death in Heb. 2:9). His prayer for life was. in fact, "heard because of his reverence" (5:7).

the "sorrowful" suffering (12:11-13). The author argues that the sons of God need to be disciplined through enduring in faith the suffering that seems to be a far cry from what God promised so that they may accomplish the change of heart by following the example of the Son, i.e. learning obedience through suffering (Heb. 5:9).

The author further points out that this change of heart is essential for obtaining the eschatological inheritance. Hebrews 2:9 states that Christ was "crowned with glory and honor" because of or through (διά) "the suffering of death" (Heb. 2:9). The second sentence of the verse, i.e. this suffering of Christ was "for everyone" (ὑπὲρ παντός), indicates that this way of obtaining glory applies to all other sons. Hebrews 2:10 declares that making "perfect the author of their salvation (i.e. the Son) through suffering" in order to bring "many sons to glory" is the divine way, i.e. "fitting for God" (NASB). Regarding to the role of suffering observed above, i.e. the opportunity through which sons of God can learn obedience, it is implied that the author considers the changed, obedient, heart as a key element to obtain the eschatological inheritance for the people of God.

When we accept that the author of Hebrews shares the eschatological framework of some apocalyptic texts, particularly the understanding of the change of heart as a key element of the eschatological inheritance observed in 4 Ezra, his notion of God's rest is reasonably explained. The author could see that the time of wilderness was intended to function as the time for the Israelites to learn obedience and to become obedient sons.[49] The wilderness people had an opportunity to experience the change of heart which is a key element for entering God's rest. This, however, did not happen. In Heb. 3:9-10, he emphasizes that God's anger was stirred up against the people who had observed God's works for forty years but "always [went] astray in their heart." Through the identical response at the second incident of Meribah in Num 20 (cf. the first incident of Meribah in Exod 17:1-7), the Israelites proved that they were as rebellious as they had been at the beginning of the forty years. In 3:18-19, he emphasizes disobedience and unbelief as the reasons why the Israelites could not enter God's rest. In the focus on an obedient heart as

---

[49] E. Käsemann's monograph, *Das wandernde Gottesvolk*, brings insights into the interpretation of Hebrews by highlighting the importance of the theme of pilgrimage in Hebrews. He argues that the author draws an analogy between his readers and the Israelites in their forty years of wilderness wandering. The author of Hebrews not only appeals to his readers to join the journey to the "rest" but also challenges them to follow Christ "outside the camp" (13:13), a reference to the time in the wilderness. Ernst Käsemann, *The Wandering People of God: An Investigation of the Letter to the Hebrews* (Minneapolis: Augsburg Pub. House, 1984), 22–23; 67-90. Käsemann's proposal of a Gnostic background to Hebrews has been reasonably criticized as methodologically and historically flawed since the concepts which he presents as Gnostic features were widely developed in various contexts, and no Gnostic document can be dated prior to Hebrews. H. Schenke opines that Käsemann constructed his view of Gnosticism from a pastiche of sources, without careful distinctions (Hans-Martin Schenke, "Erwägungen zum Rätsel des Hebräerbriefes," in *Neues Testament und christliche Existenz: Festschrift für Herbert Braun zum 70sten Geburtstag am 4 Mai 1973* (Tübingen: JCB Mohr, 1973), 421–37.). In the same vein, O. Hofius shows that the categories of "rest" and "curtain" are not limited to Gnostic texts (Hofius, *Katapausis.*, 120). Other significant critics of Käsemann's approach include Floyd V. Filson, "The Epistle to the Hebrews," *JBR*, no. 1 (1954): 20–26; Irvin Wesley Batdorf, "Hebrews and Qumran: Old Methods and New Directions," in *Festschrift to Honor F Wilbur Gingrich: Lexicographer, Scholar, Teacher, and Committed Christian Layman* (Leiden: Brill, 1972), 16–35; L. D. Hurst, *The Epistle to the Hebrews: Its Background of Thought*, Monograph Series / Society for New Testament Studies 65 (Cambridge: Cambridge University Press, 1990), 67–75; Thompson, *The Beginnings of Christian Philosophy*, 2–5.

one of the core elements of God's rest, he can conclude that the whole congregation, including the younger generation who actually entered the promised land, could not enter God's rest. Furthermore, this shared element of the obedient heart, along with God's presence, becomes the basis on which the author can see the continuity between the inheritances of the wilderness people and his readers.

5.2.4 Summary

It is true that the continuity that the author of Hebrews sees between the wilderness people's rest in the promised land and the eschatological rest is different from how pre-70 apocalyptic texts understand these issues. Hebrews' vision of the eschatological inheritance which will involve the revealed heavenly realm, similar to that of some post-70 texts, cannot be equated with the hope of Israel's simple possession of the land. Nevertheless, the wilderness people's rest in the promised land shares the two core elements of the eschatological rest of God, i.e. God's presence in the sanctuary and the changed heart of the people. Although the rest for the wilderness people is not as perfect as the eschatological rest that God's people will enjoy through God's presence in the revealed heavenly sanctuary and the cleansed heart through the blood of Jesus, their rest could be said to stand in substantial continuity with the eschatological rest.[50] In the eschatological framework observed in some apocalyptic texts, Hebrews' logic of Heb. 3:7–4:11 is most reasonably explained. In this framework, the author could say that the rebellious people who could not enter the promised land failed to enter God's rest because the core elements were not satisfied. He could say that the second wilderness generation who turned out to be disobedient could not enter God's rest in spite of the fact that they entered the promised land because they lacked the element of obedient heart. He also could say that his readers are about to enter the same rest that those previous generations failed to enter because of their disobedience since the two cases of rest share the substantial elements.

5.3 Adam's Participation in God's Rest

I have argued above that the way in which Hebrews connects Israel's entrance into the promised land and the eschatological inheritance of God's people forms a noticeable

---

[50] D. Moffitt, following Janet Martin Soskice, helpfully presents two different models for linking a subject with its source. First, the homeomorphic model, to which analogy can belong, represents its subject by copying its source. A moving toy plane is a good example of this model. Moffitt points out that the use of words such as "fly," "land," and "pilot" is understood to correspond in "a fitting way to the model's source." In an analogical relationship, the subject can have some stretches of elements of the source in new ways, but both subject and source have the same "*res significata*." Second, the paramorphic model, which relates to metaphors, connects the subject and its source in the recognition of their fundamental difference. The statement that brain is a computer is an example of this model. David M. Moffitt, "Serving in the Tabernacle in Heaven: Sacred Space, Jesus's High-Priestly Sacrifice, and Hebrews' Analogical Theology," in *Hebrews in Contexts* (Leiden: Brill, 2016), 263–67. The rest for the wilderness people which shares the core elements of the eschatological one is in an analogical relationship not a metaphorical one.

parallelism with the basic framework of a *Urzeit-Endzeit* eschatology as found in some apocalyptic texts. After connecting the two inheritances through the citation of Ps. 95, the author of Hebrews interprets this rest as their participation in the Sabbath rest of God in Gen. 2:2. This link between Ps. 95 and Gen. 2:2 suggests that the author shares a *Urzeit-Endzeit* eschatology, not only the substantial connection between Israel's historical inheritance and the eschatological inheritance, but also their meaning as the restoration of what Adam enjoyed in Eden before his sin. The parallelism between the *Urzeit-Endzeit* eschatology of apocalypses and Hebrews' eschatology is supported by some key concepts which appear in certain patterns in both. In this section, the *Urzeit-Endzeit* eschatological visions of relevant apocalyptic texts are reviewed in three patterns. First, the sanctuary is presented as a major part of the chosen people's eschatological inheritance. They will enter (or dwell in) the eternal sanctuary at the eschaton. Second, this inheritance is described as the restoration of what Adam enjoyed in the first sanctuary Eden and presented in terms of their succession to Adam's combined identity as the son/firstborn of God and his priest. Third, their inheritance includes some common elements of restoration such as glory, longevity/immortality, the restoration of the creation (subjection of creation and the restoration of fertility), and rest, which Adam enjoyed in Eden.

In certain OT traditions, the idea of the temple as the chosen people's inheritance, i.e. their eternal inhabitant, is not explicitly presented, even though some tips of the concept exist.[51] The status of Israel as God's firstborn is supposed to validate the inheritance of land. A clear example of this link appears in Jer 3:19, which states that the chosen people's status as sons of God anticipates the inheritance of the land (cf. Deut 32:8).[52] The concept of the temple as their inheritance is, however, hard to deduce simply from the notion of Israel's sonship. Meanwhile, the identity of Israel as the priestly nation exists with the notions of their service in the eschatological temple (Isa 66:22) and their right to participate in the holy things that belong to God (Exod 24:11; cf. 19:6).[53] This status of Israel is also not enough to draw the idea that the temple is their inheritance or that the temple is their dwelling place. In the *Urzeit-Endzeit* framework of some apocalyptic texts, however, the combination of the two major identities of the chosen people of Israel in the OT is observed with a further developed claim: the people of God will inherit the temple as their eternal dwelling place with God. This conceptualization is arguably derived from the understanding that the eschatological inheritance is the restoration of Adam's privilege in Eden, which is described as the primordial sanctuary; in other words, they will enjoy the restoration of Adam's identity as the firstborn and the priest and his dwelling with God in the first sanctuary Eden. After examining these patterns in the relevant apocalyptic texts, I point out some noticeable parallels in the discussions of Hebrews.

---

[51] An individual's hope to dwell in the house of the Lord appears in some Psalms (Ps. 23:6; 27:4; 84:10).

[52] Moshe Weinfeld, *Normative and Sectarian Judaism in the Second Temple Period* (London; New York: T & T Clark, 2005), 215.

[53] Some OT texts indicate that the Levites do not inherit the land like other tribes, since "the Lord is their inheritance" (Deut 18:2; cf. 10:9; Josh 13:14; 18:7). For more detailed discussion of the Levitical Status, see Menahem Haran, *Temples and Temple-Service in Ancient Israel: An Inquiry Into Biblical Cult Phenomena and the Historical Setting of the Priestly School* (Warsaw: Eisenbrauns, 1985), 58 ff.

5.3.1 The Book of Watchers

Along with the vision of the eschatological restoration of the primordial blessings in Eden in 10:16–11:2 (see section 2.2.1.2), the author envisages the transplanting of the tree of life in the eschatological sanctuary in chs. 24–25. The transplanting of the essential element of Eden implies that the eschatological sanctuary signifies the restoration of Eden.[54] Also, the fact that the place to which the tree is transplanted is the sanctuary plausibly implies that Eden, where the tree was originally located, was a sacred place.[55] The text, accordingly, envisions that the righteous will "enter" the holy place and enjoy long life by eating from the tree of life as the first human beings could do in the first sanctuary, Eden. Possible allusions to Isaiah's depiction of the new Jerusalem in terms of Edenic language in the present passage corresponds well with this typology. The Book of Parables describes "the garden of the righteous" where the chosen people will eternally dwell. The context of the passages of "the garden" (1 En 60:23; 61:12) indicates that it refers to "the garden of Eden" (see section 2.2.2). Particularly in ch. 61, the concept of angels' measuring implies that the object of the measurement, i.e. the eternal inhabitant of the righteous, alludes to the New Jerusalem and the new temple in it (Zech 2:1-5; Ezek 40:1-4; Rev 21:10-21). In sum, the Book of Parables envisions that the righteous will dwell in "the garden of life," which restores the first sanctuary, Eden.

The Book of Watchers does not present explicit ideas of Israel's filial relationship with God or of Adam's inheritance as applying to the firstborn Israel, but the Book of Parables contains the concept of the righteous as God's children (62:12; cf. 60:8). The superior status of human beings to the angels in terms of God's favoritism that the Book of Watchers describes strongly suggests the possibility of a similar understanding of the chosen people's identity.[56] The chosen people's identity as priests are not explicitly stated in the two books, but it is well implied by the vision that they will "enter into" the holy place of the eschatological sanctuary (25:6; cf. 39:5, 61:12, see section 2.2.2). Moreover, in the context of 62:12 which calls the righteous as God's children, the author envisions that they will wear "the garments of glory." The contemporary visions in some Qumran texts of Adam's glory in relation to the chosen people's priestly identity suggest the possibility that this account also similarly implies Israel's priestly status. Although the combination of the two identities of the chosen people or its influence on the concept of the eschatological inheritance does not appear explicitly as in some other apocalyptic texts, all the elements observed in the books allow an underlying idea of the inheritance of the sanctuary for God's son and his priest, Israel, as a recapitulation of Adam's dwelling in Eden. The resolution of the problem of death is presented as a part of this restoration of the primordial privileges: the chosen people

---

[54] The identity of "the holy place" in the present passage as Jerusalem, which is the holy mountain, Zion, becomes explicit in ch. 26 (cf. Isa 27:13; 56:7; 57:13; 65:11; 66:20; Dan 9:16; Joel 2:1; 4:17; Obad 16; Zech 8:3).

[55] The status of Eden as a sacred place accords with the depiction of the high mountain, Eden, as the throne room for "the Holy and Great Lord of Glory, the Eternal King" (25:3).

[56] God's pitiless judgment on the rebellious angels (12:5; 21:10) is compared with his mercy towards human beings (27:4).

will obtain the restoration to a long life through the tree of life, which will be transplanted in the eschatological sanctuary (1 En 25:6; cf. 5:9). The restoration of Edenic blessings also includes that rest and fertility of the land from which all evil and defilement will be removed (1 En 10:16–11:2; cf. 1:3-9 and 5:7-10, see section 2.2.1.2.).

5.3.2 Qumran Texts

Some Qumran texts envision that the chosen people will inherit the eschatological temple. The author of the Damascus Document argues that the temple in the promised land, which was defiled through Israel's iniquities, will be cleansed at the end. Then, the chosen community which is living a sanctified life at the present time will serve God in the eschatological sanctuary as priests inheriting "Adam's glory," which implies their succession to Adam's priesthood (CD 3:19–4:2, see section 2.3.1). 4Q171 F1-2 iii.11 further explicitly states that the chosen community will obtain "the high mountain of Israel," i.e. the eschatological temple on Zion, as their eschatological inheritance. Here the author describes the eschatological vision in primordial terms by calling the eschatological inheritance "the inheritance of Adam." This inheritance alludes in many respects to Ezekiel's vision of the eschatological temple of Zion, which recalls Eden (Ezek 40-48; see section 2.3.2). The two Qumran texts that closely connected each other (see section 2.3.2) claim that the chosen people will inherit the eschatological sanctuary and take the role of priest in it as Adam did in Eden.

The glory of the chosen community in relation to their identity as Adamic priests appears in 4QInstruction as well ("holy of holies," 4Q418 F 81 5, see section 2.3.3). Particularly in this passage, the glory of the priestly people is connected to their identity as the "firstborn son" of God. In the context of the chosen community's rulership over "the inheritance" as God's "firstborn son," the author defines their identity as priests (4Q418 F 81 1-5). Furthermore, the text indicates that this rulership is linked to Adam's stewardship over Eden which requires work to keep and till it (להמשיל, 4Q423 F1-2ii).[57] In sum, 4QInstruction claims that Adam's task in Eden will be accomplished in the eschatological inheritance by the chosen people who are priests and sons of God. It implies that Adam's task as the firstborn and priest of God in the first sanctuary will be fulfilled by Israel in the eschatological sanctuary.[58] This connection between the two identities of the chosen people arguably exists in CD as well. In the account of the chosen people's priesthood of CD, the author alludes to God's promise in 1 Sam 2:33-35 to build

---

[57] Throughout 4QInstruction, the verb המשיל is used to refer to the elect status of the chosen group. "He has made you sit among the nobility, and he has *made you master* (המשילכה) of a glorious inheritance. Seek His will always" (4Q416 F 2 iii 11-12). In 4QInstruction, the obtaining of wisdom is attained by the study of revealed mysteries, and the people who have wisdom are required to behave in an ethical manner. The author of 4QInstruction compares this way of life in which the chosen people are to live with Adam's stewardship in Eden. Goff persuasively argues that 4Q423 F 1 3 reformulates God's curse on Adam as the result of the addressees' failure in their stewardship. This interpretation is supported by the usage of the concept in Hodayot. In this text, the teacher claims that he has the power to ruin the Garden (1QH 2:25-26). Goff, *4QInstruction*, 296.

[58] The filial relationship between God and his chosen people also appears in another Qumran text, 1QH 17.35-36. Here God's faithful care and discipline as the father is contrasted with the parenthood of human parents.

a faithful house in Israel (CD 3:19), which contains the concept of a filial relationship with God: "I will be a father to him and he will be a son to me."[59]

In CD, the situation of the rebellious wilderness generation is equated with that of the people who do not join those assembled by the Teacher in Damascus. Through the time of wilderness, the rebellious, who are thus unfit to serve as priests in the sanctuary, will be removed. The Damascus Document consider the present time as the wilderness period during which the people of Israel are prepared as holy people, God's priests, to obtain their inheritance, the eschatological sanctuary (similarly argued in 4Q171 F1-2ii.5-8, see section 2.3.2). This eschatological recovery is also described in terms of reversal of curses in Gen. 3, such as the removal of evil, the restoration of the fertility of the land (CD 10.7-9; 4Q171 F1-2 ii 10; cf. 4Q416 F1 13-15; 4Q417 F2 i 12), and the restoration of immortality (CD 3:20; cf. 4Q418 F69 7; 4Q521 2ii).

5.3.3 Jubilees

Jubilees describes Eden as the first sanctuary (Jub 8:19) and envisions its restoration through the eschatological sanctuary, by defining the new creation as the time when the eschatological sanctuary is established (Jub 1:27-29, see section 2.4.2). Jubilees also shows a direct connection of Israel's eschatological possession of the promised land and the temple in it to the restoration of Eden by highlighting the fact that it is located in the land (Jub 50:5; see section 2.4.1).[60] These texts implies that the temple is the core of the inheritance, even though the concept that Israel will dwell in the temple or the temple as their inheritance is not explicit as other texts. Meanwhile, Jubilees presents the identities of Israel as God's firstborn and his priest, particularly derived from Adam's identities. On the one hand, Jubilees 2:20-23 states that God chose "the seed of Jacob" as his firstborn son, and Jub 32:19 indicates that God will give the seed of Jacob "all of the land under heaven" as their inheritance, so that they will rule in all nations.[61] Israel's inheritance as the firstborn son of God recapitulates Adam's privilege: God gave Adam dominion over everything in creation (Jub 2:13-14). On the other hand, the author points out that Israel is the descendant of the first priest Adam. The text indicates that Adam is a priestly figure. He burns incense at the gate of the Garden of Eden (Jub 3:27). The burning of incense is one of the prerogatives of priests, and the incense is burned in front of the Holy of Holies (Exod 30:7-8, 34-38; Num 16:39-40; 2 Chron 26:16-20; *Ant* 9.223-27).[62] Another piece of evidence is the covering of his nakedness, which is a condition for offering: Adam offered to God "from the day when

---

[59] James R. Davila, *The Dead Sea Scrolls as Background to Postbiblical Judaism and Early Christianity: Papers from an International Conference at St. Andrews in 2001* (Brill, 2003), 128.
[60] On the one hand, he describes Eden as a sanctuary (Jub 3:12; 4:26; 8:19), and he defines the eschaton as the "time when the temple of the Old will be created on Mt. Zion" (Jub 1:29). As Enoch's offering incense in Eden foreshadows (4:26), the first sanctuary will be restored in the eschatological temple (see section 2.4.2).
[61] Jubilees also illuminates the fact that the angels stand outside the special relationship between God and Israel (Jub 15:32, for more discussion about Israel's superiority over angels, see section 2.4.4).
[62] Levison, *Portraits of Adam in Early Judaism*, 93–95; Ruiten, *Primaeval History Interpreted*, 88; Scott, *On Earth as in Heaven*, 56–57.

he covered his shame" (Jub 3:27; cf. Exod 20:26; 28:42).⁶³ The mention that Adam is clothed in "coats of skins" (כתנות עור cf. Gen., 3:21) alludes to Exod 20:26 stating that the priests are clothed, among other things, in "coats" (כתנות) (see section 2.4.2). The text clearly places Israel in the genealogical line starting from Adam (19:24) and accordingly highlights that they are a holy, sanctified, nation (2:23, 28).

In Jubilees, the dynamics of the combined identities of Israel as God's firstborn and his priests appear in their possession of the inheritance. Their possession of the promise land as God's firstborn requires moral and cultic purity, and their purification is compared with Adam's purification before his entrance into Eden. In Jub 30:13, Israel is forbidden from marrying gentile people because it defiles the sanctuary (v.15). Israel is to be separated as "holy to the Lord" (v. 8); in other word, they are called as priestly people who need to live sanctified life so that they may keep the temple in their land from defilement. The author describes the time of wilderness as the time during which the chosen people are prepared as holy and obedient people of God by learning the commands of the Lord and purified from all their sins and defilements (Jub 50:4-5).⁶⁴ Along with the identical location of the promised land and Eden, the time in the wilderness before Israel's entrance into the promised land forms a parallelism with the time for purification of Adam and Eve before they entered Eden (section 2.4.2). In sum, the requirement that God's sons are to be purified prior to obtaining their inheritance is linked to their identity as God's priests and to the feature of the inheritance which includes the sanctuary, God's dwelling place. And Israel who will dwell in the holy land which contains the temple as God's sons and his priests will restore Adam's status in the first sanctuary Eden. Jubilees envisions that in the eschatological regaining of Eden, people will regain the original life span which began to shorten through Adam's sin (Jub 23:37), and they will enjoy rest without Satan or evil ones (Jub 23:27-30) as part of the restoration.

5.3.4 Pseudo-Philo

Pseudo-Philo describes how God shows Israel "the ways of paradise (*paradysus*)" which both Adam and the people of Noah failed to keep. In 19:10-13, "the place of sanctification" that God showed Moses as his immortal dwelling place (v. 13) most likely refers to the paradise (*paradysus*) in the vision showed to Moses (v. 10).⁶⁵ This understanding is supported by the description of paradise in 19:10 as one of the places that "are prohibited for the human race because they have sinned against me" which is congruent with the feature of the eschatological inheritance as "the place of

---

[63] The nakedness of males is considered as an offence to the sacred. See Ruiten, *Primaeval History Interpreted*, 106–7; Ego, "Heilige Zeit—Heiliger Raum—Heiliger Mensch," 215–16; Satlow, "Jewish Constructions of Nakedness in Late Antiquity."
[64] In this sense, it is interesting that, after the cultic and moral purification, the filial relationship is proclaimed as secured: "And they will all be called 'sons of the living God.' And every angel and spirit will know and acknowledge that they are my sons and I am their father in uprightness and righteousness" (1:25). The author adds that "And Zion and Jerusalem will be holy" (1:28).
[65] Jacobson, *Commentary on Pseudo-Philo's " Liber Antiquitatum Biblicarum", with Latin Text and English Translation*, vol. 2, 645. Bockmuehl and Stroumsa, *Paradise in Antiquity*, 52.

sanctification" in 19:13. The author of *LAB* envisions that the first sanctuary, Eden, which was forfeited by Adam's sin will be ultimately restored to the people of God as their eternal dwelling place.[66]

Pseudo-Philo presents the two identities of Israel (sons of God and his priests) originated from Adam, even though, like the Book of Watchers and the Book of Parables, there is no clear indication of the relationship between Israel's two identities or its connection to the eschatological inheritance. Chapter 32 presents a vivid picture of Israel's birth from the rib of Adam (*LAB* 32:15, for some Targumic parallels, see section 2.5.3). The text highlights the fact that the chosen people born from Adam are God's "firstborn" (32:17). At the same time, the text describes Israel's succession to Adam's priestly identity. Chapter 26 describes how the books and precious stones originally belonged to Adam but were taken away from him as a consequence of his sins. The text indicates the cultic role of the precious stones, more specifically as a core element of priestly garments: They are placed on the breastplate of the high priest (*LAB* 26:4).[67] Adam's priestly status does not appear explicitly in Pseudo-Philo, however, the exclusive role of the stones, which originally belonged to Adam allows the reasonable inference that Adam was a priest.[68] Restoration of the precious stones to Israel (26:13) most likely indicates Israel's priestly identity as Adam's successor (26:12; cf. 25:12). The concepts that the chosen people will inherit the paradise as their inherited dwelling place, and that it is called "the place of sanctification" (19:13) suggests a reasonable inference that the inheritance of the chosen people who are sons of God and his priests restores Adam's status in Eden the first sanctuary. The ultimate restoration of Edenic blessings includes immortality (*LAB* 3:10) as well as the renewal of creation (*LAB* 32:17).

5.4 Summary of Chapter 5

In section 5.2 of the present chapter, I have discussed the possibility that the author sees the continuity between Israel's rest in the promised land and the eschatological rest of God based on the idea that the former shares the substantial elements of the latter, i.e. God's presence and the renewal of creation (esp. the change of heart). I have pointed out that in this framework of *Urzeit-Endzeit* eschatology, the logic behind the

---

[66] The author does not equate the promised land with this eschatological inheritance. Instead, he points out core elements such as fertility and light (i.e. God's word) that the locations share. The text presents these features, of which Eden is the source, which were provided in the promised land, and which will be culminated in the eschatological inheritance (see section 2.5.2). Pseudo-Philo claims that the restoration of the primordial blessing that Israel could enjoy only partially in the promised land will be perfected in the eschaton in terms of the core elements.

[67] Interestingly, in rabbinic tradition as well, Pishon is considered to supply the precious stones for the high priest's garments (Targum *Pseudo-Jonathan* of Exodus 35:27; *T.B. Yoma* 75a; *Shemoth Rabbah* 33:8). The text of Targum *Pseudo-Jonathan* of Exodus 35:28 states that the oils, spices, and incense for the tabernacle were brought by the clouds of heaven from the Garden of Eden.

[68] Verse 26 presents the reason why the stones had to be removed from human beings: "they might have mastery over them." It indicates that Adam was not a mere beneficiary of the supernatural power of the stones but a person who mastered the sacred stones for a certain purpose.

author's citation of Ps. 95 and its application to his readers is most congruously explained. Although the author of Hebrews does not consider Israel's historical inheritance, i.e. the promised land *per se*, as the eternal inheritance as some pre-70 texts claim, in the understanding of the elements of the eternal inheritance in the given framework, he argues that the rest, which Israel could have enjoyed in the promised land albeit in a limited sense, will be culminated at the eschaton for the people of the new Joshua. I have argued next that, in his citation of Gen. 2:2, the author shares the eschatological framework which describes the eschatological inheritance in terms of protological concepts. In section 5.3, I have pointed out some further patterns that Hebrews' eschatological vision shares with that of relevant apocalyptic texts.

The first and second patterns, i.e. the sanctuary as the inheritance and the combined identities of the chosen people, are clearly observed in Hebrews. The author of Hebrews envisions the hope that the people of God will inherit the sanctuary where they will enter (Heb. 6:19-20; 10:19-20) and dwell with God (Heb. 3:6; 12:23). Addition to the statement of the house of God in Heb. 3:6, the exhortation of "holding fast" in the beginning and at the end of the present passage (Heb. 3:7–4:11) and the relevant contexts in Hebrews which contains the concept of "holding fast hope" indicate that the "hope" of dwelling with God in the sanctuary is a major focus of the present exhortation. In Hebrews, this hope is interwoven with the combined identity of God's people as sons of God and his priests. The author describes Jesus' combined identity of the Son of God and his high priest while highlighting Jesus' role as the forerunner (ἀρχηγός, 2:10; 12:2) of his brothers. The author describes Jesus' entrance into the heavenly sanctuary as the Son and the high priest (for the completion of his sacrifice, 9:23-24).[69] He also repeatedly points out that our high priest is the Son (4:14; 5:5; 7:28). In particular, Heb. 7:28 states the specific feature of the high priest, i.e. the Son is "made perfect forever" (τελειόω). The meaning of this statement becomes clearer in Heb. 5:8-10 where the author shows that Jesus has been "made perfect" (τελειόω) by learning obedience through his suffering. The sons of God need to follow the Son's example of learning obedience in order to obtain the inheritance which includes the heavenly sanctuary. During the present time of wilderness, they need to be disciplined as sons of God (12:5-13), to learn obedience through suffering as Jesus did (5:8) and to obtain a change of heart through the help of their high priest, Jesus (8:10). Accordingly, the sons of God are invited to follow Jesus into the sanctuary (6:19-20; 10:19) and take on the role of priests (13:15-16). Hebrews also contains the related themes, mentioned as the third pattern of the eschatological visions in the relevant apocalypses. Hebrews 2, which is an immediate context of the present passage, identifies two significant redemptive works that Jesus accomplished by his death. First, he was "crowned with

---

[69] Jesus sat "at the right hand of God" after he had offered a sacrifice for sins (1:3; 8:1; 10:2). The citation of Ps. 110 in the contexts, i.e. the superior status of the Son to the angels (1:13) and the discipline of the son (12:2), suggests that Jesus' sitting at God's right hand indicates his status as God's Son. For a detailed discussion on this, see Eric F. Mason, "'Sit at My Right Hand': Enthronement and the Heavenly Sanctuary in Hebrews," in *A Teacher for All Generations: Essays in Honor of James. C. VanderKam*, vol. 2, Supplements to the Journal for the Study of Judaism (Leiden; Boston: Brill, 2012), 907–12.

glory and honor" through tasting death for everyone (Heb. 2:9). Second, he "destroyed the one who has the power of death, that is, the devil" (Heb. 2:14). In this section of Jesus' redemptive works, the identity of God's people as sons of God is particularly highlighted (2:10-13), implying that the sons will enjoy the restored glory and immortality.

These parallel patterns observed above strongly support the possibility that the author shares the kind of *Urzeit-Endzeit* framework attested in the eschatological vision of some apocalyptic texts. If this is the case, we can reach some fresh understandings of Hebrews' exhortation in 3:7–4:11. As God's priests and sons, which his people become with Christ's help, the believers recapitulate Adam's identity as the firstborn son of God and his priest. The heavenly sanctuary that they can enter, following the forerunner, reflects the role of the primordial sanctuary, Eden, which has been recapitulated by the earthly temple in Israel's history. In the eschatological inheritance, consisting of the revealed heavenly sanctuary and the renewed creation (which will be discussed in the next chapter), the people of God who have learned obedience through their time of wilderness will enjoy the restoration of the glory and immortality that Adam lost through his sin. The rest that the wilderness generation of Israel could have enjoyed with God's presence in the temple and their changed heart will be fulfilled through the eschatological people. Through citing Gen. 2:2, the author indicates that this rest is other than the restoration of the primordial rest that Adam enjoyed in God's presence in Eden while he remained an obedient son, keeping God's commandment. The idea draws on this concept, but anticipates more. In the next chapter, I deal with this assumption in relation to Hebrews' vision of "the unshakable kingdom" in ch. 12, which involves the shaking of heaven and earth. More specifically, I examine how the author envision the eschatological world in the given *Urzeit-Endzeit* framework, which consists of not only the revelation of the heavenly realm but also the renewed creation.

6

The Unshakable Kingdom

In the previous chapter, I argued that the author of Hebrews envisions that God's creational intention, which he allowed Israel to enjoy in history, albeit partially, will be completely fulfilled in the eschatological world. Hebrews 12:26-29 provides the vision that the eschatological world is to be established through the shaking of heaven and earth. I argue in the current chapter that the author envisages the eschatological world that consists of not the heavenly world exclusively—as some scholars argue—but the renewed creation as well. God's rest, which Adam forfeited through his sin and which Israel were intended to enjoy when they were told to enter into the promised land, will finally be found in this unshakable kingdom where the renewed creation will be united with the revealed heaven. After examining the eschatological vision in Heb. 12:26-29 (section 6.1), I show how the suggested understanding of Heb. 12:26-29 sheds light on Heb. 12:16-17 (6.2), and then investigate the concept of the renewal of creation in the book of Hebrews (6.3).

6.1 Hebrews 12:26-29

In Heb. 12:26-29, the author envisions the unshakable kingdom that will be established after the shaking of heaven and earth. Some scholars argue that the contrast between the shaking heaven and earth and the unshakable kingdom reflects the Platonic dualism of the material and the ideal world.[1] They claim that the shaking heaven in v. 26 refers to the higher part of the created universe and not to the immediate presence of God. Accordingly, v. 27 states that the created world, heaven and earth, is "removed"— the meaning attributed to the term μετάθεσις by these scholars—in order that the unshakable, transcendent world may remain. Yet, as Koester and Cockerill correctly point out, in v. 25 the author presents the contrast between the warnings on earth and from heaven and, in v. 22, also envisages the heavenly Jerusalem.[2] The strong contrast created by the phrase, "not only the earth, but also the heaven," in v. 26 suggests that the

---

[1] Attridge, *The Epistle to the Hebrews*, 380; Ellingworth, *The Epistle to the Hebrews*, 686; Luke Timothy Johnson, *Hebrews: A Commentary*, 1st ed, The New Testament Library (Louisville: Westminster John Knox Press, 2006), 334; Thompson, *Hebrews*, 268.

[2] Craig R. Koester, ed., *Hebrews: A New Translation with Introduction and Commentary*, 1st ed, The Anchor Bible 36 (New York: Doubleday, 2001), 547; Cockerill, *The Epistle to the Hebrews*, 664.

author is maintaining the same contrast in this verse. In other words, the shaking heaven refers to the heavenly dwelling place of God, and this critically undermines the assumption of a Platonic background to the present passage. Moreover, the term μετάθεσις, which is used to present the destination of the shakable things, can mean either "removal" or "change." If the present passage does not describe the removal of the created world and the establishment of the transcendent world on the basis of Platonism, what does it envision?

I suggest, instead, that some of the Jewish apocalyptic texts that we have observed provide valuable parallel ideas and allow a fresh way of reading the present passage. Some post-70 apocalyptic writers who observed Israel's hopeless depravity and its tragic consequence, the destruction of the Temple, began to hope for the revelation of the heavenly world instead of the promised land on earth. In their minds, the heavenly world is not a transcendent place to which the chosen people will simply be transferred from an earth doomed to be destroyed. In the same vein as the previous apocalyptic texts, they believe in the faithfulness of God the creator and his eternal plan to restore the creation at the end of time. Consequently, the eschatological kingdom involves the renewal of the earth as well as heaven's coming and merging with it.

Hebrews 12:26-29 describes the unshakable kingdom that will be established through the changing of the earth and heaven, which is called their shaking. If Hebrews shares an eschatological vision similar to that of the first century apocalyptic texts previously observed, Heb. 12:26-29 might envision that the heavenly world will come, unite with the renewed earth, and form the eternal kingdom. If this is correct, Heb. 12 presents the vision that the heavenly world and the creation on earth will be transformed into the eschatological sanctuary where God will dwell among his people. In this unshakable kingdom, the believers will obtain the glory (Heb. 2:9), rest (4:9), and immortality (2:14) that Adam enjoyed in Eden. I present how this hypothesis fits into the discussion of Heb. 12 in two points: 1) The usage of the two terms, χρηματίζω and μετάθεσις, indicates that the image of shaking in Heb. 12 is related to revelation and transformation rather than to destruction and removal; 2) in the quoted OT passages, the shaking is presented as a process for the establishment of God's sanctuary among his people.

6.1.1 The usages of χρηματίζω and μετάθεσις

Concerning the image of the "shaking" in the present passage, interpreters make a connection with the concept of judgment and destruction that naturally leads to the assumption of a Platonic background of the present passage. This premise prevents them from seeing what the author intends by the image. For a correct understanding of the author's intention, first of all, the two terms χρηματίζω and μετάθεσις need to be examined. Verse 26 makes it clear that what made the shaking of the earth is "His voice," which refers to God's "warning (χρηματίζω)" in v. 25. This interpretation of the term as "to warn" becomes the basis of the connection between the shaking and the judgment theme. The term χρηματίζω, however, does not contain the specific meaning of "warning." The root noun χρῆμα has the meaning of "affair" or "business" and its verb formχρηματίζω basically means "to handle a matter," "to deal with something," or "answer." When the deity is involved as the answering authority, the verb means "to give an oracle."[3] In the LXX version of Jeremiah, the term appears to refer to the divine proclamation, including not only warning (Ezek 36:2), but also general revelations (e.g. 29:23; 30:2; 36:4). In the NT, the term is used in the case of the revelation to Jesus' parents (Mat 2:12, 22), Simeon (Lk 2:26), and Cornelius (Acts 10:22).[4] In Hebrews, the author uses the term to refer to the divine instructions to Noah (8:5) and Moses (11:7). According to the content of a revelation, it could be considered as a warning, but the term itself is not limited to the particular concept of warning.

In Heb. 12:25 χρηματίζω is used interchangeably with λαλέω ("to speak").[5] In fact, the message of Heb. 12:25 is a warning: if the believers ignore the voice from heaven, they cannot avoid judgment. Yet, the voice itself that brings forth the shaking of heaven and earth does not particularly refer to a warning message, and thus the image of shaking is not necessarily linked to judgment or destruction. The appearance of God's promise in v. 26 supports this understanding. The most frequent interpretation of the term χρηματίζω as "warning" causes exegetical incongruity with v. 26, which speaks of God's "promise" to shake heaven and earth. Ellingworth notes that the language of promise in a warning context is "at first puzzling."[6] Koester states, "the word 'promise' has connoted rest (4:1), a new covenant (8:6), and eternal inheritance (9:15; cf. 11:9), but now it warns of a final shaking," even though he does not provide a proper explanation for this inconsistency.[7]

With regard to the meaning of shaking in Heb. 12, the second term to be investigated is μετάθεσις. Hebrews 12:27 states, "the removal (μετάθεσις) of what is shaken—that is, created things—so that what cannot be shaken may remain (μένω)" (NRSV). Scholars are divided concerning the meaning of the term μετάθεσις, since it can mean either "change" or "removal."[8] In secular Greek, the verb μετατίθημι means "to bring to another place," and in some cases, it further refers to the sense "to change" or "to alter" (e.g. Jos.

---

[3] Bo Reicke, "χρηματίζω," *TDNT*, vol. 9, 480; C. Brown, "χρηματίζω," *NIDNTT*, vol. 3, 324.
[4] In two cases in the NT, the term is used of men in the sense of "appearing as something" (the disciples publicly known as "Christians" in Acts 11:26; a married woman reckoned an adulteress in Rom 7:3).
[5] Some scholars understand the person who warns on earth to be Moses (James Moffatt, *A Critical and Exegetical Commentary on the Epistle to the Hebrews*, International Critical Commentary (Edinburgh: Clark, 1924), 220; George Wesley Buchanan, ed., *To the Hebrews*, The Anchor Bible 36 (Garden City, NY: Doubleday, 1972), 224). Yet, the term χρηματίζω has never been used in NT for an opinion of a human being and v.26 indicates that the voice which shook the earth "at that time" was the divine voice that was heard at Sinai. For more discussions on this, see Juliana Casey Ihm, "Eschatology in Heb. 12: 14-29: An Exegetical Study" (Catholic University of Leuven, 1976), 512–13; William L. Lane, *Hebrews 9–13*, Word Biblical Commentary 47B (Dallas: Word books, 1991), 476.
[6] Ellingworth, *The Epistle to the Hebrews*, 686. He tries to explain this puzzling appearance of the language of promise as "the implied hope of ultimate stability for believers."
[7] Koester, *Hebrews*, 546. For his more detailed discussion of the concept promise in Heb., see p. 110.
[8] For the view that it refers to removal, cf. Attridge, *The Epistle to the Hebrews*, 380; Lane, *Hebrews 9-13*, 482; Ellingworth, *The Epistle to the Hebrews*, 1993, 687; Johnson, *Hebrews*, 335; Thompson, *Hebrews*, 2008, 268. For the view that it means transformation, cf. A. Vögtle, "Das Neue Testament und die Zukunft des Kosmos: Heb. 12,26f. und das Endschicksal des Kosmos," *Bibel und Leben*, 10 (1969): 242ff.; Hurst, "Eschatology and 'Platonism' in the Epistle to the Hebrews," 71; Thomas G. Long, *Hebrews*, Interpretation, a Bible Commentary for Teaching and Preaching (Louisville, KY: John Knox Press, 1997), 139.

Ant., 12,287; Plat. *Rep.*, I, 345b).[9] In some LXX uses of the term, the translation of someone or something could be understood as removal. The translation of Enoch can be understood as his removal from earth (Gen. 5:24), and the moving of the landmarks from their places can be understood as their removal (Deut 27:17). Yet, the term does not have the idea of the destruction of the object. Similarly, in the NT, the term refers to the "conducting across" of the dead (Acts 7:16), Enoch's translation (Heb. 11:5), or the "transformation" of God's grace into license (Jude 4), but not to the destruction of something/someone. Along with μετάθεσις, the term μένω in the same verse also needs to be investigated. Some Hebrews commentators consider this contrasting idea of "remaining" as evidence that the term μετάθεσις refers to removal,[10] and they believe this term indicates a Platonic concern with the continuation of the spiritual entities.[11] The LXX often uses μένω to translate עמד and קום, meaning "to endure" or "to be lasting." Isaiah 66:22 (LXX) uses μένω for the new heaven and earth that will endure.[12] The term does not necessarily contrast with removal.

The use of the two terms χρηματίζω and μετάθεσις in Heb. 12 indicates that the idea of destruction or removal in the present passage is not as obvious or indisputable as many interpreters assume. Rather, in light of the theme of promise in the passage, the image of shaking in association with revelation and transformation is more probable. Through this image, the author envisions the "change or relocation (μετάθεσις)" of heaven and earth: the earth will be changed, and the heavenly world will be relocated, i.e. revealed (χρηματίζω).

6.1.2 The Quotations from the OT

The author's quotation of Hag 2:6 and Exod 19:1-25 provides keys to an understanding of what exactly God is promising with the language of the shaking of heaven and earth. In God's promise of the shaking of heaven and earth in Heb. 12:26, the author is quoting Hag 2:6. In the context of the Haggai text, the prophet encourages the remnant of Israel who are disappointed by the restored post-exilic temple by giving them a vision of the future glory of the temple. Here, the shaking of heaven and earth is presented as the means by which the temple will be filled with God's glory.[13] In a number of OT texts, glory is related to God's presence in the sanctuary (Exod 29:42-43; 40:34-35; Lev 9:5-6, 23; Ezek 1:28; 8:4; 9:3; 11:22-23; 43:2-5; Zech 2:5, 8). Furthermore, by calling the temple God's "house," Haggai highlights God's "actual presence among, and his living communion with, his people."[14] In other words, Haggai envisions that God's dwelling among his people in the temple will be established through the process of shaking. Haggai 2:9 provides a more detailed picture of what the divine shaking results in: the

---

[9] C. Maurer, *TDNT*, vol. 8, 161.
[10] Lane, *Hebrews 9–13*, 482; Koester, *Hebrews*, 547.
[11] Attridge, *The Epistle to the Hebrews*, 380.
[12] Hurst, "Eschatology and 'Platonism' in the Epistle to the Hebrews," 73.
[13] Friedrich Schröger, *Der Verfasser des Hebräerbriefes als Schriftausleger*, Biblische Untersuchungen 4 (Regensburg: F. Pustet, 1968), 190–94; Lane, *Hebrews 9–13*, 480.
[14] Pieter A. Verhoef, *The Books of Haggai and Malachi*, New International Commentary on the Old Testament (Grand Rapids: Eerdmans, 1987), 36.

temple's subsequent glory will be greater than that of the former and God will give "peace" in "this place." As a number of scholars note, the term "this place" refers not only to the temple, but also to Jerusalem and Mount Zion "as the place where the temple is built."[15] Haggai envisages the eschatological culmination of the peace that Israel enjoyed in the promised land and the Solomonic temple. In his mind, Jerusalem is the capital of the world, and the new temple will be the cultic center to which all nations will come with their wealth (Hag 2:7; cf. Isa 60:5-9; Zech 14:14-16; Rev 21:26).[16] In Haggai's vision, the shaking of heaven and earth refers not to the destruction of the world but to its transformation into the place where the chosen people will dwell with God and enjoy the subjection of the nations and the abundance of the land (Hag 2:19).

The author of Hebrews modifies the Haggai text. He omits "the sea" and "the dry land" from the list of the shaking things, thus avoiding the appearance of heaven as one of the parts of the universe along with the sea and dry land. Similarly, by adding the phrase, "not only but also" (οὐ μόνον ... ἀλλὰ καί), he emphasizes the reference to heaven as distinctive from the reference to the earth. In Heb. 3–4, we can observe a parallel way of interpretation through which the author applies an OT passage to his contemporary recipients. The author applies God's proclamation of Israel's entering into the promised land in Ps. 95 to the believers' inheritance of eternal rest. The author maintains the original prophecy without changing the main meaning, while shifting the focus of the text to the eternal inheritance.[17] In sum, God's promise that the author of Hebrews presents is as follows: on one hand, as the original text prophesies, God will establish the temple where he will dwell with his people; on the other hand, it will not be the temple in the land of Canaan, but it will involve the heavenly realms as well as the earth.

Noticeably, in another OT citation in Heb. 12:18-21, Exod 19:1-25 also, the image of shaking appears with the focus on God's temple. In the context of Exod 19:18, the shaking of Mount Sinai signified God's presence on the Mount. In the scene of Moses' previous encounter with God on the same "mountain of God" (3:1), which foreshadows Israel's meeting with God, the immediate goal of God's redemption of Israel is stated: "you (pl.) shall worship (תעבדון) God on this mountain" (3:12; cf. 4:23; 7:16; 8:16; 9:1; 10:3, 7-8; 12:31). The term עבד takes on the particular force of "serve cultically as a

---

[15] Karl Friedrich Keil, Franz Julius Delitzsch, and James Martin, *Biblical Commentary on the Old Testament. The Twelve Minor Prophets*, Clark's Foreign Theological Library, vols. 17–18 (Edinburgh: T & T Clark, 1868), 195. J. L. Mackay argues that there is a play on words in the passage since Jerusalem means "city of peace." John L. MacKay, *Haggai, Zechariah & Malachi: God's Restored People*, Revised edition edition (Fearn, Ross-shire: Christian Focus, 2010), 35. R. A. Taylor points out that the expression "this place" is used as a synonym for Jerusalem (e.g. 2 Kgs 22:16; Jer 7:3; 19:3). Richard A. Taylor and E. Ray Clendenen, *Haggai, Malachi* (Nashville, TN: B&H Publishing Group, 2004), 168.

[16] Concerning Hag 2:7, P. A. Verhoef considers the new temple as the economic center (Verhoef, *The Books of Haggai and Malachi*, 107.), but in light of the similar visions of other OT texts, Hag 2:7 can be more properly understood as the hope of the nation's worship of God. Concerning the scene of war against the nations in Hag 2:22, Koole and Verhoef rightly point out that the motif of the pilgrimage of the nations is joined with the motif of the holy war (cf. Zech 14:14-16).

[17] L. D. Hurst rightly points out that Haggai's context is important in Hebrews' quotation in light of a reasonable assumption that the citation is not an "isolated proof-text." Hurst, "Eschatology and 'Platonism' in the Epistle to the Hebrews," 71.

priest" (Num 18:7), though it can refer to the work connected with one's vocation such as agricultural tasks (Exod 20:9) or to a general sense of religious service in the form of worship (Exod 23:33).[18] Other elements of the Sinai account in Exod 19 support the reference to cultic service. The people of Israel were commanded to purify themselves for three days, which bears some analogy to the ordination of the Levitical priest in Lev 8 (washing in v. 6 and waiting in vv. 33, 35).[19] The blast of the ram's horn (v.13) or trumpet (v.19) appears in priestly contexts (Lev 25:9; Num 10:8; Josh 6:1).[20] Most importantly, the people of Israel were called "a kingdom of priests and a holy nation" (v.6). In other words, they stood at the foot of the Mount as God's priests.[21] The shaking Mount became the sanctuary where God and his priests, Israel, met (קרא v.17). The author of Hebrews connects two OT texts that present the image of shaking with regard to God's presence in a sanctuary/temple and formulates an eschatological vision: not only earth but also heaven will be the temple where God will dwell among his people. Additionally, as we investigated above concerning the two terms, this eschatological sanctuary will require the process of transformation and revelation, which will cause the shaking of heaven and earth.

6.1.3 The Shaking Heavenly World

Some questions can be raised against the view suggested above, particularly regarding to the idea of the shaking heavenly realm. How can the transcendent realm of God's throne be shaken? How can the statement in v. 27 that the shaken things are "created things" be explained? To answer these questions, I shall first examine some Jewish apocalyptic texts that present the idea of the cosmic shaking of the earth as well as of the heavenly world. Second, I shall investigate the concept of the heavenly realm as itself created in the book of Hebrews.

A link between the shaking earth and the new creation appears in Pseudo-Philo. The author portrays Israel's exodus and covenant making on Mount Sinai as the new creation. God's commandment over the Red Sea is described with the image of the division of waters, which appears in the creation account of Gen. 1:9 (15:6). The Torah, which was given on Mount Sinai, is called "laws for creation." In ch. 32, the author presents Israel's reception of the Torah on Mount Sinai as causing the earth to shake along with other kinds of cosmological disturbance (flood and movement of the abyss) and the attraction of all of creation (gathering of all creatures). The text further states that "paradise gave off the scent of its fruit" on the occasion of the Mosaic covenant. These descriptions imply that Israel's status is comparable with Adam's stewardship

---

[18] BDB, 713; KB, 671.
[19] John A. Davies, *A Royal Priesthood: Literary and Intertextual Perspectives on an Image of Israel in Exodus 19.6*, Journal for the Study of the Old Testament 395 (London ; New York: T&T Clark International, 2004), 109.
[20] Jacob Milgrom, "The Priestly Consecration (Leviticus 8): A Rite of Passage," in *Bits of Honey: Essays for Samson H. Levey* (Atlanta: Scholars Press, 1993), 57–61.
[21] For a detailed discussion on the tension between the ideal (Israel's unhindered access to Yhwh on the holy mountain in a state of priestly consecration) and the result of Israel's fear (Moses' mediation), see Davies, *A Royal Priesthood*, 110–13.

over creation and Eden. Pseudo-Philo connects the shaking of the earth with the new creation and Israel's obtaining of Adamic identity. Pseudo-Philo understands the shaking of Mount Sinai as one of the phenomena signifying the restoration of Edenic elements on that location.

The idea of the shaking of the earth as the process of its transformation for the coming world appears in 4 Ezra. In the vision of the eschaton in 6:14-16, the shaking of the earth occurs, anticipating its "change." Here, Ezra is warned not to be afraid if the earth shakes:

> If the place where you are standing is greatly shaken while the voice is speaking, do not be terrified; because the word concerns the end, and the foundations of the earth will understand that the speech concerns them. They will tremble and be shaken, for they know that their end must be *changed*.

The ultimate cosmic change to come is prefigured in 6:29 by the shaking of the ground underneath Ezra. This meaning of the shaking is strongly supported by the use of the language of the "renewal of creation" (*creaturam renovare*) in 7:75 to describe the eschatological cosmic transformation. Shaking at the revelation of the heavenly world is also found in 4 Ezra. In 9:38–10:59, Ezra sees a vision of a woman who mourns the death of her son in his wedding chamber. At the end of the vision, the woman, who symbolizes Zion, appears to be a city that is revealed on earth with "glory" and "beauty" (10:50), and the earth shakes (10:26). One point to be highlighted is that this transformation of Zion into the established city is called revelation: "no work of man's building could endure in a place where the city of the Most High was to be revealed" (10:54). Chapter 13 similarly states that "Zion will come and be made manifest to all people, prepared and built, as you saw the mountain carved out without hands" (13:36). The text indicates that the revelation of the heavenly city to the human world involves shakings, even though the text does not indicate that the shaking involves heaven.

A clearer example appears in 2 Baruch, which presents the shaking of heaven in the case of its revelation:

> But also the heaven will be shaken from its place at that time; that is, the heavens which are under the throne of the Mighty One were severely shaken when he took Moses with him. For he showed him many warnings together with . . . the height of the air, the greatness of Paradise.
>
> 2 Bar 59:3

The text describes how the heavenly world where God's throne is located was shaken when God revealed the heavenly world and its truth to Moses. 2 Baruch presents the idea that the revelation of the heavenly world to a human being causes the shaking of the heavenly world. In these apocalyptic texts, cosmic shaking occurs in both cases of the transformation of earth, i.e. probably the restoration of the earth to Eden-like status, and of the revelation of the heavenly world to people on earth. The latter includes the shaking of the heavenly world itself in 2 Baruch. The shaking of heaven in Heb. 12 possibly reflects a similar idea of the revelation of heaven in the earthly sphere.

An indication that God has created the heavenly realm appears in Heb. 11:8-16 where the author discusses the "land" and the "city," which was given to Abraham as his inheritance. Here, the heavenly city is said to have God as its τεχνίτης and δημιουργός (Heb. 11:10), indicating that even the heavenly realm has been created.[22] At *Op. mund.* 146, Philo speaks of matter, "which was necessary for the *Creator* to take in order to *fashion* this visible image (ἣν ἔδει λαβεῖν τὸν δημιουργόν, ἵνα τεχνιτεύσῃ τὴν ὁρατὴν ταύτην εἰκόνα)."[23] The two terms are used to describe God, the creator of the universe. Similarly, the term τεχνίτης is used in the book of Wisdom (13:1) to refer to God the creator, and the term δημιουργός is used in Josephus (*Ant.* 1:155.272).[24] The usage of these terms in the contexts of creation suggests that, in Heb. 11:10, the author presents the creation of the heavenly city. With regard to this idea, Heb. 9:11 can be used to support a serious objection, namely, the view that the heavenly realm is spiritual and separated from the materiality of creation: "But when Christ appeared as a high priest of the good things to come, He entered through the greater and more perfect tabernacle, not made with hands, that is to say, not of this creation" (Heb. 9:11 NASB).[25] The point of the verse, however, is not to underline that the true tent is uncreated or immaterial, but to highlight that it is not made with human hands.[26] A parallel verse, Heb. 8:2, supports this understanding by stating that Jesus is the "minister of the sanctuary and in the true tabernacle, which the Lord pitched, not man." These verses imply rather that God created the heavenly sanctuary.

The author of Hebrews uses the image of shaking to present neither the destruction nor the removal of the created world. The present text does not reflect a Platonic background as a number of scholars argue. Instead, Heb. 12 presents the cosmic shaking as a way of describing transformation and revelation. Through citing two OT texts, the author of Hebrews implicitly connects the image of the shaking of a place (Mount Sinai in Exod 19 and the creation in Hag 2) with the vision of God's presence with his people in the place, turned into the temple. This image of shaking in Heb. 12 forms a notable parallel with the way the image is used in certain Jewish apocalyptic texts. The author of Hebrews possibly envisions the eschatological unshakable sanctuary, i.e. God's eternal dwelling place among his people, which will involve the transformation of the earth (the renewal of creation) and the coming/revelation of the heavenly world and its merge with the earth.

---

[22] Similarly argued in Jon Laansma, "The Cosmology of Hebrews," in *Cosmology and New Testament Theology* (London: T&T Clark, 2008), 134; O. J. Filtvedt, "Creation and Salvation in Hebrews," *ZNW* 106, no. 2 (2015): 291.

[23] Loeb 1.117. Italics are added for emphasis.

[24] For more references to the two terms in ancient literature, see Attridge, *The Epistle to the Hebrews*, 323.

[25] Ben Witherington III writes that "Hebrews 9:11 makes clear that our author is not talking about a tabernacle that is part of the material creation." Pace B. Witherington III, *Letters and Homilies for Jewish Christians: A Socio-Rhetorical Commentary on Hebrews, James and Jude* (Downers Grove, IL: IVP Academic, 2007), 268–69.

[26] Filtvedt, "Creation and Salvation in Hebrews," 290. Lane aptly points out the fact that the author uses a demonstrative pronoun, even though he unconvincingly interprets "not of ordinary building" (William L. Lane, *Hebrews 9-13*, Word Biblical Commentary 47B (Dallas: Word books, 1991), 230. The verse says that the heavenly tabernacle does not belong to "this creation," instead just of "creation."

6.2 The Warning from Esau's Example

The Jewish apocalyptic background allows a fresh reading of the account of Esau in Heb. 12:16-17 as well. Hebrews 12:14-17 contains pastoral exhortations for the present lives of the believers, first, encouraging virtuous behavior (v. 14) and, second, warning against sinful behavior (vv. 15-17). It is widely noted that the author connects the sections, vv. 14-17 and vv. 18-24, as a whole by the inferential γάρ in v.18.[27] The role of substantiating γάρ in v.17, however, is easily missed or misunderstood as connecting v.17 only with v.16.[28] Yet, the conjunction γάρ in v.17 serves to introduce a warning as a support for the whole section of pastoral exhortation in vv.14-16.[29] The stern warning that they have no chance to repent with the example of Esau in v.17 is not presented as only the destiny of the immoral or godless in v.16, but it acts as a pivot that combines and reinforces the whole exhortation of vv.14-16. Subsequently, γάρ in v. 18 connects vv. 18-25 specifically to v. 17 on which vv. 14-16 converge and explains why, like Esau, the believers who fall away have no chance to repent because, in their case, they have experienced the heavenly city.[30] Why does the author suddenly bring up Esau? Does he connect Esau's case with believers simply based on the same concept of "firstborn" (12:16; 12:23) or might there also be some consideration of a deeper theological link between what Esau lost and what believers will inherit?

6.2.1 The Pivotal Role of Esau's Case

Cockerill interestingly points out a plausible allusion to Deut 29:15-20 in Heb. 12:15-17.[31] The threefold warning in Deut 29:18 shows notable similarities to Heb. 12:15-16.[32] The third warning in Deut 29:18-20 portrays a person who deliberately boasts about the curses against disobedience and goes his own way, and God, who refuses to forgive this person. Esau's willingness to abandon his inheritance for the pleasure of this world and the consequence in Heb. 12:16-17 corresponds well with the bold apostasy and God's response to it in the Deuteronomy text. Noticeably, this case of apostasy in Deut 29:18-20 functions as the climax of the section of 29:15-20. The first two "lest any"

---

[27] Ihm, "Eschatology in Heb. 12," 308–9; Lane, *Hebrews 9–13*, 1991, 459; Ellingworth, *The Epistle to the Hebrews*, 670; Allen, *Hebrews*, 642.
[28] Ellingworth further understands that γάρ in v. 18 links vv.18-24 with the whole section of vv. 14-17 not specifically with the example of Esau. Ellingworth, *The Epistle to the Hebrews*, 666, 670.
[29] Lane, *Hebrews 9–13*, 459. A detailed discussion of γάρ that functions to support the whole section of exhortation in vv. 14-16 will follow.
[30] Thompson and Cockerill similarly link the case of Esau with the following discussion in vv. 18-25. Thompson, *Hebrews*, 267; Cockerill, *The Epistle to the Hebrews*, 642.
[31] Cockerill, *The Epistle to the Hebrews*, 631.
[32] The first clauses of Deut and Heb. do not have much verbal resemblance: μή τίς ... ἀπὸ κυρίου τοῦ θεοῦ (Deut 29:18); μή τις ὑστερῶν ἀπὸ ... τοῦ θεοῦ (Heb. 12:15). Yet the contents of the warning correspond well. Short of God's grace in Heb. 12:15 is reminiscent of drawing near to God's 'throne of grace' in Heb. 4:15, which forms a contrast to the idea of turning away from God in Deut 29:18. The warning of a bitter root in the second clauses clearly show that the author of Heb. depends on the Deut text. Cockerill points out that A text of LXX for Deut 29:18 agrees with Heb. 12:15 except for a phrase:μή τις ῥίζα πικρίας ἄνω φύουσα ἐνοχλῇ (Heb. 12:15b); μή τις ἔστιν ἐν ὑμῖν ῥίζα πικρίας ἄνω φύουσα ἐνοχλῇ (Deut 29:17 LXX, A text). Cockerill, 635.

warnings in Deut 29:15-17 are connected to this apostasy case with the conjunction (ἢ, καί in the LXX text). Accordingly, Deuteronomy warns that if God's people turn away from God (the first "lest any" clause), and thus a bitter root springs up in the community (the second "lest any" clause), then deliberate apostasy may occur. In light of the allusions to the Deuteronomy passage, the author of Hebrews most likely presents a similar flow of thought: Esau's case in 12:16-17 is given as the climax of his warnings in 12:15-17.[33] As γάρ in v.17 indicates, the irretrievable decision of Esau is presented as the end result of preceding steps in v. 15.

The thematic connection between Esau's irretrievable mistake, i.e. selling his birthright to inherit the heirloom, and the stern warning in vv.18-25 against the possible apostasy of the firstborn sons of God that may cause their loss of the inheritance (i.e. the unshakable kingdom) suggests the idea that Esau's case in 12:16-17 is not presented as a general example of a faulty decision that results in forfeiture of divine blessings. I argue that, in a supposition that the present chapter shares a similar eschatological framework of some apocalyptic texts, we may see a substantial connection between what Esau forfeited and what the readers are expecting to obtain. The right of the firstborn that Esau handed over to his brother Jacob/Israel in exchange for food was not simply the right to inherit the possessions of his father, Isaac, but the right to "God's rest" in the promised land, which will culminate in the eschatological inheritance. Noticeably, the logic of the present exhortation shows remarkable similarity with that of Heb. 3:12-13: they need to encourage each other (3:13; 12:12-14) so that their falling away from God (3:12; 12:15a) may not cause them to harden their hearts (3:13; 12:15b) through "the deceitfulness (ἀπάτη) of sin" (3:13; 12:16). As pointed out in my discussion of Heb. 3:7–4:11, the term ἀπάτη is used in other biblical texts to refer to the desire for the world's riches or pleasure (e.g. Mt 13:22/Mk 4:19; Eph 4:22; 2 Pet 2:13).[34] The author most likely understands Esau's case in the same way that he comprehends the case of the wilderness generation, i.e. as an example of the forfeiture of the eschatological inheritance for the sake of worldly things. In this understanding, the author connects the case of Esau with his discussion of the eschatological inheritance in the following verses, 12:18-29, with the inferential γάρ in v.18.

6.2.2 Adam and Edom

In the given *Urzeit-Endzeit* framework, the inheritance that Esau forfeited, and that thus became Israel's, is described with the language of the primordial bliss in Eden. In other words, the connection between what Esau forfeited and Adam's privilege in Eden is implied. Additionally, in this section, I examine some Jewish traditions of Esau that

---

[33] Immorality and godlessness as the climax of sins against which the author warns requires some explanation. Especially, Esau has not committed the sin of immorality. Scholars explain this sexual unfaithfulness as a figure of speech for covenant disloyalty (Philip Edgcumbe Hughes, *A Commentary on the Epistle to the Hebrews* (Grand Rapids: Eerdmans, 1977), 540; Lane, *Hebrews 9–13*, 451; Johnson, *Hebrews*, 324), or as a demonstration that Esau's selling his birthright for nothing more than one meal is similar to selling oneself for buying pleasure from a prostitute (Cockerill, *The Epistle to the Hebrews*, 639.). Either can be a reasonable explanation.

[34] According to BDAG, the term ἀπάτη has the meaning of "seduction which comes from pleasure."

contain more direct connections between what Esau lost and the Adamic blessings in order to highlight a reason that the author specifically mentions Esau in his exhortation. First, I investigate some OT texts that show noticeable comparisons between Edom's judgment and Israel's Adamic blessings. The ideas that Esau's firstborn right for the land had the meaning of the restoration of Adam's privilege and that Israel inherited it instead of Edomites as the result of Esau's despise of his inheritance aptly explain the dynamic in these OT text between Israel's inheritance of Adamic blessings and Edom's judgment for its covetousness of the inheritance that does not belong to them any more. Second, I examine some Targumim and rabbinic texts which show that an Adamic concept of Esau's inheritance was known in Jewish tradition.

The connection between the Adamic blessings and Edom is observed in some OT texts. Ezekiel 35 and 36 show an interesting parallel between Edom's desolation and Israel's restoration that is described in terms of Adam's multiplication.[35] Chapter 35 contains Edom's claim to be the owner of Israel and its land (vv. 10, 12) and God's judgment on Edom, which takes advantage of "the desolation" of "the house of Israel," i.e. their exile from Jerusalem (v.15). Chapter 36 states that Israel will be multiplied, and the land will be restored to them by using the language of Gen. 1. God promises in Ezek 36:11 as follows:

> I will multiply human beings (אדם) and animals upon you. They shall increase and be fruitful; and I will cause you to be inhabited as in your former times, and will do more good (והטבתי) to you than ever before (מראשתיכם). Then you shall know that I am the LORD.
>
> NRSV

The phrases, "I will multiply you Adam" and "they shall ... be fruitful," allude to God's blessing on Adam in Gen. 1:28.[36] The verb והטבתי suggests the adjective טוב in Gen. 1. The noun ראשה, translated as "beginning," is most likely intended as a connection to ראשית in Gen. 1:1.[37] Additionally, verse 35 envisions that Israel's desolated land will "become like the garden of Eden." Some prophetic texts that contain a similar parallel between Israel's blessing and Edom's judgment, such as Obad 10 and Mal 1:1-4, show that these prophecies are not only derived from the politically motivated hatred between Judah

---

[35] Ezekiel prophesies that "Mount Seir and all Edom, all of it" will become a desolation (35:15; 36:5), and the Lord will multiply "Adam, all the house of Israel, all of it" upon the mountains of Israel (36:12). For more parallels between chs. 35 and 36, see Tracy McKenzie, "Edom's Desolation and Adam's Multiplication," in *Text and Canon: Essays in Honor of John H. Sailhamer* (Eugene, OR: Pickwick, 2017), 96–102; Johan Lust, "Edom-Adam in Ezekiel, in the MT and LXX," in *Studies in the Hebrew Bible, Qumran, and the Septuagint Presented to Eugene Ulrich* (Boston: Brill, 2006).

[36] Walther Zimmerli, Frank Moore Cross, and Klaus Baltzer, *Ezekiel: A Commentary on the Book of the Prophet Ezekiel*, Hermeneia: A Critical and Historical Commentary on the Bible (Philadelphia: Fortress Press, 1979), vol. 2, 230; Block, *The Book of Ezekiel*, vol. 2, 334.

[37] Ashley S. Crane, *Israel's Restoration: A Textual-Comparative Exploration of Ezekiel 36–39*, Supplements to Vetus Testamentum, v. 122 (Leiden; Boston: Brill, 2008), 53; Jake Stromberg, "Observations on Inner-Scriptural Scribal Expansion in MT Ezekiel," *VT*, no. 1 (2008): 73–74.

and Edom, but also based on the tradition of Gen. 27.[38] Regarding this, the way in which Ezekiel places Edom and Israel in a relation of rivalry for the promised inheritance and operates Adamic language to describe the inheritance suggests the following possibility: he considers the biblical tradition of the tension between Esau and Jacob surrounding the firstborn right and especially the identity of what Esau delivered to Jacob for a bowl of food, i.e. its connection to the primordial privileges of Adam.

Another OT text that shows a similar connection between Edom and Adam is Amos 9:12. The present passage most likely alludes to Num 24:17-19.[39] In the prophecy of Balaam in Num 24, Israel's dominion over other nations is described as the fulfillment of the Abrahamic promise. The text mentions the multiplication of "seed" (24:7) and contains a verbatim quotation of Gen. 12:3: "Blessed is everyone who blesses you, and cursed is everyone who curses you." More interestingly, Num 24 depicts how Israel's "tabernacle" will be like "palm trees that stretch out, like gardens," echoing the first sanctuary, the Garden of Eden.[40] As G. K. Beale notes, Amos 9 presents a similar prophecy about the "raising up of the tabernacle of David."[41] It is quite plausible that Amos 9 reflects this idea of the restoration of the first sanctuary, Eden, in its allusion to Num 24:17-19. Like Ezek 35–36, Amos similarly implies the identity of what Esau handed over to Jacob.

In addition to this, Amos develops the idea that Israel will possess Edom. Related to the link between Edom and Adam/Israel, some scholars notice the phonological correspondence between Adam and Edom. They think the author of Ezekiel might have chosen the names Adam (אדם) or Edom (אדום) on the basis of their phonological similarity.[42] Nevertheless, the LXX translator of Amos 9:12 suggests a different possibility by reading "Adam" (τῶν ἀνθρώπων) for "Edom" in the Hebrew *Vorlage*.[43] R. Bauckham

---

[38] In Obadiah, Jacob and Esau are presented as representatives of the two peoples ("house of Jacob" and "house of Esau," vv. 6, 10, 18). The divine verdict against Edom, "you shall be utterly despised" (בזה), alludes to Gen. 25:34: "Thus did Esau despise (בזה) the birthright." In Mal 1:1-4, the author equates the two peoples of Israel and Edom, with their representatives, Jacob and Esau. In the introduction of the notion of their brotherhood, the verses bring the Genesis narrative of Jacob and Esau into play. See also Joachim J. Krause, "Tradition, History, and Our Story: Some Observations on Jacob and Esau in the Books of Obadiah and Malachi," *JSOT* 32, no. 4 (2008): 475–86.

[39] Numbers 24:17-19   Amos 9:11-12
And a scepter shall *rise* from Israel   I will *raise* up the fallen tabernacle
...And *Edom shall be a possession*   of David ... that they may *possess*
...One from Jacob shall have   *the remnant* of *Edom* and all the nations ...
dominion, and shall destroy *the remnant* ...

John Sailhamer, *Introduction to Old Testament Theology: A Canonical Approach* (Grand Rapids: Zondervan, 1995), 250–51; Gundry Stanley, *Three Views on the New Testament Use of the Old Testament* (Grand Rapids: Zondervan, 2008), 70.

[40] Beale, *The Temple and the Church's Mission*, 123–26, 242–43.

[41] Ibid., 243. For the discussion of the meaning of "David's tent" as the Temple, see John Anthony Dunne, "David's Tent as Temple in Amos 9:11-15: Understanding the Epilogue of Amos and Considering Implications for the Unity of the Book," *WTJ* 73, no. 2 (2011): 363–74.

[42] T. McKenzie argues that Edom was used as a representative for all enemies of Israel based on the phonological similarity with Adam. Tracy McKenzie, "Edom's Desolation and Adam's Multiplication," 92. J. Lust insists that Adam is used in order to form a contrast with "the whole of Edom, all of it." Johan Lust, "Edom-Adam in Ezekiel, in the MT and LXX," 394.

states that the type of reading observed in Amos 9:12 LXX was conceivably "a deliberate alternative reading of the text," which is "quite comparable with many examples of deliberate 'alternative readings' in the Qumran pesharim."[44] G. K. Beale also points out that some scholars too quickly assume that the Greek text of Amos 9:12 erroneously translates the MT.[45] In light of the connection between Edom and the Adamic blessings observed above, the LXX translation of Amos 9:12 arguably suggests Edom's status that came out of Adam by interpreting the remnant of "Edom" as that of "Adam."

More explicit connections between what Esau lost and Adamic bliss appear in some later Jewish and Christian texts that contain the idea of Esau's priesthood, particularly having descended from Adam the first priest. In some texts, the best garments that Rebekah took from Esau's belongings and Jacob put on to deceive his father were priestly garments. Isaac's words in Gen. 27:27 are taken to allude to the temple: "and he smelled the scent of his garments and blessed him and said, 'See, the scent of my son is as the scent of a field which the Lord had blessed.'" Targum Neofiti 27:27 interprets the text as follows: He said, "See! The smell of my son is as the smell of incense of choice perfumes which will be offered upon the altar on the mountain of the sanctuary, that is, the mountain which he who lives and endures for all ages has blessed."[46] Genesis Rabbah contains a similar reading: "This teaches that God showed him [Isaac] the [future] temple ... [about which it says], "my sweet savor" [Num. 28:2]" (Gen. Rab. 65:23).[47] J. L. Kugel aptly states that if the scent of the garment suggested the future site of the Temple, it is a reasonable inference that the garments were priestly ones.[48] Midrash Tanhuma further claims that the priestly garments of Esau were handed over from the first high priest, Adam.

> God clothed Adam with the garments of the high priesthood, since he was the firstborn of the world, then came Noah and [passed them on to Shem, and Shem] passed them on to Abraham, and Abraham passed them on to Isaac, and Isaac passed them on to Esau, who was his firstborn. But when Esau saw his wives worshipping other gods he left them [the priestly garments] with his mother. Since Jacob had bought the birthright from Esau, Rebekah said, "Jacob has bought the birthright from Esau, it is only right that he should wear these clothes," as it is written, "And Rebekah took the best garments of Esau, her older son..." [Gen. 27:15].[49]

---

[43] The term ἄνθρωπος appears three times in Amos. Unlike the other two cases of 4:13 and 5:19, the term in 9:12 appears with the article.
[44] Richard Bauckham, "James and the Gentiles (Acts 15:13-21)," in *History, Literature, and Society in the Book of Acts* (Cambridge: Cambridge University Press, 1996), 160–61.
[45] Beale, *The Temple and the Church's Mission*, 242.
[46] Martin McNamara, ed., *Targum Neofiti 1: Genesis: Translated, with Apparatus and Notes*, The Aramaic Bible, vol. 1A (Edinburgh: T&T Clark, 1992), 135.
[47] H. Freedman, Maurice Simon, and Isidore Epstein, eds., *Midrash Rabbah* (London: Soncino, 1939), vol. 2, 600.
[48] James L. Kugel, *Traditions of the Bible: A Guide to the Bible as It Was at the Start of the Common Era*, rev. and augm. ed. (Cambridge: Harvard University Press, 1998), 368.
[49] Salomon Buber, ed., *Midrash Tanḥuma* (Tel-Aviv: s.n., 1963), 133.

The text states that the priestly garments are passed down to the firstborns, who are in charge of the high priesthood that began with Adam the first high priest, and they are handed over to Jacob when Esau sold his priesthood, i.e. one of the privileges of his birthright.[50] It is further interesting that mentions of Esau's priestly garments in some rabbinic texts link Esau's selling of his birthright to his denial of the world to come. Targum Neofiti reads Gen. 25:34 as follows: "And Jacob gave bread and a dish of lentils to Esau and he ate ... Esau despised his birthright, and [made denial] concerning the vivification of the dead and denied the life of the world to come" (Ta. Neof. Gen. 25:34; Gen. Rab. 63:11 as well).[51] A similar addition to Esau's account of Gen. 25 appears in another Targum text (Ta. Ps.-J. Gen. 25:29) and some other rabbinic texts (b. B. Bat. 16b; Exod. Rab. 1.1).

The warning depending on Esau's example in vv. 16-17 functions as the climax of the warning part of the exhortation in vv. 14-17, and as the pivot, it connects vv. 14-17 with the eschatological vision in vv. 18-27. Esau's selling of his birthright forms a clear parallel with the birthright of the firstborn in the heavenly city in v. 23. The unfortunate consequence of Esau's offense, i.e. no chance to repent, is obviously placed in tandem with the stern warning in v.25. The multivalent thematic connection between Esau's example and the readers' situation is reasonably explained in the supposition that the author shares a similar eschatological vision with his contemporary apocalyptic texts. In the *Urzeit-Endzeit* eschatological framework, the author sees a continuity between the inheritance that Israel could have possessed and the eschatological inheritance that believers will inherit with the help of their high priest Jesus. In other words, what Esau sold for a bowl of food is in substantial continuity with what Hebrews' readers will enjoy in the unshakable kingdom, and thus, the author warns his readers by connecting their situation with the example of Esau: do not forfeit the inheritance as Esau did. Particularly, in this eschatological framework, Israel's inheritance that will be eschatologically culminated through Christ is the restoration of the primordial privileges that Adam enjoyed in Eden. Here, we can find the other reason that the author might bring Esau into his account. Some Jewish and early Christian traditions of Esau observed above show the distinctive idea that Esau forfeited the bliss that was Adam's. Esau stands out as an obvious example of someone who forfeited the primordial bliss for the delights of the world. In his *Urzeit-Endzeit* framework, the author admirably exhorts the believers who are in danger of committing apostasy even after experiencing

---

[50] Jerome also notes a similar idea by saying, "And Rebecca took with her in the house the garments of Esau her elder son, which were most desirable. Now in respect of this verse the Hebrews hand on a tradition that first-born sons performed the duty of the priests and possessed the priestly raiment, in which they were clothed as they were offering the victims to God, before Aaron was chosen for the priestly office." (Questions in Genesis 27:15). Jerome, *Saint Jerome's Hebrew Questions on Genesis*, trans. Robert Hayward, Oxford Early Christian Studies (Oxford; New York: Clarendon Press, 1995), 63.

[51] McNamara, *Targum Neofiti 1: Genesis*, 130. Both *Targum Pseudo-Jonathan* and *Targum Neofiti 1* on Gen. 4 expand Genesis' story of Cain and Abel, claiming that Cain killed Abel because of their differing theological opinions on the existence of the world to come. Michael Maher, *Targum Pseudo-Jonathan, Genesis* (Collegeville, MN: Liturgical Press, 1992), 33. McNamara, *Targum Neofiti 1: Genesis*, 65–68.

the heavenly world, i.e. a part of the eschatological inheritance, by warning them not to reiterate Esau's mistake that, on the one hand, forfeited the primordial bliss that they are hoping to restore as their eternal inheritance, and on the other hand, further back, recapitulates Adam's irrevocable mistake ("no chance to repent" 12:17; 12:25).

6.3 The Renewal of Creation

Criticism of the *Urzeit-Endzeit* eschatology in Hebrews is possibly based on the view that there is no concept of the renewal of creation in the book of Hebrews. H. Windisch, for example, maintains that Hebrews contains no concept of a renewal of the created world, but that Hebrews reckons with its annihilation instead.[52] Similarly G. Theissen insists that in Hebrew's eschatology, the "realm of creation" will be removed in order to make room for an eternal and immaterial "realm of salvation."[53] Cosmological dualism is argued by scholars who read Hebrews against a Platonic background.[54] More recently, K. Schenck argues that, in contrast with the unshakable dwelling place of God, the created realm of the old age will ultimately be removed.[55]

There is no explicit mention of the new heaven and earth in the book of Hebrews. Nevertheless, there are a good number of hints in Hebrews that allow an inference of the concept, the renewal of creation. The author repeatedly shows his deep interest in the world's creation and God as the Creator. E. Adams aptly lists the various references to the creation in Hebrews (1:2, 10; 2:10; 3:4; 4:3-4, 10; 9:26; 11:3).[56] In the introduction of the book, in 1:2-3, Christ is said to be the one "through whom" God made the world and who sustains all things in the universe by "the word of His power."[57] The wording of v. 2 defines God as creator and the Son as his agent for creation. A few verses later in Heb. 1:10, the author quotes Ps. 102, during his discussion of the Son's superiority to the angels. Here the Son is said to be responsible for the establishment of the earth and the heavens: "In the beginning, Lord, you founded the earth, and the heavens are the

---

[52] Hans Windisch, ed., *Der Hebräerbrief*, Handbuch zum Neuen Testament, Bd.4, Tl.3 (Tübingen: J. C. B. Mohr, 1913), 115.
[53] Gerd Theissen, *Untersuchungen zum Hebräerbrief*, Studien zum Neuen Testament, Bd. 2 (Gütersloh: Gütersloher Verlagshaus Gerd Mohn, 1969), 121.
[54] See, in particular, Thompson, *Hebrews*.
[55] Kenneth Schenck, *Cosmology and Eschatology in Hebrews: The Settings of the Sacrifice*, Society for New Testament Studies Monograph Series 143 (Cambridge; New York: Cambridge University Press, 2007), 142. Wilfried Eisele, in his attempt to sketch the putative Platonic background of Hebrews, argues that the shaking of the created realm in Heb. 12:26-27 is connected to the idea of the transition of the individual soul from earth to heaven at death. Wilfried Eisele, *Ein unerschütterliches Reich: die mittelplatonische Umformung des Parusiegedankens im Hebräerbrief*, Beihefte zur Zeitschrift für die neutestamentliche Wissenschaft und die Kunde der Älteren Kirche, Bd. 116 (Berlin; New York: de Gruyter, 2003), 428.
[56] Adams, "The Cosmology of Hebrews," 124–30.
[57] Weiss convincingly argues that the phrase refers to Jesus as sustaining creation. See Hans-Friedrich Weiss, *Der Brief an die Hebräer: Übersetzt und Erklärt*, 15. Aufl, Kritisch-exegetischer Kommentar über das Neue Testament 13 (Göttingen: Vandenhoeck & Ruprecht, 1991), 146.

work of your hands."⁵⁸ In Heb. 2:10-18, where the redemptive work of Christ is discussed, God is identified as the one "for whom and through whom all things exist."⁵⁹ As E. Adams points out, God is presented as both agent and cause (δι' ὅν) of the world.⁶⁰ In 3:1-6, God is again acknowledged as the creator of the world: "For every house is built by someone, but the builder of all things is God (ὁ δὲ πάντα κατασκευάσας θεός)." In Heb. 4:3-4, God's creative work is followed by his rest on the seventh day. The expression, "from the foundation of the world" (ἀπὸ καταβολῆς κόσμου, Heb. 4:3), appears again in Heb. 9:26. In the discussion of the topic of faith in ch.11, the author of Hebrews states his faith and that of his readers: "By faith we understand that the world was established by the word of God, so that what is seen was made from what is not visible" (Heb. 11:3). Apart from these examples, the author also mentions the createdness of the world (9:12; 12:27).

Furthermore, Hebrews implies the idea that the renewed creation will be part of the eschatological inheritance of the sons of God. Hebrews 1:2 indicates that the Son was appointed "heir of all things" (κληρονόμον πάντων), and 2:6-8 interprets Ps. 8 as meaning that God's intention for humanity within the created order will be fulfilled in the Son and his followers, the sons of God: "all things" (πάντα) will be put "in subjection under his feet." A. T. Lincoln aptly understands that the text points out the consummation that will embrace "created existence and its environment."⁶¹ In this regard, 1:10-12 presents an intriguing idea of the change of creation. The author of Hebrews quotes Ps. 102 in this passage to affirm the Son's creatorship and sovereign deity. Psalm 102 is not about creation's end but about it being changed. Some interpreters connect Ps. 102:26-27 with the new creation idea of Isa 65:17 and 66:22.⁶² Laansma interestingly sees the

---

⁵⁸ The citation of Ps. 102:26-27 in Heb. 1:11 is considered by a number of scholars as a text that shows Hebrews' anticipation of the dissolution of the universe: "they will perish, but you remain; they will all wear out like clothing (Heb. 1:11)" (e.g. David Arthur DeSilva, *Perseverance in Gratitude: A Socio-Rhetorical Commentaryon the Epistle "to the Hebrews"* (Grand Rapids: Eerdmans, 2000), 100; Koester, *Hebrews*, 203; Alan Christopher Mitchell and Daniel J. Harrington, *Hebrews*, Sacra Pagina Series, v. 13 (Collegeville, MN: Liturgical Press, 2009), 50). Nevertheless, Philip Church well proposes that Hebrews' quotation of Ps. 102 anticipates the renewal of the creation instead of its dissolution. He points out the verb רבד is used to refer to God's judgment on Jerusalem and the towns of Judea, which are not permanent destroyed but will be restored after the exile (Jer 9:12; 48:8). The imperfect tense of the verb possibility indicates that the psalm makes a hypothetical statement: if they do come to an end, YHWH will outlast them. Church also proposes that the semantic range of the term ἀπόλλυμι that the LXX renders includes not permanent destruction (e.g. the antediluvian world "perishes" in 2 Pet 3:6). Lastly, he points out that, in the context of Heb. 1, there is no suggestion that God will discard the creation. Rather the author highlights that the son upholds all things by his word (1:3). Philip Church, "Hebrews 1:10-12 and the Renewal of the Cosmos," *TynBul* 67, no. 2 (2016): 269–86.

⁵⁹ Filtvedt aptly indicates that the phrase "all things" refers back to everything that was created by God through Jesus (1:2-3). According to him, "the proctological πάντα in 2:10 picks up on the eschatological πάντα in 2:8, just as the proctological πάντα in 1:3 picks up on the eschatological πάντα in 1:2." Filtvedt, "Creation and Salvation in Hebrews," 283.

⁶⁰ Edward Adams, "The Cosmology of Hebrews," 125.

⁶¹ Andrew T. Lincoln, *Hebrews: A Guide* (London: T&T Clark, 2006), 100; Edward Adams, "The Cosmology of Hebrews," in *The Epistle to the Hebrews and Christian Theology* (Grand Rapids; Cambridge: Eerdmans, 2009), 137.

⁶² Mitchell Dahood, *Psalms III: 101–150* (New York: Doubleday, 1970), 22.

possibility that a similar kind of interpretation is based on Hebrews' quotation of Ps. 102.[63]

Hebrews 12:27 presents the contrast between the change/revelation(μετάθεσις) of the "things which can be shaken" (τῶν σαλευομένων) and the remaining/lasting (μένω) of "the things which cannot be shaken" (τὰ μὴ σαλευόμενα). Furthermore, the former are called "things created/made" implying that the latter are "things not created/made." Nevertheless, cosmological dualism is not the only way to explain this dichotomy as some scholars insist.[64] In Hebrews, among that which "remains" are a better possession (10:34) and a lasting city (13:14). The things that cannot be shaken in 12:27, which the author calls as the unshakable kingdom in the next verse, possibly refer to the dwelling place for God and his people, not as a physical location but as the abstract idea of a place for the union of God and his people. In the Haggai passage cited by Hebrews, Yahweh provides the people, who are disappointed in their rebuilt temple, with the promise of his house that will consist of the whole creation. He speaks about the latter glory of this house that will be greater than the former (2:9). Although the present and the future temples are distinctive entities in different locations, God considers them as the same house which has different extents of glory according to its point in time. In a similar way, the author of Hebrews points out that, at the eschaton, the renewed creation and the revealed heavenly world as the created places will become the venue of the house of God that has the unshaken quality.

The apocalyptic texts observed in previous chapters commonly share the idea of the renewal of creation that will occur at the eschaton. More specifically, they understand the removal of sufferings, death, sins, and defilement from the creation as the reversal of the curses caused by Adam's sin, and they also envision that the chosen people will exercise dominion over the creation as Adam was originally intended to do. 1 Enoch 10:16–11:2 alludes to Trito-Isaiah's vision of the new heaven and earth while connecting the postdiluvian restoration with the eschatological vision (see section 2.2.1.2). The Enochic text envisions that all iniquity and defilement will be removed from the earth along with all plague and sufferings (1 En 10:20-22) and that the earth will have the heavenly blessing, such that it will produce abundantly adhering to the people's will (1 En 10:19; 11:1). Jubilees describes "the day of the new creation" at the eschaton when "the heaven and earth and all of their creatures shall be renewed" (Jub 1:29). All sins, defilement, Satan, and evil ones will be removed from the land (Jub 50:5), and all creatures will obey the chosen people which was partially restored in the subjection of crows to Abram (11:18-24; cf. Adamic dominion over creation in 2:14; 6:5). In light of Jubilees' eschatological vision of restoration of what Adam forfeited, such as the lifespan

---

[63] Jon Laansma, "Hidden Stories in Hebrews: Cosmology and Theology," in *A Cloud of Witnesses: The Theology of Hebrews in Its Ancient Context* (London; New York: T&T Clark, 2008), 11. According to Laansma, "[i]n these chapters where the cosmos is directly thematicized an entirely positive view is taken of the cosmos and of the cosmos' destiny." According to him, the fact that Hebrews' discussion is fused to Ps. 95's theme of rest in 3:7–4:11 is not surprising.

[64] For the view that considers this dichotomy as a support for the cosmological dualism in Hebrews, see Attridge, *The Epistle to the Hebrews*, 381; George H. Guthrie, "Hebrews," in *Commentary on the New Testament Use of the Old Testament* (Grand Rapids; Nottingham: Baker Academic; Apollos, 2007) 423; Johnson, *Hebrews*, 269; Thompson, *Hebrews*, 2008, 335.

to the original length (Jub 4:30; 23:27) and his priesthood in the sanctuary (see section 2.4.2), the renewed creation most likely reflects the reversal of the curses that Adam caused through his sin. Pseudo-Philo states that the new creation at the eschaton will be an eternal dwelling place for the chosen people (*LAB* 3:10, see section 2.5.1). While it is stated that the earth was cursed through Adam's sin (37:3),[65] the author implies that, in the new creation at the eschaton, Eden's fertility, which was partially granted in the promised land, will be restored in a perfect form.[66] The author envisions that in this renewed creation, i.e. their dwelling place (19:13), the chosen people's dominion over "all things," which Adam forfeited through his sin (13:8).[67]

In the recognition of the hopeless present world, 4 Ezra envisions the coming world. Nevertheless, the coming world shows obvious features of continuity with the first world. 4 Ezra mentions the bodily resurrection indicating "material continuity" between two worlds. Furthermore, it highlights God's ongoing love for his creation (8:47, see section 3.2.1.3). 4 Ezra describes the shaking of the earth, which is connected to its change or renewal (4 Ezra 6:14-16). This idea is supported by the language of the "renewal of creation" in 7:75. 2 Baruch portrays the reversal of Adam's curses that will take place in the messianic kingdom. Untimely death, tribulation, illness, and lamentation will disappear (2 Bar 73:2-4; cf. 56:6). The products of the land will "shoot out speedily" so that "the reapers will not become tired, and the farmers will not wear themselves out" (73:7–74:1). The author also highlights that all creatures will be subject to human beings, alluding to Isaiah's vision of the new creation (2 Bar 73:6; cf. Is 65:25, see section 3.2.2.2).

As we observed in ch. 5, the author of Hebrews claims that God intended for the Israelites to enjoy God's rest in the promised land. The understanding that what Israel could enjoy in its history on the earth does not function as a metaphor or type of the transcendent and spiritual reality but shares substantial elements of the eschatological inheritance allows a reasonable inference: the author does not see creation as something to be destroyed and removed at the advent of the heavenly world. All apocalyptic texts observed above, including post-70 texts that hope for the revelation of the heavenly realm, uniformly envision the renewal of creation at the eschaton. The author of Hebrews does not explicitly mention the renewal of creation. In light of his consistent interest in creation and the eschatological vision of the Son's dominion over all creation, however, the following implication is not hard to draw: the renewed creation that Israel could enjoy in the promised land in a partial form, such as fertility of the land (Deut 7:13), subjection of nations (Deut 2:25; 11:25; cf. Gen. 9:2), or absence of plague (Deut 7:15), will be expanded to the whole creation and culminated to the perfect level at the eschaton. As followers of the Son, God's people will fulfill the Adamic task to rule over

---

[65] In the context, the statement of the result of Adam's sin, i.e. thorns and thistles, is used as an analogy for Abimelech's ruling over Israel though.

[66] For the relation between the three locations (i.e. Eden, the promised land, and the eschatological world) in terms of fertility and light, see section 2.5.2. Along with the fertility, the original lifespan and God's word (expressed as "light") that Adam enjoyed in Eden will be restored at the new creation (3:10; cf. 26:13, see sections 2.5.2 and 2.5.3).

[67] Concerning the equality of the references to paradise in chs. 13 and 19, see section 2.5.2.

all things in the renewed creation (Heb. 2:7-8), from which sin, suffering, and death will be removed (Heb. 2:14-16).

6.4 Summary of Ch. 6

In Hebrews 12, the author envisions the establishment of the eschatological kingdom through the shaking of heaven and earth. He points out that God's voice for "revelation" (χρηματίζω) from heaven causes the shaking, and through this shaking, the "created things" in heaven and earth will undergo some kind of "change" (μετάθεσις). By citing the OT passages that describe the establishment of a sanctuary on the earth or the mountain that experienced "shaking," the author presents his vision of the eschatological dwelling place for God and his priestly people that encompasses the earth and the heavenly realm. The eschatological visions in the parallel apocalyptic texts formulated with the notion of shaking provide a clearer understanding of Hebrews' vision: the unshakable kingdom will consist of the union of the revealed heavenly realm and the renewed creation. In this understanding, the exhortation depending on Esau's example, which is seemingly arbitrary, turns out to contain a crucial connection with the text's discussion of the eschatological kingdom. In the same vein in which he sees the continuity between Israel's inheritance of the promised land with the eschatological inheritance in Heb. 3–4, the author places the danger for his readers to forfeit their eschatological inheritance in tandem with Esau's loss of his birthright to the inheritance of the promised land. Some OT and Jewish traditions that connect Esau's inheritance, which he delivered to Jacob/Israel, with Adamic privileges well align with this supposed background of Hebrews, i.e. the *Urzeit-Endzeit* eschatology, since it operates Israel's history in the framework of God's creational intention and the culmination of its restoration at the eschaton. Hebrews 12:26-29 does not refer to the final judgment through which creation will be shaken to be ultimately destroyed. It discusses instead God's "promise" that he will prepare the earth and the heavenly realms to become the eternal dwelling place for him and his people. The author, accordingly, envisions that all things will become subject to the sons of God in the renewed creation, as they did to Adam in the beginning (Heb. 2:8; cf. Ps. 8:6-8).

7

Conclusion

As discussed in the first chapter of this monograph, many scholars of Hebrews hold the view that the author envisions the eschatological inheritance of the people of God in terms of the transcendent, heavenly world. This view was basically derived from the understanding that the author's cosmology reflects a dualism between the spiritual/heavenly and the material/earthly, which existed historically in various theo-philosophical forms under the influence of Middle Platonism. In their views, the author cites Gen. 2:2 in Heb. 3:7–4:11 to shed light on the transcendence of the rest that the people of God will possess eschatologically. In Hebrews' discussion, the function of Israel's historical possession of the land of Canaan, their earthly sanctuary and Levitical priests is to foreshadow or to highlight the metaphysical meaning of the true, heavenly inheritance. In the same vein, these scholars also tend to interpret the author's vision in Heb. 12:18-29 as the description of the transcendent world that will be granted to God's people at the eschaton: the material world, heaven and earth, will be shaken and destroyed, and the heavenly world, which has no substantial connection with the historical categories of Israel, will ultimately be given to God's people through Jesus' redemptive works.

If this is the case, however, why does the author of Hebrews emphasize Jesus' role in creation and, in particular, his inheritance of all creation? Is it reasonable that an author who wants to highlight the invisible, unshakable world that will come after the destruction of creation, should describe the redeemer as the creator and the heir of all creation? Moreover, how could he say that his readers are expecting to obtain the rest that the wilderness people forfeited in their disobedience? In what sense can he place these two unmingled earthly and heavenly inheritances in tandem, encouraging his readers to obtain the bliss unlike the previous generation who failed due to lack of faith and obedience?

I argue that an *Urzeit-Endzeit* eschatological framework, as observed in some Jewish apocalyptic texts, offers a plausible background against which the arguments of Hebrews are developed. Like some contemporary Jewish writers, the author envisions the eschatological world as the culmination of God's creational intention, which has been experienced by the previous generation of Israel, albeit partially. The argument was presented in three steps. First, in Chapters 2 and 3, which grouped pre-70 and post-70 texts respectively, I examined some apocalyptic texts with regard to how they envision the eschatological inheritance of the chosen people as reminiscent of the protological bliss of Adam in Eden. Second, in Chapter 4, I highlighted the two common elements of the *Urzeit-Endzeit* eschatological visions in the given texts, i.e. the restoration of God's presence and the renewal of creation, and I also pointed out the distinctions between the three groups, pre-70, post-70, and Revelation, with regard to how they understand the venue of God's presence. While the pre-70 texts envision the restored Jerusalem temple as the location of the restoration of God's presence, the post-70 apocalyptic texts hope for the revelation of the heavenly realms through which God will dwell among his people. Revelation, on the one hand, contains a similar hope of the coming heavenly realm. But, on the other hand, it re-appreciates the historical sanctuary of Israel as a venue of God's presence among his people, as implied in its description of the eschatological world as the holy of holies and the chosen people's identity as priests in the eschatological sanctuary.

Third, in Chapters 5 and 6, I showed that this framework of *Urzeit-Endzeit* aligns better with Hebrews' discussions than do other scholarly views. In the discussion of Heb. 3:7–4:11 in Chapter 5, I argued that, through the citation of Ps. 95, the author claims that God's rest, which an earlier generation of Israel forfeited, remains open for his readers not because Israel's historical inheritance merely foreshadows or symbolizes the eschatological inheritance, but because it shares core elements of the eschatological inheritance. Israel's rest in the promised land was not perfect and temporal, but in substantial continuity with the eschatological rest at the eschaton. I suggested the possibility that, while retaining a similar *Urzeit-Endzeit* eschatological framework, the author of Hebrews shared contemporary interpretations of the elements of such eschatological visions (i.e. the Jerusalem temple as a venue of God's presence in Rev and the change of heart as a core element of the renewal of creation in 4 Ezra). Accordingly, the author could consider that the older generation of Num 14, who could not enter the promised land and obtain God's presence among them, could not enter God's rest. He could claim that the younger generation of Num 20 was not able to enter God's rest, even though they actually entered the promised land, since their heart had not been changed into an obedient one. He could also encourage his readers to enter God's rest, which the previous generations of Israel forfeited, and thus remains open for them. The author makes the *Urzeit-Endzeit* framework relatively explicit through connecting Ps. 95 to Gen. 2:2. He implies that the rest which the wilderness generation could have enjoyed in the promised land and which will culminate in the eschaton is nothing other than the recapitulation of Adam's participation in God's Sabbath rest in Eden. In his *Urzeit-Endzeit* framework, the author's interpretation of Ps. 95 and his link between Ps. 95 and Gen. 2:2 are most reasonably explained on a thematic and theological level.

This understanding allows some implications about Hebrews' description of his readers' situation in comparison with that of Israel in the wilderness. The author does not use Israel's historical categories as metaphors for the spiritual realities, which have no substantial connections with the historical categories. The corresponding descriptions of the earthly and heavenly categories suggest rather that he presents the fulfillment and consummation through Christ of what partially functioned and was in a limited, temporal way provided in Israel's history. In light of the understanding of the connection between Israel's rest in the promised land and the eschatological rest that God's people will enjoy in the eschatological world, the author places the present time of his readers in tandem with the wilderness period of the Israelites. He claims that his readers are in the wilderness, waiting to enter into the promised inheritance which lies in front of them. During the time of wilderness, just as the Israelites could come closer to God's presence through the high priest, who was allowed to enter the holy of holies in the tabernacle once a year, the readers are coming close to God's presence through their high priest, who serves in the heavenly tabernacle. Unlike the service of human priests, Jesus' "once for all" sacrifice and his continuous intercession in the heavenly holy of holies make the people cleansed and perfect for ever. When the Joshua *par excellence* comes back, the people will be led into the eternal inheritance that consists of the revealed heavenly temple and the renewed creation. There, they will enjoy God's rest in the culminated form, the rest in which Adam could participate before his sin, and the Israelites could enjoy in the promised land, albeit partially.

In Chapter 5, I further supported the argument with some noticeable patterns shared by *Urzeit-Endzeit* eschatologies in some apocalyptic texts and Hebrews. The relevant apocalyptic texts envisage that the chosen people will obtain the eschatological sanctuary as their inheritance, where they will dwell with God eternally. This vision appears in relation to Israel's combined identities as God's firstborn and his priests, priests in the Adamic succession. In other words, they formulate the eschatological status of the chosen people as recapitulating the status of Adam in Eden. This background noticeably parallels the way in which the author of Hebrews both describes Jesus' combined identities as the Son of God and his high priest in the discussion of his entrance into the heavenly sanctuary to sit at God's right hand and also encourages his readers to follow the forerunner, Jesus, entering the true sanctuary and inheriting the glory of the Son (Heb. 2:8).

As regards Heb. 12:18-29, the language of the shaking of heaven and earth, and the vision of the unshakable kingdom are often considered to reflect the dualism between the material and spiritual worlds. In ch. 6, however, I argued that Hebrews' vision of the accomplishment of the eschatological world in the present passage can most reasonably be explained by an *Urzeit-Endzeit* apocalyptic eschatology. The contrast between the earthly realm and the heavenly space of God's presence in v. 25 and the statement of the heavenly Jerusalem in v. 22 suggest that the same contrast between the earthly and heavenly realms continues in v. 26 and thus that the shaking of heaven refers to the heavenly dwelling place of God. I showed that the usage of the two terms, χρηματίζω and μετάθεσις, suggests that the image of shaking in Heb. 12 is related to revelation and transformation rather than to destruction or removal. I also pointed out that, in the quoted OT passages of Haggai and Exodus, the shaking of heaven and earth is presented as a process for the establishment of God's sanctuary among his people. The parallel contexts of these OT passages indicate that the author envisages that the establishment of the eschatological sanctuary where God's people will dwell with God, will involve the shaking of not only the creation, but also the heavenly realms.

In light of this evidence, scholarly assumptions that the language of shaking in the present passage denotes the idea of destruction and that the author envisages the transcendent world which will be established through the destruction of the creation are not compelling. Instead, I argued that, in the present context of God's "promise" (12:26), the author describes the eschatological world that consists of the transformed creation and the revealed heavenly realms, similar to what one finds in apocalyptic *Urzeit-Endzeit* visions. The idea is supported by some contemporary apocalyptic texts in which the image of shaking is related to the transformation of the earth or the revelation of heavenly realms, particularly in connection to the eschatological vision described in terms of the primordial bliss. 2 Bar 59:3, especially, contains the idea of the shaking of the heavens through its revelation to human beings. On the question of whether the heavenly realm can belong to "created things" (12:27), I highlighted some passages which show that Hebrews understands the heavenly realm as created by God.

I claimed that the mention of Esau in Heb. 12:16-17 is also comprehensible in an *Urzeit-Endzeit* framework. The possible link of Esau's example with the wilderness generation in Heb. 3:7–4:11 and the thematic connection between Esau's case and the situation of the readers in Heb. 12:18-29 (i.e. firstborn, loss of inheritance, and danger of an irretrievable sin) strongly suggest that Esau is not presented as a general example of someone making a faulty decision. I argued that, in a framework of *Urzeit-Endzeit* eschatology, the author sees the substantial connection between what Esau forfeited, i.e. the right to God's rest in the promised land, and what the readers are expecting to obtain, i.e. God's rest in the eschatological inheritance. In other words, the author presents Esau as the one who made a mistake similar to that of the wilderness generation discussed in Heb. 3:7–4:11. Esau and the wilderness generation are parallel examples of the forfeiture of the eschatological inheritance through the process of falling away from God/God's grace (3:12; 12:15a), hardening his heart/having bitter root in his heart (3:13; 12:15b), and thus deliberately forsaking the eternal inheritance for the pleasures of the world (3:13; 12:16-17). Accordingly, with the inferential γάρ in v.18 he connects Esau's example to his discussion in 12:18-29 of the eschatological world that will be given as the inheritance of God's people, warning them not to repeat the same mistake as Esau, in the same way that he exhorted them concerning God's rest with the example of the wilderness generation in Heb. 3:7–4:11.

Some biblical and Jewish traditions that show a more direct connection between what Esau lost and what Adam enjoyed in Eden suggest an additional reason why the author mentions Esau in particular in his exhortation of the eschatological inheritance. In some OT texts, the dynamics between Israel's inheritance of Adamic blessings and Edom's judgment for coveting the inheritance describe the concept of Esau's right as the firstborn in terms of Adamic bliss. Some Targumim and rabbinic texts contain the more developed idea that Esau handed over to Jacob his priesthood, which had been passed on to firstborns since Adam. These texts interestingly connect Esau's selling of his birthright to his denial of the world to come. Such relatively direct connections between Esau's inheritance and the bliss of Adam in some Jewish traditions help to explain how the author of Hebrews' exhortation, which uses Esau's example, could be an effective warning for his readers not to forfeit the eschatological inheritance, a reference to the culmination of the primordial bliss in the *Urzeit-Endzeit* framework. In Chapter 6, additionally, I highlighted parallel patterns in some apocalyptic texts which suggest the possibility that Hebrews contains the idea of new creation even though there is no explicit mention of new creation.

In Heb. 12:18-29, the author states that, while they wait to receive the eschatological inheritance, the readers can experience the heavenly realms through their high priest,

Jesus (cf. Heb. 6:4-5), as the wilderness generation had experienced God's presence on the holy mountain, Sinai, though in a more full and direct way. He presents the vision that the eschatological inheritance will be established with the revealed heavenly realms and the renewed creation. In this unshakable, eternal world, they will enjoy the consummated forms of God's rest, glory, the submission of all creation, and the life that Adam enjoyed in Eden and the Israelites could enjoy in the promised land, albeit in a partial and temporal form. The author states that, if the wilderness generation, who experienced the holy mountain and rebelled, could not obtain their inheritance, how could they, who even experienced the heavenly realms, have a chance to repent. He sternly warns his readers that they cannot repent just as Esau could not when he sold his firstborn right to the inheritance, reiterating Adam's irretrievable sin. The author asks an implicit question in this warning: could Adam repent after his willful choice rejecting the heavenly bliss in Eden?

Scholarly reluctance to recognize the notions of Adam, Eden, or the new creation in Hebrews very likely derives from the fact that Hebrews never explicitly mentions any of them. For example, among four possible references of the term ἑνός in Heb. 2:11— God, Adam, Abraham, or humanity—some scholars confidently set aside the option of Adam mainly because there is no explicit occurrence of the name "Adam" in Hebrews. Ellingworth describes the proponents of this view in patristic writings and expounds on the theological view of Adam as the single common ancestor of the human race in the New Testament, rabbinic writings and patristic writings.[1] He dismisses, however, any Adamic influence simply because of the absence of an explicit mention of Adam in Hebrews.[2] Cockerill similarly drops the option of Adam for the reason that "Hebrews never mentions Adam."[3]

Nevertheless, the argument of this monograph suggests that the lack of an explicit mention of primordial categories is insufficient ground for excluding the possibility of underlying protological notions in Hebrews. The absence of an explicit mention can rather be understood in light of the cultural backgrounds that the author and his readers share. Given their shared "cultural encyclopedia,"[4] when the author brings up particular combinations of the concepts, such as sonship, the firstborn, inheritance, glory, superiority to angels, and the priesthood and temple, people could plausibly recall the underlying concepts of the primordial bliss that Adam lost and the hope of the eschatological culmination. In the cultural background of the *Urzeit-Endzeit* framework that I have argued Hebrews shares with some apocalyptic texts, the descriptions of Jesus in Heb. 1:2-6, i.e. as the image of God (1:3) and God's firstborn

---

[1] Sedulius Scotus, *PL* 103.255; c. Valentinum, *PG* 26.1224; Erasmus, *TDNT* 1.
[2] Ellingworth, *The Epistle to the Hebrews*, 165.
[3] Cockerill, *The Epistle to the Hebrews*, 140.
[4] Umberto Eco highlighted the larger socio-cultural context, called 'encyclopedia,' apart from which language cannot be analyzed. According to him, such a cultural encyclopedia is the theoretical pool of a society's knowledge such as codes, rules, conventions, history, literature, truth claims, and discourses. As readers or audiences interpret texts, they refer to the cultural encyclopedia to decode that which the author has coded in the text. Umberto Eco, *Semiotics and the Philosophy of Language* (Bloomington: Indiana University Press, 1984), 68–84. For a similar discussion related to the biblical texts, see Leroy A. Huizenga, *The New Isaac: Tradition and Interpretation in the Gospel of Matthew* (Leiden: Brill, 2009), 24–29.

(1:2, 6; Ps. 2:7), reflect his Adamic identity. He restores Adam's glory, authority over the creation, and superiority to the heavenly beings (2:5-9; Ps. 8:4-6). Through obeying even to death, he overcame the power of death which had been activated through Adam's sin. As the high priest, Jesus serves God in the heavenly sanctuary as the first priest Adam did in Eden. The other sons are promised that they will enjoy God's rest that Adam could participate in (Gen. 2:2) and enter the heavenly sanctuary following the high priest (e.g. Heb. 4:16; 6:19; 10:19-22). This will be part of the eschatological kingdom, which will be combined with the renewed creation (Heb. 12:28).

The conclusion can be summarized thus: the way in which the author of Hebrews unfolds his eschatological visions suggests that he shares apocalyptic *Urzeit-Endzeit* eschatologies which place Israel's history in between the corresponding beginning and renewal of the present world. God's intention toward the creation and his people, which Adam forfeited through his sin, has been experienced, at least partially, throughout Israel's history and its earthly categories, and it will ultimately be fulfilled in a culminated form in the eschatological renewal of the world through what Jesus has done. Hebrews' logic in Heb. 3:7–4:11 and 12:18-29 is, in other words, most coherently explained in this framework of *Urzeit-Endzeit*.

This understanding of Hebrews' eschatology carries an implication regarding the recipients of the epistle. The identity of the recipients of Hebrews is as mysterious as that of the author, and I am not attempting to argue for a specific group as the exclusive recipients of the epistle. The understanding of Hebrews' eschatological view in the framework that I suggested, however, can imply a significance that Hebrews' exhortation would have for Jewish Christians, particularly those who might be wondering about God's covenantal faithfulness to Israel or the meaning of the historical categories that God provided for them (e.g. promised land, sacrificial system, priesthood, and temple). How could God let his chosen people be scattered away from the promised land and the temple be destroyed by the hands of the Gentiles (in the case that the book was written after 70 CE)? Did all the historical categories that Israel had held throughout its history mean nothing? In his *Urzeit-Endzeit* framework of eschatology, the author places Israel's history in between the corresponding beginning and end of God's salvation history. God will eventually accomplish his intention toward humanity and the creation at the eschaton. He allowed his chosen people to experience anticipatory bliss similar to what Adam enjoyed in Eden, such as the rest in the promised land, priesthood, sacrifice, and temple, the bliss which will be granted to God's people in a complete form at the eschaton. Then, what Hebrews would have attempted is not to prevent Jewish Christians' relapse into Judaism by devaluing Israel's earthly categories. Rather, the author seeks to highlight the meaning of these categories as Israel's privileges through which they genuinely experienced, even if only partially, the divine bliss that God originally intended and that will ultimately culminate in the world to come. The author thus claims that in Jesus God is indeed faithful and is keeping his promises to Israel.

Bibliography

Adams, Edward. *Constructing the World: A Study in Paul's Cosmological Language*. Studies of the New Testament and Its World. Edinburgh: T&T Clark, 2000.

Adams, Edward. *The Stars Will Fall from Heaven: Cosmic Catastrophe in the New Testament and Its World*. Library of New Testament Studies 347. London; New York: T&T Clark, 2007.

Adams, Edward. "The Cosmology of Hebrews." in *The Epistle to the Hebrews and Christian Theology*, 122–39. Grand Rapids; Cambridge: Eerdmans, 2009.

Allen, David Lewis. *Hebrews*. New American Commentary 35. Nashville: B & H Publishing Group, 2010.

Anderson, Gary. "Celibacy or Consummation in the Garden? Reflections on Early Jewish and Christian Interpretations of the Garden of Eden." *Harvard Theological Review* 82, no. 2 (1989): 121–48.

Attridge, Harold W. "'Let Us Strive to Enter That Rest' the Logic of Hebrews 4:1-11." *The Harvard Theological Review* 73, no. 1/2 (1980): 279–88.

Attridge, Harold W. *The Epistle to the Hebrews: A Commentary on the Epistle to the Hebrews*. Hermeneia: A Critical and Historical Commentary on the Bible. Philadelphia: Fortress Press, 1989.

Aune, David E. and Eric Stewart. "From the Idealized Past to the Imaginary Future: Eschatological Restoration in Jewish Apocalyptic Literature." In *Restoration: Old Testament, Jewish, and Christian Perspectives*, 147–77. Leiden: Brill, 2001.

Aune, David Edward. *Revelation 1–5*. Word Biblical Commentary 52. Dallas: Word Books, 1997.

Aune, David Edward. *Revelation 17–22*. Word Biblical Commentary 52C. Nashville: T. Nelson, 1998.

Bachmann, V. "Rooted in Paradise? The Meaning of the 'Tree of Life' in 1 Enoch 24–25 Reconsidered." *Journal for the Study of the Pseudepigrapha* 19, no. 2 (2009): 83–107.

Barker, Margaret. *The Gate of Heaven: The History and Symbolism of the Temple in Jerusalem*. London: SPCK, 1991.

Barnard, Jody A. *The Mysticism of Hebrews: Exploring the Role of Jewish Apocalyptic Mysticism in the Epistle to the Hebrews*. Wissenschaftliche Untersuchungen zum Neuen Testament 331. Tübingen: Mohr Siebeck, 2012.

Batdorf, Irvin Wesley. "Hebrews and Qumran: Old Methods and New Directions." In *Festschrift to Honor of Wilbur Gingrich: Lexicographer, Scholar, Teacher, and Committed Christian Layman*, 16–35. Leiden: Brill, 1972.

Bauckham, Richard. *The Theology of the Book of Revelation*. New Testament Theology. Cambridge; New York, NY: Cambridge University Press, 1993.

Bauckham, Richard. "James and the Gentiles (Acts 15:13-21)." In *History, Literature, and Society in the Book of Acts*. Cambridge: Cambridge University Press, 1996.

Baumgarten, Joseph. "Purification after Childbirth and the Sacred Garden in 4Q265 and Jubilees." In *New Qumran Texts and Studies*, 3–10. Leiden: Brill, 1994.

Baumgarten, Joseph and Michael Davis. "Cave IV, V, VI Fragments." In *Damascus Document, War Rule, and Related Documents*, 59–79. Tübingen, Germany: Mohr Siebeck, 1995.

Baumgarten, Joseph, Jόzef T. Milik, Stephen J. Pfann, and Ada Yardeni, eds. *Discoveries in the Judaean Desert. 18, Qumran Cave 4, XIII, The Damascus Document (4Q266-273)*. Oxford: Clarendon Press, 1996.

Baumgarten, Joseph and D. R. Schwartz. *The Dead Sea Scrolls, Volume 2: Damascus Document, War Scroll, and Related Documents*. Edited by James H. Charlesworth. Tübingen; Louisville: Westminster John Knox Press, 1996.

Bautch, Kelley Coblentz. *A Study of the Geography of 1 Enoch 17–19: "No One Has Seen What I Have Seen."* Supplements to the Journal for the Study of Judaism 81. Leiden; Boston: Brill, 2003.

Bautch, Kelley Coblentz. "Situating the Afterlife." In *Paradise Now: Essays on Early Jewish and Christian Mysticism*, 249–64. Atlanta: Society of Biblical Literature, 2006.

Beale, G. K. *The Temple and the Church's Mission: A Biblical Theology of the Dwelling Place of God*. New Studies in Biblical Theology 17. Downers Grove, IL: InterVarsity Press, 2004.

Beale, G. K. *A New Testament Biblical Theology: The Unfolding of the Old Testament in the New*. Grand Rapids: Baker Academic, 2011.

Beale, G. K. *The Book of Revelation: A Commentary on the Greek Text*. The New International Greek Testament Commentary. Grand Rapids: Eerdmans, 2013.

Beasley-Murray, George R., ed. *The Book of Revelation*. Century Bible. London: Oliphants, 1974.

Berg, Shane. "Ben Sira, the Genesis Creation Accounts, and the Knowledge of God's Will." *Journal of Biblical Literature* 132 (2013): 139–57.

Bergmeier, R. "Quellen vorchristlicher Gnosis?" In *Tradition und Glaube: Das Frühe Christentum in seiner Umwelt: Festgabe für Karl Georg Kuhn zum 65. Geburtstag*. Göttingen: Vandenhoeck & Ruprecht, 1971.

Black, Matthew, and James C. VanderKam, eds. *The Book of Enoch or 1 Enoch: A New English Edition*. Studia in Veteris Testamenti Pseudepigrapha 7. Leiden: Brill, 1985.

Bloch, René S. "Methodological Note for the Study of Rabbinic Literature." In *Approaches to Ancient Judaism: Theory and Practice*, 51–75. Missoula: Scholars Press, 1978.

Block, Daniel Isaac. *The Book of Ezekiel*. The New International Commentary on the Old Testament. Grand Rapids: Eerdmans, 1997.

Boccaccini, Gabriele, ed. *Enoch and Qumran Origins: New Light on a Forgotten Connection*. Grand Rapids: Eerdmans, 2005.

Bockmuehl, Markus, and Guy G. Stroumsa. *Paradise in Antiquity: Jewish and Christian Views*. Cambridge: Cambridge University Press, 2010.

Bogaert, Pierre, ed. *Apocalypse de Baruch*. Sources Chrétiennes, 145. Paris: Éditions du Cerf, 1969.

Boring, M. Eugene. *Revelation*. Interpretation, a Bible Commentary for Teaching and Preaching. Louisville: John Knox Press, 1989.

Boring, M. Eugene and Fred B. Craddock. *The People's New Testament Commentary*. Louisville, KY: Westminster John Knox Press, 2010.

Bousset, Wilhelm. *Die Offenbarung Johannis*. Kritisch-exegetischer Kommentar über das Neue Testament, Abt. 16. Göttingen: Vandenhoeck und Ruprecht, 1896.

Boxall, Ian. *The Revelation of Saint John*. Black's New Testament Commentaries 18. Peabody, MA; London; New York: Hendrickson Publishers; Continuum, 2006.

Boyarin, Daniel. *Intertextuality and the Reading of Midrash*. Indiana Studies in Biblical Literature. Bloomington: Indiana University Press, 1990.

Breech, Earl. "These Fragments I Have Shored against My Ruins: The Form and Function of 4 Ezra." *Journal of Biblical Literature* 2 (1973): 267–74.

Brooke, George J. "Biblical Interpretation in the Wisdom Texts from Qumran." In *Wisdom Texts from Qumran*, 201–20. Leuven: Leuven University Press, 2002.

Brooke, George J. "Miqdash Adam, Eden and the Qumran Community." In *Gemeinde ohne Tempel/ Community without Temple: Zur Substituierung und Transformation des Jerusalemer Tempels und seines Kults im Alten Testament, Antiken Judentum und Frühen Christentum*, 285–301. Tubingen: Mohr, 1999.

Bruce, F. F. *The Epistle to the Hebrews*. Rev. ed. The New International Commentary on the New Testament. Grand Rapids: Eerdmans, 1990.

Buber, Salomon, ed. *Midrash Tanḥuma*. Tel-Aviv: Ortsel, 1963.

Buchanan, George Wesley, ed. *To the Hebrews*. The Anchor Bible 36. Garden City, NY: Doubleday, 1972.

Bultmann, Rudolf. *History and Eschatology*. Edinburgh: The University Press, 1957.

Bultmann, Rudolf. *The Presence of Eternity: History and Eschatology*. New York: Harper and Brothers, 1957.

Bunta, Silviu N. "The Convergence of Adamic and Merkabah Traditions in the Christology of Hebrews." In *Searching the Scriptures: Studies in Context and Intertextuality*. Studies in Scripture in Early Judaism and Christianity 19. London: Bloomsbury T&T Clark, 2015.

Calaway, Jared C. *The Sabbath and the Sanctuary: Access to God in the Letter to the Hebrews and Its Priestly Context*. Wissenschaftliche Untersuchungen zum Neuen Testament. 2. Reihe 349. Tübingen: Mohr Siebeck, 2013.

Campbell, Jonathan G. *The Use of Scripture in the Damascus Document 1-8, 19-20*. Beihefte zur Zeitschrift für die alttestamentliche Wissenschaft, 228. Berlin; New York: W. de Gruyter, 1995.

Caquot, A. "Les Textes de Sagesse de Qoumrân (Aperçu Préliminaire)." *Revue d'Histoire et de Philosophie Religieuses* 76, no. 1 (1996): 1–34.

Cavin, Robert L. *New Existence and Righteous Living: Colossians and 1 Peter in Conversation with 4QInstruction and the Hodayot*. Beihefte zur Zeitschrift für die neutestamentliche Wissenschaft,197. Berlin: De Gruyter, 2013.

Charles, R. H., ed. *The Apocalypse of Baruch: Translated from the Syriac, Chapters I-LXXVII from the Sixth Cent. Ms. in the Ambrosian Library of Milan: And Chapters LXXVIII-LXXXVII-The Epistle of Baruch from a New and Critical Text Based on Ten Mss. and Published Herewith*. London: Adam & Charles Black, 1896.

Charles, R. H., ed. *The Book of Enoch*. Oxford: Clarendon, 1912.

Charles, R. H., ed. *A Critical and Exegetical Commentary on the Revelation of St. John*. The International Critical Commentary. Edinburgh: T&T Clark, 1920.

Charlesworth, James H., P. Dykers, and M. J. H. Charlesworth. *The Pseudepigrapha and Modern Research with a Supplement*. Septuagint and Cognate Studies Series, no. 7S. Chico, CA: Scholars Press, 1981.

Charlesworth, James H., ed. *The Old Testament Pseudepigrapha*. Anchor Bible Reference Library. New York: Doubleday, 1983.

Childs, Brevard S. *Myth and Reality in the Old Testament*. London: SCM Press, 1962.

Church, Philip. "Hebrews 1:10-12 and the Renewal of the Cosmos." *Tyndale Bulletin* 67, no. 2 (2016): 269–86.

Church, Philip. *Hebrews and the Temple: Attitudes to the Temple in Second Temple Judaism and in Hebrews*. Leiden: Brill, 2017.

Cockerill, Gareth Lee. *The Epistle to the Hebrews*. The New International Commentary on the New Testament. Grand Rapids; Cambridge: Eerdmans, 2012.

Collins, John J. "Likeness of the Holy Ones." In *the Provo International Conference on the Dead Sea Scrolls: Technological Innovations, New Texts, and Reformulated Issues.* Leiden; Boston; Köln: Brill, 1999.

Collins, John J. *Apocalypticism in the Dead Sea Scrolls.* The Literature of the Dead Sea Scrolls. London; New York: Routledge, 1997.

Coloe, Mary L. *God Dwells with Us: Temple Symbolism in the Fourth Gospel.* Collegeville, MN: Liturgical Press, 2001.

Crane, Ashley S. *Israel's Restoration: A Textual-Comparative Exploration of Ezekiel 36–39.* Supplements to Vetus Testamentum, 122. Leiden; Boston: Brill, 2008.

Dacy, Marianne. "Attitude to the Temple in the Damascus Document and the Temple Scroll." *Australian Journal of Jewish Studies,* 2009, 44–52.

Dahl, N. A. "Christ, Creation and the Church." In *the Background of the New Testament and Its Eschatology.* Cambridge: Cambridge University Press, 1956.

Dahood, Mitchell. *Psalms III: 101–150.* New York: Doubleday, 1970.

Davenport, Gene L. *The Eschatology of the Book of Jubilees.* Studia Post-Biblica, 20. Leiden: Brill, 1971.

Davidson, Richard M. *Flame of Yahweh: Sexuality in the Old Testament.* Peabody, MA: Baker Academic, 2007.

Davies, John A. *A Royal Priesthood: Literary and Intertextual Perspectives on an Image of Israel in Exodus 19.6.* Journal for the Study of the Old Testament 395. London; New York: T&T Clark International, 2004.

Davies, Philip R. *The Damascus Covenant.* Journal for the Study of the Old Testament 25. Sheffield: JSOT Press, 1983.

Davila, James R. *The Dead Sea Scrolls as Background to Postbiblical Judaism and Early Christianity: Papers from an International Conference at St. Andrews in 2001.* Leiden: Brill, 2003.

Dempster, Stephen G. *Dominion and Dynasty: A Biblical Theology of the Hebrew Bible.* New Studies in Biblical Theology 15. Downers Grove: InterVarsity Press, 2003.

Descamps, A. "La Structure de l'Épître Aux Hébreux." *Revue Diocésaine de Tournai* 9 (1954): 251–58.

DeSilva, David Arthur. *Perseverance in Gratitude: A Socio-Rhetorical Commentary on the Epistle "to the Hebrews."* Grand Rapids: Eerdmans, 2000.

Deutsch, C. "Transformation of Symbols: The New Jerusalem in Rev 21:1–22:5." *Zeitschrift für die neutestamentliche Wissenschaft* 78, no. 1 (1987): 106–26.

Dillmann, August, ed. *Das Buch Henoch.* Leipzig: Fr. Chr. Wilh. Vogel, 1853.

Docherty, Susan E. *The Use of the Old Testament in Hebrews: A Case Study in Early Jewish Bible Interpretation.* Wissenschaftliche Untersuchungen zum Neuen Testament. 2. Reihe 260. Tübingen: Mohr Siebeck, 2009.

Doering, Lutz. "Urzeit-Endzeit Correlation in the Dead Sea Scrolls and Pseudepigrapha." In *Eschatologie-Eschatology.* Tübingen: Mohr Siebeck, 2011.

Dumbrell, William J. *Covenant and Creation: An Old Testament Covenantal Theology.* Exeter: Paternoster, 1993.

Dunne, John Anthony. "David's Tent as Temple in Amos 9:11-15: Understanding the Epilogue of Amos and Considering Implications for the Unity of the Book." *The Westminster Theological Journal* 73, no. 2 (September 2011): 363–74.

Eco, Umberto. *Semiotics and the Philosophy of Language.* Bloomington: Indiana University Press, 1984.

Ego, Beate. "Heilige Zeit—heiliger Raum—heiliger Mensch: Beobachtungen zur Struktur der Gesetzesbegründung in der Schöpfungs- und Paradiesgeschichte des

Jubiläenbuches." In *Studies in the Book of Jubilees*, 207–19. Tübingen: Mohr Siebeck, 1997.

Eisele, Wilfried. *Ein unerschütterliches Reich: die mittelplatonische Umformung des Parusiegedankens im Hebräerbrief*. Beihefte zur Zeitschrift für die neutestamentliche Wissenschaft und die Kunde der älteren Kirche, 116. Berlin; New York: W. de Gruyter, 2003.

Elgvin, Torleif. "An Analysis of 4QInstruction." Hebrew University of Jerusalem, 1997.

Ellingworth, Paul. *The Epistle to the Hebrews: A Commentary on the Greek Text*. The New International Greek Testament Commentary. Grand Rapids; Carlisle, England: Eerdmans; Paternoster Press, 1993.

Enns, P. E. "Creation and Re-creation: Psalm 95 and Its Interpretation in Hebrews 3:1–4:13." *Westminster Theological Journal* 55, no. 2 (1993): 255–80.

Farrer, Austin. *The Revelation of St. John the Divine: Commentary on The English Text*. Oxford: Clarendon Press, 1964.

Filson, Floyd V. "The Epistle to the Hebrews." *Journal of Bible and Religion* 22, no. 1 (1954): 20–26.

Filtvedt, O. J. "Creation and Salvation in Hebrews." *Zeitschrift für die neutestamentliche Wissenschaft und die Kunde der alteren Kirche* 106, no. 2 (2015): 280–303.

Fletcher-Louis, Crispin H. T. *All the Glory of Adam: Liturgical Anthropology in the Dead Sea Scrolls*. Studies on the Texts of the Desert of Judah 42. Leiden; Boston; Köln: Brill, 2002.

Fraade, Steven D. *Enosh and His Generation: Pre-Israelite Hero and History in Postbiblical Interpretation*. Society of Biblical Literature Monograph Series 30. Chico, CA: Scholars Press, 1984.

Freedman, H., Maurice Simon, and Isidore Epstein, eds. *Midrash Rabbah*. London: Soncino, 1939.

Fuller, Michael E. *The Restoration of Israel: Israel's Re-Gathering and the Fate of the Nations in Early Jewish Literature and Luke-Acts*. Berlin; New York: Walter de Gruyter, 2006.

Georgi, Dieter. "Die Visionen vom himmlischen Jerusalem in Apk 21 u 22." In *Kirche: Festschrift für Günther Bornkamm zum 75 Geburstag*, 351–72. Tübingen, Germany: J C. B. Mohr, 1980.

Giblin, Charles Homer. *The Book of Revelation: The Open Book of Prophecy*. Collegeville: Michael Glazier Inc, 1991.

Giesen, Heinz. *Die Offenbarung des Johannes*. Regensburger Neues Testament. Regensburg: F. Pustet, 1997.

Gilders, William K. "Blood and Covenant: Interpretive Elaboration on Genesis 9.4-6 in the Book of Jubilees." *Journal for the Study of the Pseudepigrapha* 15, no. 2 (2006): 83–118.

Gilders, William K. "The Concept of Covenant in Jubilees." In *Enoch and the Mosaic Torah: The Evidence of Jubilees*, 178–92. Grand Rapids: Eerdmans, 2009.

Goff, Matthew J. *The Worldly and Heavenly Wisdom of 4QInstruction*. Studies on the Texts of the Desert of Judah, v. 50. Leiden; Boston: Brill, 2003.

Goff, Matthew J. *4QInstruction*. Wisdom Literature from the Ancient World 2. Atlanta: Society of Biblical Literature, 2013.

Gore-Jones, Lydia. "The Unity and Coherence of 4 Ezra: Crisis, Response, and Authorial Intention." *Journal for the Study of Judaism: In the Persian Hellenistic & Roman Period* 47, no. 2 (2016): 212–35.

Grässer, Erich. *Der Glaube im Hebräerbrief*. Marburg: Elwert, 1965.

Grelot, Pierre. "La Géographie Mythique d'Hénoch et Ses Sources Orientales." *Revue Biblique* 65, no. 1 (1958): 33–69.

Grossman, Maxine L. *Reading for History in the Damascus Document: A Methodological Study*. Studies on the Texts of the Desert of Judah, v. 45. Leiden; Boston; Köln: Brill, 2002.

Gruenwald, Ithamar. *Apocalyptic and Merkavah Mysticism*. 2nd rev. ed. Ancient Judaism and Early Christianity 90. Leiden; Boston: Brill, 2014.

Gundry, Stanley. *Three Views on the New Testament Use of the Old Testament*. Grand Rapids: Zondervan, 2008.

Gunkel, Hermann, Heinrich Zimmern, and Friedrich Hügel. *Schöpfung und Chaos in Urzeit und Endzeit: Eine religionsgeschichtliche Untersuchung über Gen. 1 und Ap. Joh. 12*. Göttingen: Vandenhoeck und Ruprecht, 1895.

Hahne, Harry. *The Corruption and Redemption of Creation: Nature in Romans 8.19-22 and Jewish Apocalyptic Literature*. London; New York: T&T Clark, 2006.

Haran, Menahem. *Temples and Temple-Service in Ancient Israel: An Inquiry into Biblical Cult Phenomena and the Historical Setting of the Priestly School*. Warsaw: Eisenbrauns, 1985.

Harrington, D. G. "Two Early Jewish Approaches to Wisdom: Sirach and Qumran Sapiential Work A." In *the Wisdom Texts from Qumran and the Development of Sapiential Thought*, 263–75. BETL 159. Leuven: Leuven University Press, 2002.

Harrington, Daniel J., J. Cazeaux, C. Perrot, and Pierre Bogaert. *Pseudo-Philon: Les antiquités bibliques*. Sources chrétiennes 229, 230. Paris: Éditions du Cerf, 1976.

Harrington, Daniel J. *Wisdom Texts from Qumran*. London; New York: Routledge, 1996.

Hartman, Lars. "'Comfort of the Scriptures'—an Early Jewish Interpretation of Noah's Salvation, 1 En 10:16-11:2." *Svensk Exegetisk Årsbok* 41–42 (1977): 87–96.

Hayward, C. T. R. "The Figure of Adam in Pseudo-Philo's Biblical Antiquities." *Journal for the Study of Judaism* 23, no. 1 (1992): 1–20.

Hayward, C. T. R. *Targums and the Transmission of Scripture into Judaism and Christianity*. Studies in the Aramaic Interpretation of Scripture 10. Leiden; Boston, Mass: Brill, 2010.

Heide, Gale. "What Is New about the New Heaven and the New Earth? A Theology of Creation from Revelation 21 and 2 Peter 3." *Journal of the Evangelical Theological Society* 40, no. 1 (1997): 37–56.

Hobbins, John F. "The Summing up of History in 2 Baruch." *The Jewish Quarterly Review*, no. 1/2 (1998): 45.

Hofius, Otfried. *Katapausis: Die Vorstellung vom endzeitlichen Ruheort im Hebräerbrieff*. wissenschaftliche Untersuchungen zum Neuen Testament. Tübingen, Germany: J. C. B. Mohr, 1970.

Hughes, Philip Edgcumbe. *A Commentary on the Epistle to the Hebrews*. Grand Rapids: Eerdmans, 1977.

Hughes, Philip Edgcumbe. *The Book of the Revelation: A Commentary*. Leicester: Grand Rapids: InterVarsity Press; Eerdmans, 1990.

Huizenga, Leroy A. *The New Isaac: Tradition and Interpretation in the Gospel of Matthew*. Leiden: Brill, 2009.

Hurst, Lincoln D. "Eschatology and 'Platonism' in the Epistle to the Hebrews." *Society of Biblical Literature Seminar Papers* 23 (1984): 41–74.

Hurst, Lincoln D. *The Epistle to the Hebrews: Its Background of Thought*. Monograph Series / Society for New Testament Studies 65. Cambridge: Cambridge University Press, 1990.

Hurtado, L. W. "Revelation 4–5 in the Light of Jewish Apocalyptic Analogies." *Journal for the Study of the New Testament* 25 (1985): 105–24.

Ihm, Juliana Casey. "Eschatology in Heb. 12: 14-29: An Exegetical Study." Catholic University of Leuven, 1976.

Jacobson, Howard. *Commentary on Pseudo-Philo's "Liber Antiquitatum Biblicarum," with Latin Text and English Translation*. Arbeiten zur Geschichte des antiken Judentums und des Urchristentums 31. Leiden: Brill, 1996.

Jefferies, Daryl F. *Wisdom at Qumran: A Form-Critical Analysis of the Admonitions in 4QInstruction*. New Jersey: Gorgias Press, 2002.

Jerome. *Saint Jerome's Hebrew Questions on Genesis*. Translated by Robert Hayward. Oxford Early Christian Studies. Oxford, England: New York: Clarendon Press; Oxford University Press, 1995.

Johnson, Luke Timothy. *Hebrews: A Commentary*. The New Testament Library. Louisville: Westminster John Knox Press, 2006.

Jonge, Marinus de. *Jewish Eschatology, Early Christian Christology and the Testaments of the Twelve Patriarchs: Collected Essays*. Brill, 1990.

Kampen, John. "The Significance of the Temple in the Manuscripts of the Damascus Document." In *Dead Sea Scrolls at Fifty: Proceedings of the 1997 Society of Biblical Literature Qumran Section Meetings*, 185–97. Atlanta: Scholars Press, 1999.

Katzin, David. "'The Time of Testing': The Use of Hebrew Scriptures in 4Q171's Pesher of Psalm 37." *Hebrew Studies* 1 (2004): 121–62.

Keil, Karl Friedrich, Franz Julius Delitzsch, and James Martin. *Biblical Commentary on the Old Testament. The Twelve Minor Prophets*. Clark's Foreign Theological Library 17–18. Edinburgh: T & T Clark, 1868.

Kiddle, Martin. *The Revelation of St. John*. 4th reprint of 1st edition published 1940. The Moffatt New Testament Commentary. London: Hodder and Stoughton, 1947.

Kirschner, Robert. "Apocalyptic and Rabbinic Responses to the Destruction of 70." *Harvard Theological Review* 78, no. 1–2 (January 1985): 27–46.

Kistemaker, Simon. *The Psalm Citations in the Epistle to the Hebrews*. Eugene, OR: Wipf & Stock Publishers, 2010.

Kister, Menahem. "Two Formulae in the Book of Jubilees." *Tarbiz* (2001): 289–300.

Klein, Michael L., ed. *The Fragment Targums of the Pentateuch According to Their Extant Sources*. Analecta Biblica 76. Rome: Biblical Institute Press, 1980.

Klijn, Albertus Frederik Johannes. "Recent Developments in the Study of the Syriac Apocalypse of Baruch." *Journal for the Study of the Pseudepigrapha* 4 (1989): 3–17.

Knibb, M. A. "The Date of the Parables of Enoch: A Critical Review." *New Testament Studies* 25, no. 3 (1979): 345–59.

Knowles, Michael. *Jeremiah in Matthew's Gospel: The Rejected Prophet Motif in Matthean Redaction*. London: Bloomsbury Publishing, 2015.

Koester, Craig R., ed. *Hebrews: A New Translation with Introduction and Commentary*. The Anchor Bible 36. New York: Doubleday, 2001.

Kosmala, Hans. *Hebräer—Essener—Christen: Studien zur Vorgeschichte der frühchristlichen Verkündigung*. Studia Post-Biblica 1. Leiden: Brill, 1959.

Krause, Joachim J. "Tradition, History, and Our Story: Some Observations on Jacob and Esau in the Books of Obadiah and Malachi." *Journal for the Study of the Old Testament* 32, no. 4 (2008): 475–86.

Krispenz, Jutta. "Wie viele Bäume braucht das Paradies? Erwägungen zu Gen. II 4B-III 24." *Vetus Testamentum*, no. 3 (2004): 301–18.

Kugel, James L. *A Walk through Jubilees: Studies in the Book of Jubilees and the World of Its Creation*. Supplements to the Journal for the Study of Judaism 156. Leiden; Boston: Brill, 2012.

Kugel, James L. *Traditions of the Bible: A Guide to the Bible as It Was at the Start of the Common Era*. Cambridge: Harvard University Press, 1998.

Kuhn, Heinz-Wolfgang. *Enderwartung und gegenwärtiges Heil: Untersuchungen zu den Gemeindeliedern von Qumran mit einem Anhang über Eschatologie und Gegenwart in der Verkündigung Jesu*. Studien zur Umwelt des Neuen Testaments 4. Göttingen: Vandenhoek & Ruprecht, 1966.

Laansma, Jon. "The Cosmology of Hebrews." In *Cosmology and New Testament Theology*, 125–43. London: T&T Clark, 2008.

Laansma, Jon. "Hidden Stories in Hebrews: Cosmology and Theology." In *A Cloud of Witnesses: The Theology of Hebrews in Its Ancient Context*, 9–18. London; New York: T & T Clark, 2008.

Lambden, Stephen N. "From Fig Leaves to Fingernails: Some Notes on the Garments of Adam and Eve in the Hebrew Bible and Select Early Postbiblical Jewish Writings." In *Walk in the Garden: Biblical, Iconographical and Literary Images of Eden*, 74–90. Sheffield, England: JSOT, 1992.

Lane, William L. *Hebrews 1–8*. Word Biblical Commentary 47A. Dallas: Word Books, 1991.

Lane, William L. *Hebrews 9–13*. Word Biblical Commentary 47B. Dallas: Word books, 1991.

Lange, Armin. *Weisheit und Prädestination: weisheitliche Urordnung und Prädestination in den Textfunden von Qumran*. Studies on the Texts of the Desert of Judah 18. Leiden; New York: Brill, 1995.

Lee, Pilchan. "The New Jerusalem in the Book of Revelation: A Study of Revelation 21–22 in the Light of Its Background in Jewish Tradition." University of St. Andrews, 1999.

Leuenberger, Martin. "Ort und Funktion der Wolkenvision und ihrer Deutung in der syrischen Baruchapokalypse: eine These zu deren thematischer Entfaltung." *Journal for the Study of Judaism in the Persian, Hellenistic and Roman Period* 36, no. 2 (2005): 206–46.

Levison, John R. *Portraits of Adam in Early Judaism: From Sirach to 2 Baruch*. Journal for the Study of the Pseudepigrapha 1. Sheffield: JSOT, 1987.

Lied, Liv Ingeborg. *The Other Lands of Israel: Imaginations of the Land in 2 Baruch*. Supplements to the Journal for the Study of Judaism 129. Leiden; Boston: Brill, 2008.

Lincoln, Andrew T. "Sabbath, Rest, and Eschatology in the New Testament." In *From Sabbath to Lord's Day: A Biblical, Historical and Theological Investigation*, 198–220. Grand Rapids: Zondervan, 1982.

Lincoln, Andrew T. *Hebrews: A Guide*. London: T&T Clark, 2006.

Loisy, Alfred Firmin, and Friedrich Hügel. *L'Apocalypse de Jean*. Paris: Nourry, 1923.

Long, Thomas G. *Hebrews*. Interpretation, a Bible Commentary for Teaching and Preaching. Louisville, KY: John Knox Press, 1997.

Lust, Johan. "Edom-Adam in Ezekiel, in the MT and LXX." In *Studies in the Hebrew Bible, Qumran, and the Septuagint Presented to Eugene Ulrich*. Boston: Brill, 2006.

Macaskill, Grant. *Revealed Wisdom and Inaugurated Eschatology in Ancient Judaism and Early Christianity*. Supplements to the Journal for the Study of Judaism 115. Leiden; Boston: Brill, 2007.

MacKay, John L. *Haggai, Zechariah & Malachi: God's Restored People*. Revised edition. Ross-shire: Christian Focus, 2010.

Mackie, Scott D. *Eschatology and Exhortation in the Epistle to the Hebrews*. Wissenschaftliche Untersuchungen zum Neuen Testament 223. Tübingen: Mohr Siebeck, 2007.

MacRae, G. W. "Heavenly Temple and Eschatology in the Letter to the Hebrews," *Semeia*, 12 (1978): 179–99.

Maher, Michael. *Targum Pseudo-Jonathan, Genesis.* Collegeville, MN: Liturgical Press, 1992.
Malina, Bruce J. *The Palestinian Manna Tradition: The Manna Tradition in the Palestinian Targums and Its Relationship to the New Testament Writings.* Leiden: Brill, 1968.
Marcus, J. "Son of Man as Son of Adam: Exploring an Adamic Eschatology within the Pre-Gospel Jewish-Christian Tradition." *REVUE BIBLIQUE* 110, no. 1 (2003): 38–61.
Martínez, Florentino García. "Man and Woman: Halakhah Based upon Eden in the Dead Sea Scrolls." In *Paradise Interpreted: Representations of Biblical Paradise in Judaism and Christianity.* Leiden; Boston; Köln: Brill, 1999.
Martínez, Florentino García. "Wisdom at Qumran: Worldly or Heavenly?" In *Wisdom and Apocalypticism in the Dead Sea Scrolls and in the Biblical Tradition.* Leuven: University Press, 2003.
Martínez, F. García, and A. S. van der Woude. "A 'Groningen' Hypothesis of Qumran Origins and Early History." *Revue de Qumrân* 14, no. 4 (56) (1990): 521–41.
Mason, Eric F. *"You Are a Priest Forever": Second Temple Jewish Messianism and the Priestly Christology of the Epistle to the Hebrews.* Studies on the Texts of the Desert of Judah, v. 74. Leiden; Boston: Brill, 2008.
Mason, Eric F. "Cosmology, Messianism, and Melchizedek: Apocalyptic Jewish Traditions and Hebrews." In *Reading the Epistle to the Hebrews: A Resource for Students*, 53–76. Atlanta: Society of Biblical Literature, 2011.
Mason, Eric F. "'Sit at My Right Hand': Enthronement and the Heavenly Sanctuary in Hebrews." In *A Teacher for All Generations: Essays in Honor of James. C. VanderKam*, 2:901–16. Supplements to the Journal for the Study of Judaism. Leiden; Boston: Brill, 2012.
McKenzie, Tracy. "Edom's Desolation and Adam's Multiplication." In *Text and Canon: Essays in Honor of John H. Sailhamer*, 90–119. Eugene, OR: Pickwick, 2017.
McNamara, Martin, ed. *Targum Neofiti 1: Genesis: Translated, with Apparatus and Notes.* The Aramaic Bible 1A. Edinburgh: T & T Clark, 1992.
Ménégoz, Eugène. *La théologie de l'épitre aux Hébreux.* Fischbacher, 1894.
Metzger, B. M. "The Fourth Book of Ezra: A New Translation and Introduction." In *The Old Testament Pseudepigrapha*, 1:516–59. Garden City, NY: Doubleday, 1983.
Michaels, J. Ramsey. *Revelation.* InterVarsity Press, 1997.
Milgrom, Jacob. "The Priestly Consecration (Leviticus 8): A Rite of Passage." In *Bits of Honey: Essays for Samson H. Levey*, 57–61. Atlanta: Scholars Press, 1993.
Milik, Józef T., and Matthew Black, eds. *The books of Enoch: Aramaic fragments of Qumrân Cave 4.* Oxford: Clarendon Press, 1976.
Mitchell, Alan Christopher, and Daniel J. Harrington. *Hebrews.* Sacra Pagina Series 13. Collegeville, MN: Liturgical Press, 2009.
Moffatt, James. *A Critical and Exegetical Commentary on the Epistle to the Hebrews.* International Critical Commentary. Edinburgh: Clark, 1924.
Moffitt, David M. *Atonement and the Logic of Resurrection in the Epistle to the Hebrews.* Supplements to Novum Testamentum 141. Leiden: Brill, 2011.
Moffitt, David M. "Serving in the Tabernacle in Heaven: Sacred Space, Jesus's High-Priestly Sacrifice, and Hebrews' Analogical Theology." In *Hebrews in Contexts*, 259–79. Leiden: Brill, 2016.
Moo, Douglas J. *The Old Testament in the Gospel Passion Narratives.* Sheffield: Almond, 1983.
Morris, Leon. *Revelation: An Introduction and Commentary.* The Tyndale New Testament Commentaries 20. Downers Grove, IL: IVP, 2007.

Motyer, Steve. "The Temple in Hebrews: Is It There?" In *Heaven on Earth*, 177–89. Carlisle: Paternoster Press, 2004.

Mounce, Robert H. *The Book of Revelation*. Rev. ed. The New International Commentary on the New Testament. Grand Rapids: Eerdmans, 1997.

Mueller, James R. "The Apocalypse of Abraham and the Destruction of the Second Jewish Temple." *Society of Biblical Literature Seminar Papers* 21 (1982): 341–49.

Murphy, Frederick James. *The Structure and Meaning of Second Baruch*. Dissertation Series / Society of Biblical Literature, no. 78. Atlanta: Scholars Press, 1985.

Murphy, Frederick James. "The Temple in the Syriac Apocalypse of Baruch." *Journal of Biblical Literature* 106, no. 4 (1987): 671–83.

Murphy, Frederick James. *Pseudo-Philo: Rewriting the Bible*. Oxford University Press, 1993.

Murphy-O'Connor, J. "Essene Missionary Document: CD II, 14-VI, 1." *Revue Biblique* 77, no. 2 (1970): 201–29.

Nickelsburg, George W. E. *Resurrection, Immortality, and Eternal Life in Intertestamental Judaism*. Harvard Theological Studies 26. Cambridge: Harvard University Press, 1972.

Nickelsburg, George W. E. "Apocalyptic and Myth in 1 Enoch 6–11." *Journal of Biblical Literature* 96, no. 3 (1977): 383–405.

Nickelsburg, George W. E. *Jewish Literature between the Bible and the Mishnah: A Historical and Literary Introduction*. 2nd ed. London: SCM Press, 1981.

Nickelsburg, George W. E. *1 Enoch. 1, A Commentary on the Book of 1 Enoch, Chapters 1-36; 81-108*. Hermeneia—a Critical and Historical Commentary on the Bible. Minneapolis, MN: Fortress Press, 2001.

Nickelsburg, George W. E. "Where Is the Place of Eschatological Blessing?" In *Things Revealed: Studies in Early Jewish and Christian Literature in Honor of Michael E. Stone*, 53–71. Leiden: Brill, 2004.

Nickelsburg, George W. E., James C. VanderKam, and Klaus Baltzer. *1 Enoch. 2, A Commentary on the Book of 1 Enoch, Chapters 37-82*. Hermeneia—a Critical and Historical Commentary on the Bible. Minneapolis: Fortress Press, 2012.

Nitzan, Bilha. *Pesher Habakkuk: A Scroll from the Wilderness of Judaea (1QpHab)*. Jerusalem: Bialik Institute, 1986.

Osborne, Grant R. *Revelation*. Baker Exegetical Commentary on the New Testament. Grand Rapids: Baker Academic, 2002.

Oswalt, John. *The Book of Isaiah. Chapters 40–66*. The New International Commentary on the Old Testament. Grand Rapids; Cambridge: Eerdmans, 1998.

Ounsworth, Richard Joseph. *Joshua Typology in the New Testament*. Wissenschaftliche Untersuchungen zum Neuen Testament 328. Tübingen: Mohr Siebeck, 2012.

Pannenberg, Wolfhart. "Die weltgründende Funktion des Mythos und der christliche Offenbarungsglaube." In *Mythos und Rationalität*. Gütersloh: Gütersloher Verlagshaus Gerd Mohn, 1988.

Pardee, Dennis. "Restudy of the Commentary on Psalm 37 from Qumran Cave 4." *Revue de Qumran* 8, no. 2 (1973): 163–94.

Parry, Donald W. *Temples of the Ancient World: Ritual and Symbolism*. Salt Lake City, UT: Deseret Book Company, 1994.

Pattemore, S. W. "How Green Is Your Bible? Ecology and the End of the World in Translation." *Bible Translator* 58, no. 2 (2007): 75–85.

Pfeiffer, Henrik. "Der Baum in der Mitte des Gartens: zum überlieferungsgeschichtlichen Ursprung der Paradieszählung (Gen. 2,4b-3,24)—Teil I: Analyse." *Zeitschrift für die alttestamentliche Wissenschaft* 112, no. 4 (2000): 487–500.

Poupko, Yehiel E. *Pesikta Derab Kahana*. Edited by William G. Braude. Translated by Israel J. Kapstein. 2nd edition. Philadelphia: The Jewish Publication Society, 2002.

Quek, Tze-Ming. "The New Jerusalem as God's Palace-Temple: An Exegetical Study of the Eden-Temple and Escalation Motifs in Revelation 21:1–22:5." Regent College, 2004.

Rabin, Chaim, ed. *The Zadokite Documents*. Oxford: Clarendon Press, 1954.

Rad, Gerhard von. *The Problem of the Hexateuch, and Other Essays*. London; Edinburgh: Oliver & Boyd, 1966.

Ravid, Liora. "The Relationship of the Sabbath Laws in 'Jubilees' 50:6-13 to the Rest of the Book." *Tarbiz* (2000): 161–66.

Reddish, M. G. "Followers of the Lamb: Role Models in the Book of Revelation." *Perspectives in Religious Studies* 40, no. 1 (2013): 65–79.

Reed, Annette Yoshiko. "Enochic and Mosaic Traditions in Jubilees: The Evidence of Angelology and Demonology." In *Enoch and the Mosaic Torah: The Evidence of Jubilees*. Grand Rapids; Cambridge: Eerdmans, 2009.

Rey, Jean-Sébastien. *4QInstruction: sagesse et eschatologie*. Studies on the texts of the desert of Judah 81. Leiden; Boston: Brill, 2009.

Roloff, Jürgen, and John E. Alsup. *The Revelation of John: A Continental Commentary*. 1st Fortress Press ed. A Continental Commentary. Minneapolis: Fortress Press, 1993.

Rössler, Dietrich. *Gesetz und Geschichte: Untersuchungen zur Theologie der jüdischen Apokalyptik und der pharisäischen Orthodoxie*. Kreis Moers: Neukirchener Verlag, 1962.

Ruiten, J. van. "The Intertextual Relationship between Isaiah 65,17-20 and Revelation 21,1-5b." *Estudios Bíblicos* 51, no. 4 (1993): 473–510.

Ruiten, J. van. "Eden and the Temple: The Rewriting of Genesis 2:4–3:24 in the Book of Jubilees." In *Paradise Interpreted: Representations of Biblical Paradise in Judaism and Christianity*. Leiden, Boston, Köln: Brill, 1999.

Ruiten, J. van. *Primaeval History Interpreted: The Rewriting of Genesis 1-11 in the Book of Jubilees*. Supplements to the Journal for the Study of Judaism 66. Leiden: Brill, 2000.

Russell, D. S. *The Method & Message of Jewish Apocalyptic, 200 BC-AD 100*. London: SCM Press, 1964.

Sailhamer, John. *Introduction to Old Testament Theology: A Canonical Approach*. Grand Rapids: Zondervan, 1995.

Samely, Alexander. *Rabbinic Interpretation of Scripture in the Mishnah*. Oxford: Oxford University Press, 2002.

Samely, Alexander. *Forms of Rabbinic Literature and Thought: An Introduction*. Oxford: Oxford University Press, 2007.

Satlow, Michael L. "Jewish Constructions of Nakedness in Late Antiquity." *Journal of Biblical Literature*, 1997.

Sayler, Gwendolyn B. *Have the Promises Failed?: A Literary Analysis of 2 Baruch*. Dissertation Series / Society of Biblical Literature 72. Chic: Scholars Press, 1984.

Schechter, Solomon and Anan ben David, eds. *Documents of Jewish Sectaries*. Cambridge: The University Press, 1910.

Schechter, Solomon. *Fragments of a Zadokite Work*. Cambridge: Harvard University Press, 1910.

Schenck, Kenneth. *A Brief Guide to Philo*. Louisville: Westminster John Knox Press, 2005.

Schenck, Kenneth. *Cosmology and Eschatology in Hebrews: The Settings of the Sacrifice*. Society for New Testament Studies Monograph Series 143. Cambridge; New York: Cambridge University Press, 2007.

Schenke, Hans-Martin. "Erwägungen zum Rätsel des Hebräerbriefes." In *Neues Testament und christliche Existenz: Festschrift für Herbert Braun zum 70sten Geburtstag am 4 Mai 1973*, 421–37. Tübingen: J. C. B. Mohr, 1973.

Schimanowski, Gottfried. "Connecting Heaven and Earth." In *Heavenly Realms and Earthly Realities in Late Antique Religions*, 67–84. Cambridge; New York: Cambridge University Press, 2004.

Schofer, J. "The Redaction of Desire: Structure and Editing of Rabbinic Teachings Concerning Yeser ('Inclination')." *Journal of Jewish Thought and Philosophy* 12, no. 1 (2003): 19–53.

Schröger, Friedrich. *Der Verfasser des Hebräerbriefes als Schriftausleger*. Biblische Untersuchungen 4. Regensburg: F. Pustet, 1968.

Schürer, Emil, C. H. Cave, Geza Vermes, Fergus Miller, and Martin Goodman. *The History of the Jewish People in the Age of Jesus Christ, Volume 3, Part 1*. New English version. Edinburgh: T&T Clark, 1986.

Scott, James M. *On Earth as in Heaven: The Restoration of Sacred Time and Sacred Space in the Book of Jubilees*. Supplements to the Journal for the Study of Judaism 91. Leiden; Boston: Brill, 2005.

Segal, Michael. *The Book of Jubilees: Rewritten Bible, Redaction, Ideology and Theology*. Supplements to the Journal for the Study of Judaism, v. 117. Leiden; Boston: Brill, 2007.

Smalley, Stephen S. *The Revelation to John: A Commentary on the Greek Text of the Apocalypse*. Downers Grove: InterVarsity Press, 2005.

Smit, P. B. "Reaching for the Tree of Life: The Role of Eating, Drinking, Fasting, and Symbolic Foodstuffs in 4 Ezra." *Journal for the Study of Judaism* 45, no. 3 (2014): 366–87.

Smith, Mark S., and Simon B. Parker, eds. *Ugaritic Narrative Poetry*. Writings from the Ancient World / Society of Biblical Literature 9. Atlanta: Scholars Press, 1997.

Spicq, Ceslas. *L'Épitre aux Hébreux*. Études Bibliques. Paris: Gabalda, 1952.

Stemberger, Günter. *Der Leib der Auferstehung: Studien zur Anthropologie und Eschatologie des palästinischen Judentums im neutestamentlichen Zeitalter (ca. 170 v. C[h]r.-100 n. Chr.)*. Analecta Biblica 56. Rome: Biblical Institute Press, 1972.

Stephens, Mark B. *Annihilation or Renewal?: The Meaning and Function of New Creation in the Book of Revelation*. Wissenschaftliche Untersuchungen zum Neuen Testament 307. Tübingen: Mohr Siebeck, 2011.

Sterling, Gregory E. "Ontology versus Eschatology: Tensions between Author and Community in Hebrews." *The Studia Philonica Annual* 13 (2001): 190–211.

Sterling, Gregory E. "The Place of Philo of Alexandria in the Study of Christian Origins." In *Philo und das Neue Testament. Wechselseitige Wahrnehmungen. I. Internationales Symposium zum Corpus Judaeo-Hellenisticum*, 21–52. Tübingen: Mohr Siebeck, 2004.

Steyn, Gert J. *A Quest for the Assumed LXX Vorlage of the Explicit Quotations in Hebrews*. Forschungen zur Religion und Literatur des Alten und NeuenTestaments, 235. Göttingen: Vandenhoeck & Ruprecht, 2011.

Stone, Michael E., and Frank Moore Cross. *Fourth Ezra: A Commentary on the Book of Fourth Ezra*. Hermeneia-a Critical and Historical Commentary on the Bible. Minneapolis: Fortress Press, 1990.

Stordalen, T. *Echoes of Eden: Genesis 2–3 and Symbolism of the Eden Garden in Biblical Hebrew Literature*. Contributions to Biblical Exegesis and Theology 25. Leuven, Belgium: Peeters, 2000.

Stromberg, Jake. "Observations on Inner-Scriptural Scribal Expansion in MT Ezekiel." *Vetus Testamentum*, no. 1 (2008): 68–86.

Strugnell, John, Daniel Harrington, and Torleif Elgvin. *Qumran Cave 4. XXIV: 4QInstruction (Musar LeMevin): 4Q415 Ff. (DJD 34)*. Oxford: Clarendon, 1999.

Svendsen, Stefan N. *Allegory Transformed: The Appropriation of Philonic Hermeneutics in the Letter to Hebrews*. Tübingen: Mohr Siebeck, 2009.

Tavo, Felise. *Woman, Mother, and Bride: An Exegetical Investigation into the "Ecclesial" Notions of the Apocalypse*. Biblical Tools and Studies 3. Leuven; Dudley: Peeters, 2007.

Taylor, Richard A., and E. Ray Clendenen. *Haggai, Malachi*. Nashville: B & H Publishing Group, 2004.

Testuz, Michel. *Les Idées Réligieuses Du Livre des Jubilés*. Genève: Droz, 1960.

Theissen, Gerd. *Untersuchungen zum Hebräerbrief*. Studien zum Neuen Testament 2. Gütersloh: Gütersloher Verlagshaus Gerd Mohn, 1969.

Thiessen, M. "Hebrews 12.5-13, the Wilderness Period, and Israel's Discipline." *New Testament Studies* 55, no. 3 (2009): 366–79.

Thomas, John Christopher, and Frank D. Macchia. *Revelation (THNTC)*. Grand Rapids: Eerdmans, 2016.

Thompson, Alden Lloyd. *Responsibility for Evil in the Theodicy of IV Ezra: A Study Illustrating the Significance of Form and Structure for the Meaning of the Book*. Dissertation Series—Society of Biblical Literature 29. Missoula, MT: Scholars Press, 1977.

Thompson, James W. *The Beginnings of Christian Philosophy: The Epistle to the Hebrews*. The Catholic Biblical Quarterly 13. Washington, D.C: Catholic Biblical Association of America, 1981.

Thompson, James W. *Hebrews: Commentaries on the New Testament*. Paideia: Commentaries on the New Testament. Grand Rapids: Baker, 2008.

Thompson, James W. "What Middle Platonism Has to Do with Hebrews." In *Reading the Epistle to the Hebrews: A Resource for Students*, 31–52. Atlanta: Society of Biblical Literature, 2011.

Tigchelaar, Eibert J. C. "Eden and Paradise." In *Paradise Interpreted: Representations of Biblical Paradise in Judaism and Christianity*. Leiden; Boston; Köln: Brill, 1999.

Tronier, H. "The Corinthian Correspondence between Philosophical Idealism and Apocalypticism." In *Paul beyond the Judaism/Hellenism Divide*, 165–96. Westminster: John Knox Press, 2001.

Uhlig, Siegbert. *Das äthiopische Henochbuch*. Jüdische Schriften aus hellenistisch-romischer Zeit, Lfg. 6. Gütersloh: Mohn, 1984.

Urbach, Efraim Elimelech. *The Sages, Their Concepts and Beliefs*. Publications of the Perry Foundation in the Hebrew University of Jerusalem. Jerusalem: Magnes Press, Hebrew University, 1975.

VanderKam, James C. "The Origins and Purposes of the Book of Jubilees." In *Studies in the Book of Jubilees*, 3–24. Tübingen: Mohr Siebeck, 1997.

VanderKam, James C. "Covenant and Biblical Interpretation in Jubilees 6." In *the Dead Sea Scrolls*, 92–104. Jerusalem: Israel Exploration Society, 2000.

VanderKam, James C. *The Book of Jubilees*. Guides to Apocrypha and Pseudepigrapha. Sheffield: Sheffield Academic Press, 2001.

VanderKam, James C. "The Scriptural Setting of the Book of Jubilees." *Dead Sea Discoveries* 1 (2006): 61.

Vanhoye, Albert. "Ľοἰχουμένη dans l'épître aux Hébreux." *Biblica*, no. 45 (1964): 248–253.

Vanhoye, Albert. *La Structure Littéraire de l'Épître Aux Hébreux*. Paris: Desclée de Brouwer, 1976.

Vanhoye, Albert. *Structure and Message of the Epistle to the Hebrews*. Rome: Editrice Pontificio Istituto Biblico, 1989.

Verhoef, Pieter A. *The Books of Haggai and Malachi*. New International Commentary on the Old Testament. Grand Rapids: Eerdmans, 1987.

Vermès, Géza. *Scripture and Tradition in Judaism: Haggadic Studies*. 2nd ed. Studia Post-Biblica, 4. Leiden: Brill, 1973.

Violet, Bruno. *Die Apokalypsen des Esra und des Baruch in deutscher Gestalt*. Leipzig: Hinrichs, 1924.

Vögtle, A. "Das Neue Testament und die Zukunft des Kosmos: Heb. 12,26f. und das Endschichsal des Kosmos," Bibel und Leben, 10 (1969).

Volz, Paul. *Die Eschatologie der jüdischen Gemeinde im neutestamentlichen Zeitalter*. Repr. Hildesheim: Georg Olms, 1966.

Wacholder, Ben Zion. "The Teacher of Righteousness Is Alive, Awaiting the Messiah: חסאה in CD as Allusion to the Siniatic and Damascene Covenants." *Hebrew Union College Annual*, 1999.

Wacholder, Ben Zion. *The New Damascus Document: The Midrash on the Eschatological Torah of the Dead Sea Scrolls: Reconstruction, Translation and Commentary*. Studies on the Texts of the Desert of Judah, v. 56. Leiden: Brill, 2007.

Wallace, H. N. "Tree of Knowledge and Life." In *Anchor Bible Dictionary*, 6:656–60, 1992.

Walton, John H. *Genesis*. The NIV Application Commentary. Grand Rapids: Zondervan, 2001.

Walton, John H. *Zondervan Illustrated Bible Backgrounds Commentary*. Grand Rapids: Zondervan, 2009.

Weinfeld, Moshe. *Normative and Sectarian Judaism in the Second Temple Period*. London; New York: T&T Clark, 2005.

Weiss, Herold. "Sabbatismos in the Epistle to the Hebrews." *Catholic Biblical Quarterly*, 1996, 674–89.

Weiss, Hans-Friedrich. *Der Brief an die Hebräer: Übersetzt und Erklärt*. 15. Aufl. Kritisch-Exegetischer Kommentar über das Neue Testament 13. Göttingen: Vandenhoeck & Ruprecht, 1991.

Whitney, K. William. *Two Strange Beasts: Leviathan and Behemoth in Second Temple and Early Rabbinic Judaism*. Harvard Semitic Monographs, no. 63. Winona Lake, IN: Eisenbrauns, 2006.

Wilcke, Hans-Alwin. *Das Problem eines messianischen Zwischenreichs bei Paulus*. Zürich: Zwingli Verlag, 1967.

Willet, T. W. *Eschatology in the Teodocies of 2 Baruch and 4 Ezras*. Sheffield: JSOT, 1989.

Windisch, Hans, ed. *Der Hebräerbrief*. Handbuch zum Neuen Testament. Tübingen: J. C. B. Mohr, 1913.

Wise, Michael Owen. "4QFlorilegium and the Temple of Adam." *Revue de Qumran* 15, no. 1–2 (1991): 103–32.

Wise, Michael Owen, Martin G. Abegg, and Edward M. Cook, eds. *The Dead Sea Scrolls: A New Translation*. 1st ed. London; San Francisco: HarperSanFrancisco, 1996.

Witherington III, Pace B. *Letters and Homilies for Jewish Christians: A Socio-Rhetorical Commentary on Hebrews, James and Jude*. Downers Grove, IL: IVP Academic, 2007.

Witte, Eberhard. *Untersuchungen zur Machtverteilung im Unternehmen*. Sitzungsberichte/ Bayerische Akademie der Wissenschaften. Philosophisch-historische Klasse, Jahrg. 1978, Heft 1. München: Bayerische Akademie der Wissenschaften, 1978.

Wright, B. G. "The Categories of Rich and Poor in the Qumran Sapiential Literature." In *Sapiential Perspectives: Wisdom Literature in Light of the Dead Sea Scrolls, Proceedings of the Sixth International Symposium of the Orion Center for the Study of the Dead Sea Scrolls and Associated Literature*, 101–25. Leiden: Brill, 2004.

Wright, N. T. *The Climax of the Covenant: Christ and the Law in Pauline Theology*. Edinburgh: T&T Clark, 1991.

Yamauchi, Edwin Masao. *Pre-Christian Gnosticism: A Survey of the Proposed Evidences*. London: Tyndale Press, 1973.

Zimmerli, Walther, Frank Moore Cross, and Klaus Baltzer. *Ezekiel: A Commentary on the Book of the Prophet Ezekiel*. Hermeneia: A Critical and Historical Commentary on the Bible. Philadelphia: Fortress Press, 1979.

Index of References

ANCIENT SOURCES

Dead Sea Scrolls (Qumran Texts)

Hymns / Hodayot (1QH)
8:10-13	45
9:25	39
11:10-12	89
11:21-3	43

Community Rule / Manual of Discipline (1QS)
2:9	89
3:13	40
3:15-17	40
3:17-18	40
4:7	42
8	90
8:5-6	43
11:7-8	43

Psalms Pesher 4QpPs37 (4Q171)
F1-2 I	90
F1-2 i.18	37
F1-2 ii.2-3	37
F1-2ii.5-8	35–6, 90, 121
F1-2 ii.7	37
F1-2 ii.9-10	37
F1-2 ii 10	121
F1-2 ii.18	37
F1-2 ii.24-25	37
iii.1-2	37
iii.8-12	37, 43, 62, 90
iii.10-11	37
F1-2 iii.11	120

Damascus Document (4Q265–4Q273)
CD 1.1-2.1	31
CD1:6	89
CD 1.7	31
CD 1.14-15	37
CD 2.2–2.13	31
CD 2:8	32
CD 2:11-12	31, 62
CD. 2.14–4.12a	32
CD 2:18	32
CD 2.21	32
CD 3:1	35
CD 3.5	32
CD 3.6	32
CD 3.7	32
CD 3:9	121
CD 3.10	32
CD 3.11	32
CD 3.12	32
CD 3:12–4:4	31–5, 89
CD 3:17	39
CD 3:19–4:2	120
CD 3:20	33, 89, 121
CD 3.20-21	43
CD 3:21–4:4	33, 62, 113
CD 4:1	32
CD 4.8	35
CD 4:15	37
CD 4:17-18	34, 35
CD 5.6-8	34
CD 6:11-14	34, 89
CD 6:14	34, 35
CD 6.15-16	34
CD 6.16-18	34
CD 8.13	37
CD 9:14	34
CD 10:7-9	33, 121
CD 11:18-19	34
CD 11:21–12:2	47
CD 12:1-2	34
CD 15:1-2	37
CD 15:4-5	37
CD 15:9	37
CD 15:12	37
CD 16:13	34
CD 19:26	37

Index of References

CD 20:13b-15a	36	*Temple Scroll* (11QT^a)	
CD 20:15	37	45:11-12	47

Damascus Document (4Q268)
Frag. 1.7-8   31

Purities (4Q274)   47

Non-Canonical Psalms B (4Q381)
46.5   39

Songs of the Sabbath Sacrifice (4Q400)
f2   43

Sapiential Work A^{a-e} / The Children of Salvation 4QInstruction (4Q415–4Q418, 4Q423)

4Q415
1 ii   42
2 i   42

4Q416
F1 13-15   121
2 ii 6-7   42
F2 ii17-18   43

4Q417
F1 i 4-5   43
F1 i.13-18   39
F2 I 10-12   42
F2 i 12   121

4Q418
F69 ii   89
F69 7   121
F 81   41
F 81 1-5   41, 43, 62, 113, 120
F 81 5   120
F88 8   41
236 3   42

4Q423
F 1-2 1-4   41, 62
F1-2ii   120
9 3   42

Messiah of Heaven and Earth (4Q521)
2ii   121

Josephus

Antiquities of the Jews
1:155.272   134
12,287   130

Miscellaneous Jewish and Christian Literature

Cave of Treasures
2:10-14   18 n. 76

Liber Antiquitatum Biblicarum
3   90
3:8   59
3:10   55, 56, 57, 61, 89, 123, 144
4:10   59
7:4   55
8:3   55
9:1   59
9:8   56
10:5   57
10:5-6   93
11:1   56
11:15   56
12:4   55
13   60, 90
13:1-7   90
13:7   60
13:8-10   55, 60, 61, 90, 144
13:9   60
13:10   55, 56, 60, 90
15:6   57, 92, 93, 132
16:3   57
17:5   59
18:12   56
19   54, 90
19:7   54, 55
19:10   56, 122
19:10-13   55, 56, 90, 122
19:12-13   54
19:13   56, 60, 62, 122, 123, 144

21:1	55	5:9	120
21:17	55	10–11	21, 30
25–26	57, 90	10:13-15	89
26	59	10:16–11:2	25–7, 90, 119, 120, 143
26:4	59	10:16–19	25, 74
26:6	57, 59	10:17	26
26:8	56	10:19	26, 143
25:12	60, 123	10:20	89
26:12	60, 123	10:20–11:2	25, 62
26:13	55, 57, 60, 62, 123	10:20-22	143
28:2	55	11:1	26, 143
30:7	55	18	22, 23, 24
32	132	18:6-16	22
32:7	57, 58	18:9	24
32:8	58, 72, 93	24	29
32:15	59, 123	24–25	21–5, 119
32:17	59, 62, 123	24–27	21
37:3	56, 61, 144	24:2	24
		25	24
Philo		25:3	24
Allegorical Interpretation		25:4	3, 22, 25, 72
3.82	17	25:5	23
		25:6	22, 25, 30, 62, 90, 113, 119, 120
De confusion linguarum			
75-78	5	32	22, 23, 24
		37–71	27
Legum allegoriae		39:5	30, 119
3.97-99	6	39:6	29
		40:10	29
De migration Abrahami		45:4	30
1	11	46:4	29
1:2	11	51	27
		51:1	29
De opificio mundi		51:5	30
146	134	60	28
		60:8	27, 30, 119
De somniis		60:23	27, 30, 119
1.181	5	61	28, 119
1.188	6	61:4	28
		61:5	29
Pseudepigrapha		61:12	28, 29, 30, 62, 113, 119
1 Enoch			
1:3-9	89, 120	62:12	119
1:4	24	70:3	29
5:7-10	120	84:6	74
5:8	22, 23	108	22

2 Baruch

Ref	Page
3:5-7	94
4	70, 93
4–5	93
4:1-3	12, 92
4:1-7	16
4:3	71
4:4	70, 92
5:3	94
10:9-12	94
14:13	70
21	70, 71
21–34	28
21:19	70
21:22	70
21:22-23	71
22:25	70
29	72
29:4	27
32:2	94
32:3-5	94
32:4	16, 73, 93
32:6	95
36–37	74, 95
37	74
39–40	72
39:3-6	74
40:1-2	72
40:3	73
40:3-4	72
40:15	70
44:8	93
49:2	74
50	74
50–1	75
51	70, 74
51:1	74
51:3	70, 74
51:5-6	75
51:7	75
51:8	75, 93
51:9	75
51:11	71, 93
51:12	86
52:7	93
55–74	71
56:6	71, 144
57	70
59:3	93, 133, 150
59:4	12, 93
73	71
73:2-4	144
73:6	71, 144
73:7–74:1	71, 144
74:2	73
78:3-4	86
83:4	70
83:6	70

4 Ezra

Ref	Page
3:2	64
3:4	66
3:8	64, 65
3:12	65
3:14	92
3:14-15	66
3:18	92
3:20-22	64
3:27	65
4:7-8	68
4:23	64
4:24	64
4:28-29	65
4:30	65
4:32	65
4:42	69
4:43	66
5:1-2	67
5:2	65
5:28-30	64
5:29	66
5:40	66
5:42-45	66
5:54	65
6	28
6:1-6	66
6:6	66, 69
6:14-16	66, 133, 144
6:22	67, 115
6:26	68
6:27-28	67
6:29	67, 133
6:38-54	67
6:49-52	27
6:54	68
6:55	70
6:58	86

6:59	68	*Joseph and Asenath*	
7:6-9	68	16:16	74
7:10-11	67		
7:12	65	*Jubilees*	
7:13	65, 115	1	45
7:14	68	1:17	16
7:17-18	64	1:17-18	88
7:18	68	1:18	51
7:26	93	1:22-25	45
7:29-30	67	1:24-25	51
7:30	69	1:25	53
7:31	69, 93	1:26	54
7:31-32	66	1:26-29	88
7:36	92	1:27	47
7:50	64	1:27-29	121
7:58	65	1:28	16
7:75	67, 69, 133, 144	1:29	47, 62, 88, 143
7:119	66	2:7	72
7:121	66, 68	2:13-14	121
7:121-123	93	2:14	143
7:123	66, 68, 92	2:18	52
7:125	115	2:19-20	52
7:129	66	2:20	52
8:1-2	65	2:20-23	121
8:2	65	2:21-22	52
8:15-16	64	2:23	52, 122
8:31	64	2:28	122
8:35	65	2:30	52
8:47	66, 144	3	46
8:49	65	3:6	47
8:51-52	86	3:8-14	88
8:52	16, 92	3:9	46
8:52-55	68	3:12	46
9–10	93	3:27	49, 121, 122
9:14	64		
9:32	115	3:28	49
9:38–10:59	133	3:32–4:33	49
10	94	3:34	47
10:26	133	4	47, 49
10:44-46	12	4:17	50
10:50	133	4:17-26	49
10:54	93, 133	4:19	50
13:32-36	66	4:23	49
13:35-36	12, 69	4:24	50
13:36	16	4:26	45, 46, 47–8, 88
13:37-38	66		
13:44	66	4:30	50, 144
13:46	66	5	52

Index of References

5:10	53, 62	BIBLICAL	
5:11	53		
5:18	53, 62	Old Testament	
5:19	53		
6:1	51	*Genesis*	
6:5	143	1	29, 137
6:11	51	1:1	137
6:17	51	1:9	57, 132
6:18	52	1:26-28	1
8:16	47	1:27-28	31, 43, 85
8:19	46, 88, 121	1:28	59, 84, 137
8:21	88	1:35	137
10:31-34	47	2	24
10:33	88	2–3	24
11:18-24	143	2:2	1, 2, 12, 14, 99, 100–2, 103, 118, 124, 125, 147, 148, 152
14:1	51		
14:20	51		
15:1	51		
15:27	52	2:9	83, 95
15:32	53, 62	2:10	83
19:24	48, 122	2:10-12	59
23	45	2:10-14	29, 56
23:15	50	2:17	50
23:27	50, 88, 122, 144	3	67, 83, 121
		3:6	41
23:27-30	122	3:8	84
30:8	122	3:16-19	33, 71
30:13	122	3:18	41
30:15	122	3:21	49, 122
30:18	52	3:22	22
32:19	121	4:12	41
33:20	50, 53, 62, 113	5:1-4	1 n. 3
		5:5	50
50	44, 45, 46, 88	5:9	78
		5:24	130
50:4	45	6	32
50:4-5	122	6–9	55
50:5	44, 121, 143	6:3	52
50:11	45	9	26
		9:2	144
Sibylline Oracles		9:12-17	78
3:290	16	12:1	11
		12:2	84
Testament of Moses		12:3	138
1:12	70	14:17-20	10
		15	70, 92
Testament of Levi		17:2	84
18:10	3	22:16	84
18:10-11	25	25:34	140

Index of References

26:3	84	9:23	130
26:24	84	15:18	47
27	137	22:4-7	47
27:15	139	25:9	132
27:27	139	26:10-13	85
28:3	84	26:12	84
35:11f	84		
47:27	84	*Numbers*	
48:3f	84	3:7-8	84
		8:25-26	84
Exodus		10:8	132
1:7	85	14	103, 105, 107, 108, 110, 114
3:1	131		
3:12	131	14:2	108
4:23	131	14:3	108
7:16	131	14:11	108
8:16	131	14:21	105
9:1	131	14:27	105
10:3	131	14:28	105
10:7-8	131	14:30	105, 106, 107, 108, 110
12:31	131		
16:4	72	14:31	105
17:1-7	116	14:32-33	105
19	132	14:33	105
19:1-25	130, 131	14:43	108
19:6	118	16:39-40	49, 121
19:15	47	18:5-6	84
19:18	131	18:7	132
20:9	132	18:20	41, 42, 43
20:26	49, 122	20	107, 108, 110, 116
23:33	132		
24	45	20:3	108
24–31	44, 50	20:4	108
24:11	118	20:10-11	107
24:12-18	44	20:12	108
25:34	140	24	138
28:42	49, 122	24:6	16
29:42-43	130	24:7	138
30:7-8	49, 121	24:17-19	138
30:34-38	49, 121	28:2	139
40:34-35	130		
		Deuteronomy	
Leviticus		1:35-37	108
8:6	132	2:14	36
8:13	132	2:25	144
8:19	132	7:13	144
8:33	132	7:15	144
8:35	132	11:25	144
9:5-6	130	23:14	84

27:17	130	95:7b-11	99
28	27, 30, 90	95:11	100, 105
28:12	26	96	8
29:15-17	136	96:1-13	78
29:15-20	135	96:9-11	8
29:18	135	97	8
29:18-20	135	102	141, 142–3
30:19	66	102:26-27	142
32:8	118	103:15-16	74
32:51	108	106:32	108
		110	17
Joshua		110:4	10
6:1	132	114:4	27
		149:1-9	78
1 Samuel			
2:33-35	120	*Proverbs*	
		3:18	22
2 Samuel			
7:6-7	84	*Isaiah*	
		4:5-6	85
1 Kings		6	16
6:18-35	84	42:5-13	78
6:20	83, 95, 114	49:16	70
7:18-20	84	51:3	26
		53:5	16
I Chronicles		60:5-9	131
23:32	84	65:17	142
		65:20-23	26
2 Chronicles		65:25	24, 26, 72,
3:8-9	83, 95, 114		144
26:16-20	49, 121	66:14	24
		66:20-23	26
Job		66:22	118, 130
14:1	74		
		Jeremiah	
Psalms		3:16-17	85
2:7	1, 152	3:19	118
8	1, 18, 19, 142	29:23	129
8:4-6	152	30:2	129
8:6-8	145	31:33	115
33:1-22	78	36:4	129
40	10		
74	57	*Ezekiel*	
89	57	1	16
90:4	50	1:28	130
93	8	8:4	130
95	1, 2, 8, 12, 100,	9:3	130
	101, 102–18,	11:22-23	130
	131, 148	17:23	37

20:40	37, 38	2:1-5	29, 119
28	24	2:5	130
28:13-14	38	2:8	130
28:13-15	38	14:8	83, 95
28:14	24, 84	14:14-16	131
28:16	24	14:17-18	29
34:14	37		
35	137	*Malachi*	
35–36	138	1:1-4	137
35:10	137	1:10	34, 35
35:12	137		
35:15	137		

Apocrypha or Deutero-Canonical Books

36	137		
36:2	129		
36:11	137	*Wisdom*	
37:25-27	82	2:7-8	74
37:26-28	85	13:1	134
40–48	33, 38, 120		
40:1-4	29, 119	*Sirach*	
43:2-5	130	17:7	40
44	33		

New Testament

44:14	84		
44:15	33		
47–48	95	*Matthew*	
47:1-12	83, 84, 95	2:12	129
47:8-9	29	2:22	129
		6:28-30	74
Daniel		13:22	109, 136
2:34-35	85		
2:44-45	85	*Mark*	
		4:19	109, 136
Joel			
3:18	84	*Luke*	
		2:26	129
Amos			
9	138	*Acts*	
9:12	138–9	7:16	130
		7:48	16
Obadiah		10:22	129
10	137	17:24	16
Haggai		*1 Corinthians*	
2:6	8, 130	11:7	1 n. 2
2:7	131		
2:9	143	*2 Corinthians*	
2:19	131	5:1	16
Zechariah		*Ephesians*	
1:16–2:13	85	4:22	109, 136

Colossians
1:15-18   1

Hebrews
1   1 n. 3
1–2   18, 19
1:2   1, 7, 9, 10, 16,
                    141, 142, 152
1:2-3   141
1:2-6   151
1:2–2:9   18 n. 76
1:3   1, 151
1:6   7, 8, 17, 18 n. 76
1:10   7, 10, 141
1:10-12   142
2   18, 19, 124
2:3   9
2:5   8, 17
2:5–9   18 n. 76, 152
2:6-8   142
2:6-10   1
2:8   10, 145, 149
2:9   1, 116, 125, 128
2:10   7, 9, 10, 115, 116, 124, 141
2:10-13   125
2:10-18   142
2:11   151
2:14   125, 129
2:15   9
3–4   11, 12, 106, 112, 131, 145
3:1–4:14   111, 112
3:1-6   142
3:4   7, 10, 141
3:6   109, 111, 112, 124
3:7–4:11   2, 5, 9, 13, 14, 15, 19, 99, 104, 111, 117, 124, 125, 136, 147, 148, 150, 152
3:7–4:13   1
3:7-14   106, 107–9
3:7-19   105–11
3:9   107

3:9-10   110, 116
3:10   107
3:12   105, 112, 136, 150
3:12-13   136
3:12-14   109
3:12-19   105
3:13   102, 109, 136, 150
3:14   9
3:15-19   106, 109–10
3:16   110
3:16-19   109–10
3:17   105, 110
3:18   108, 110, 150
3:18-19   13, 106, 108, 110, 116
3:19   106, 108
4:1   102, 129
4:3   142
4:3-4   7, 10, 141, 142
4:4   103, 112
4:6   106, 152
4:6-7   102
4:6-9   13
4:8   103, 106
4:9   128
4:10   7, 10, 141
4:11   106
4:14   124
4:14-16   112
4:15-16   112
4:16   2, 112
5   115
5:5   124
5:8-10   124
5:9   116
6:4-5   151
6:5   16
6:9-20   112
6:19   2, 112, 152
6:19-20   124
6:20–7:17   10
7:2   109
7:9   109
7:19   112
7:24   16
7:25   115

7:28	124	12:11	109
8:1	7, 109	12:11-13	116
8:2	6, 7, 16, 134	12:12-14	136
8:5	7, 129	12:14	135
8:6	115	12:14-16	135
8:10	115	12:14-17	135, 140
9–10	9	12:15	136
9:11	2, 6, 15–16, 13	12:15a	150
9:12	142	12:15b	136, 150
9:15	129	12:15-16	135
9:21	109	12:15-17	135, 136
9:23-24	124	12:16	135, 136
9:23-26	7	12:16-17	135, 136, 140, 150
9:24	6, 15		
9:26	7, 10, 141, 142	12:17	135, 136, 141
9:27	109		
9:27-28	7, 8	12:18	16, 135, 136
10:1	6	12:18-21	131
10:1-10	10	12:18-24	13, 135
10:10	10	12:18-25	135, 136
10:19	112, 124	12:18-27	140
10:19-20	124	12:18-29	136, 147, 149, 150, 152
10:19-22	2, 152		
10:19-25	112	12:22	16, 111, 127, 149
10:22	112		
10:23	109	12:23	124, 135, 140
10:25	7	12:25	127, 128, 129, 140, 141, 149
10:34	143		
10:35	112		
10:36-39	7	12:25-29	7, 8
11	106	12:26	127, 128, 129, 130, 149
11:1	109		
11:1–12:2	13, 14, 15	12:26-27	7–8
11:3	7, 10, 141, 142	12:26-29	2, 19, 127–34, 145
11:5	130		
11:7	129	12:27	16, 127, 129, 142, 143, 150
11:8-16	134		
11:9	129	12:28	16, 152
11:10	16, 134	13:1	17
11:13-16	14	13:14	16, 17, 143
11:16	106, 111	13:15-16	124
11:39	106	13:20	109
11:39-40	14		
12	115, 133, 134, 145	*2 Peter*	
		2:13	109, 136
12:2	115, 124		
12:5-10	115	*Jude*	
12:5-13	124	4	130

Revelation

1:5	78	21:10	82, 95
1:6	78, 85, 114	21:10-21	29, 119
2–5	83	21:12-14	82
2:5	82	21:22	82, 83, 114
2:7	78, 83, 98	21:23-24	83
2:10	78	21:26	131
2:11	78	22	79, 83
2:17	78	22:1-4	98
2:26	78, 85	22:2	29
3:5	78	22.3	83, 95
3:8	79	22:4	79, 85
3:12	78, 79, 81, 98, 114	22:14	79
		22:14-15	83
3:21	78	22:14-19	79
4–5	76	22:15	79
4–22	76	22:19	82
4:3	78		
4:8	77		
4:11	77, 78		
5:9b-10	77		
5:10	95		
5:12	77		
5:12-13	78		
5:13	77		
7:15-17	82		
11:1-2	82, 97		
12	2, 82		
12:6	82, 97		
12:14	82, 97		
13:6	82, 97		
14:2-3	82		
14:3	78		
19:7	81		
20:6	79		
21–22	83		
21:1–22:5	79, 95		
21:1	80, 81		
21:1-2	78		
21:1-5	80		
21:2	80, 81, 82, 95		
21:2-3	81		
21:4	81, 95, 114		
21:5	78		
21:9	81		
21:9-27	83		

OTHER SOURCES

Babylonian Talmud

Arakhin

13b	78

Bava Batra

16b	140

Classic Greek/Latin texts

Historia Ecclesiae (Eusebius)

5.1.36	74

Octavius (Minucius Felix, Marcus)

38	74

Republic (Plato)

I, 345b	130
7.515 AB	6

Midrash

Genesis Rabbah

63:11	140
65:23	139

Exodus Rabbah

1.1	140

Numbers Rabbah
15:11   78

Midrash Tanhuma Genesis
1.32   78
27:15   139

Targums

Targum Neofiti Genesis
25:34   140
27:27   139

Targum Pseudo-Jonathan Genesis
25:29

Subject Index

1 Enoch 21
    Book of Watchers 21–7, 30, 89–91, 113, 119–20
    Book of Parables 27–30, 119
2 Baruch 63, 69–76, 86, 91–5, 96, 97, 113
4 Ezra 63–9, 75–6, 86, 91–5, 96, 97, 111, 113, 115
4QInstruction 39–43, 120
4QpPs37 (4Q171) 35–9

Abraham 84
Adam 1–2, 18 n. 76, 19, 40, 151
    Abraham, parallel with 84
    creation 58
    Edom 138–9
    Garden of Eden 41
    glory of 119, 120
    God's rest, participation in 117–23
    heaven 70–1
    inheritance 37, 41, 120
    Israel 48, 57, 58–9, 68, 122
    lifespan 50
    nakedness 49, 121–2
    priesthood 35, 42, 43, 49, 59–60, 85, 120, 121, 139
    repentance 151
    restoration of 118–23
    reversing the curse of 61, 68, 71, 85, 91, 140, 143–4
    sexual relationship 47
    sin 32–3, 43, 59, 60–1, 65, 67, 71
    tasks 43
Adamic blessings 137, 139, 150
allegorical interpretation 11–13
analogy 117 n. 50
angels 52
    sin 52–3
    measuring 28–9, 119
apocalyptic backgrounds 15–20
apocalypticism 11
apostasy 135–6

Attridge, Harold W. 9–10, 103
Aune, David E. and Steward, E. 4

Bachmann, V. 22–3
Bautch, Kelley Coblentz 22
Beale, G. K. 1 n. 3, 18 n. 76, 77–8
Behemoth 27
Black, Matthew 23–4
blessings 25, 26–7
Book of Parables 27–30, 119
Book of Watchers 21–7, 30, 89–91, 113, 119–20
Bultmann, Rudolf 3 n. 8
Bunta, Silviu N. 18 n. 76

Calaway, Jared C. 13–15
Canaan 55, 103, 113
Cave of the Treasures, The 18 n. 76
change 129–30
Chaoskampf myth 2
chosen people 41–3
Christ. *See* Jesus Christ
chronology 50
Cockerill, Gareth Lee 104
cosmological dualism 9–15, 127, 141, 143, 147
covenants 58, 60
    Abraham 66
    renewal 50–3
creation 6–7, 52 n. 111, 57–8, 141 *see also* creation renewal/restoration
    Adam 58
    corrupted 71
    Israel 58
    sea monster 58
    shaking of the earth 66–7 *see also* unshakeable kingdom
creation renewal/restoration 4, 27, 87, 141–5
    2 Baruch 71, 73, 76, 86
    4 Ezra 66–7, 76, 86

Beale, G. K. 77–8
Book of Watchers 30
change of heart and 115–17
at day of judgment 89–91
Jubilees 47–8, 53
Liber Antiquitatum Biblicarum 61
new song 78–9
Revelation 77–9, 85, 86
Trito-Isaiah 26, 30
Zion's renewal, link with 94–5
cults 60

Dahl, N. A. 4
Damascus Document (CD 3:12–4:4) 31–5, 43, 120–1
day of judgment 89–91
De migration Abrahami (Philo) 11
death 9 n. 38, 61
second death 79
decontextualizing/recontextualizing 9, 10
dew 72
disobedience 105–6, 107–10, 117, 121
Docherty, Susan A. 10
Doering, Lutz 23–4

earth *see also* world
dualism with heaven 9-15, 127, 141, 143, 147
gradual transformation of 88–9
New Jerusalem as new earth 82, 84–5
shaking 2, 5, 7–8, 66–7, 132–4, 149–50
see also unshakeable kingdom
Eden. *See* Garden of Eden
Edom 137–9
Eisele, Wilfried 7–8
Ellingworth, Paul 151
Enoch 39–40, 47–8, 49–50
Esau 135–41, 145, 150, 151
eschaton, the 3, 5, 111–17
eschatological hope 64–6
eschatological visions 87, 127–34
post-70 91–8
pre-70 87–91, 97–8
eternal life 29, 42
Eve, sexual relationship 47
evil 2, 115
good and 39–40
seed 65

Exodus, the 57–8
Ezekiel 38

faithfulness 9
lack of 67
fertility 56, 61
lack of 67–8
floods 25–6, 57
flowers 74
food 72, 94
fornication 34
fruit 68 n. 14, 72

Garden of Eden 22, 23–5, 27, 29, 30, 53
Adam 41
expansion 85, 86
holy mountain and 38
paradise, connection with 55–7
promised land, connection with 55–7
restoration 71–2, 82, 83–6, 138
restoration of Adam in 118–23, 140
as sanctuary of God 46–9, 84, 88–9
temple, connection with 89–91
garden of life 28–9, 30
garden of the righteous 27, 28–9, 30
gardens 27, 28, 29
Genesis 2:2 100–1
gĕzērâ šāwâ (connection of two verses) 100–1
glory 119, 130
Gnosticism 116 n. 49
God *see also* God's rest
covenant renewal 50–3
as creator 141–2
filial relationship with Israel 50–3, 59, 61, 86, 118, 119, 120–3
image of 1
mercy of 53
presence in the temple 87–91, 113
presence of, concept of 96, 97–8, 111–14
presence restored 87
promise of 70, 129, 130–2 *see also* promised land
sovereignty of 66
voice. *See* unshakeable kingdom
warning of 128–9, 135

God's rest 99–100, 111–13, 148
    Adam's participation in 117–23
    Genesis 2:2 100–1
    Israelite's failure to enter 105–11
    Psalm 95 102–17
    Urzeit-Endzeit eschatology 111–17
good (and evil) 39–40
Gräßer, E.
    "wanderende Gottesvolk, Das" 7
Grelot, P. 23
Gunkel, H.
    Schöpfung und Chaos in Urzeit und Endzeit 2–3

heart, change of 111–17
heaven 6, 7, 17–18 *see also* New Jerusalem
    Adam 70–1
    dualism with earth 9–15, 127, 141, 143, 147
    messianic era 69
    New Jerusalem as new heaven 82, 84–5
    οἰκουμένη 8
    righteous, the 74–5
    shaking 128, 132–4, 149–50 *see also* unshakeable kingdom
    tent 15–16
heavenly city. *See* New Jerusalem
heavenly realms 87, 91–8, 113–14
    creation 134
    shaking 128, 132–4, 149–50 *see also* unshakeable kingdom
Hebrew, translations of 109
Hofius, Otfried 104
holiness 42
holy mountain 24, 38 *see also* Garden of Eden
hope, holding firm to 112, 124
humanity 39, 42–3
    hopeless 64–6
Hurst, Lincoln D. 15–16

immortality 65, 68, 74
incense 49, 121
infertility 67–8
inheritance 37, 38, 41–2, 118, 151 *see also* promised land
    Adam 37, 41, 120
    connection between historical and eschatological 54–5
    Esau 136, 137–40, 145, 150, 151
    imminent possession of 44–5
    Israel 136–8, 140
Israel/Israelites 4, 14, 53, 88, 144, 152
    see also inheritance
    Adam 48, 57, 58–9, 68, 122
    covenant renewal 50–3
    creation 58
    cult 60
    disobedience 105–6, 107–10, 117
    Edom 138
    failure to enter God's rest 105–11, 112–13
    filial relationship with God 51–3, 59, 61, 86, 118, 119, 120–3
    history of 31–2
    identities of 123
    inheritance 136–8, 140
    priesthood of 53, 60, 118, 131–2
    promised land 90–1, 102–5, 114–14
    religious service 131–2
    rest. *See* God's rest
    sin 53, 55
    vindication 71–2
    wilderness 148–9

Jacob 52
Jeremias, J. 3–4
Jerusalem 16, 24, 131 *see also* New Jerusalem
    destruction 63, 66
Jesus Christ 9, 124–5, 149
    Adamic identity 152
    death and resurrection 78
    heart, change of 115
    as humanity's representative 17, 18–19
    messianic era 66
    nature of 1
    priesthood 17, 152
    redemption of 77–9
    second coming 8
    suffering of 10, 124
Jubilees 44–54, 88–9, 113, 121–2

Kadesh rebellions 107–8, 110
Kampen, J. 34–5
Käsemann, E. 116 n. 49

land, infertile 67-8 *see also* promised land
Lange, A. 39-40
letters for the seven churches 78-9
Leviathan 27
Liber Antiquitatum Biblicarum 54-62, 89-91, 113, 122-3
Life of Adam and Eve 18 n. 76, 19
life span. *See* longevity
light 56-7, 60, 61
longevity 33, 42, 43, 50, 53

Mackie, Scott D. 16-17
manna 72
marital imagery 81
Mason, Eric F. 16, 17
material, the, dualism with the spiritual 9-15, 127, 141, 143, 147
measuring 28-9
Melchizedek 10, 17
merkabah mysticism 18 n. 76
messianic era 66, 67, 69, 74, 75
 as bridge between two worlds 73-5
 concepts of 92-7
 Israel's vindication 71, 72
 restoration of Eden 71-2
Moffitt, David M. 17-19, 117 n. 50
Moses 54, 60
Mount Sinai 93
 shaking 131-3
Mount Zion. *See* Zion
mountains 21-2, 23, 24, 25, 37-8
 holy mountain 24, 38 *see also* Garden of Eden
multiplying 84-5

New Jerusalem 16, 24, 29, 79-86
new song 78
Nickelsburg, George W. E. 23-4
Noah 48 n. 94
 Flood, and the 25-6, 60
Numbers 14 105-6
Numbers 20 106-11

obedience 115-17, 124
οἰκουμένη (world) 8, 17 *see also* world
Old Testament 9, 130-2

pain 75
paradise 23, 55-7, 61, 68, 122 *see also* heavenly realms
 revelation of 92-3
Parousia 7, 8
Philo 12
 De migration Abrahami 11
pilgrimage 116 n. 49
pillars 79
Platonic background 5-8, 11, 15-16
post-70 Second Temple literature
 2 Baruch 63, 69-76, 86, 91-5, 96, 97, 113
 4 Ezra 63-9, 75-6, 86, 91-5, 96, 97, 111, 113, 115
 Revelation 76-86, 95-8, 113, 114
pre-70 literature 87-91, 97-8, 113
precious stones 57, 59-60, 123
priesthood 10, 33, 41-2, 50, 120-1, 132, 149
 Adam 35, 42, 43, 49, 59-60, 85, 120, 121, 139
 Esau 139-40
 incense 121
 inheritance 140
 Israel 53, 60, 118
 Jesus Christ 17, 124
 temple, the 79
primordial world 2-5
proctology 101
promised land, the 11-12, 26-7, 36-7, 70 *see also* inheritance
 creation, restoration of 62
 fertility 56
 Garden of Eden 47, 55-7
 God's rest 114
 Israel 90-1, 102-5, 113-14
 light 56-7
 as metaphor 102-5
 paradise, connection with 55-7
 Psalm 95 102-5
Psalm 37 35-9
Psalm 95, 100, 101, 102-17, 118, 124
Pseudo-Philo. See *Liber Antiquitatum Biblicarum*
purification 26, 44-50, 53, 122

Subject Index

Qumran texts 17, 30, 89–91, 120–1
    4QInstruction 39–43, 120
    4QpPs37 (4Q171) 35–9
    Damascus Document (CD 3:12–4:4) 31–5, 120–1

recipients 152
Red Sea, dividing 57
redeemed, the 82–3
removal 129–30
repentance 135, 151
rest 12–14, 15 *see also* God's rest
resurrection 60, 66, 75
    Jesus Christ 78
revelation 93–5, 128–9, 133
Revelation 76–86, 95–7, 111, 113, 114
    Christ's redemption and the new creation 77–9
    New Jerusalem 79–85
righteous, the 25–6, 28–9, 74–5, 86
    garden of 27–9
    temple, the 79
rivers, life-giving 29, 56
rulership 41–2

Sabbath, the 13–14, 45, 52
sanctuary 13–14, 17, 79, 124 *see also* Garden of Eden
    concepts of 96
    hope 112, 124
    on the mountain 38–9
Schöpfung und Chaos in Urzeit und Endzeit (Gunkel, H.) 2–3
second death 79
service, religious 131–2 *see also* priesthood
sexual relationships 47
shaking 2, 5, 7–8, 66–7, 128–30 *see also* unshakeable kingdom
Shebuot, festival of 51
Shem 48 n. 94
sin 32–3, 43
    Adam 32–3, 43, 59, 60–1, 65, 67, 71
    angels 52–3
Sinai, event of 93
Songs of the Sabbath Sacrifice 13, 14
sonship 1, 18 n. 76
spiritual, the
    dualism with the material 9–15, 127, 141, 143, 147

suffering 116
Svendsen, Stefan N. 11–13

tabernacle 12 n. 52
temple, the 33–5, 43–4, 81–2, 131
    building 16
    concepts of 92–7
    defilement 34–5
    destruction 63
    expansion 85
    Garden of Eden, connection with 89–91
    God's presence 87–91, 113, 114, 130, 131
    as inheritance 118, 121
    measuring 28–9
    pillars 79
    redeemed, the 82–3
    righteous, the 79
    shaking 130–2
tent 15–16
Thompson, James 5–7, 16, 102–3
Torah, the 22
transformation 128–30
translation differences 109
tree of life 22, 23, 24–5, 29, 30, 83, 119–20
two monsters, account of 27–8, 30, 72
two world concept 64–6, 73–5, 79–85

μετάθεσις (change; removal) 129–30
unshakeable kingdom 127–34, 143, 145, 149–50
Urzeit-Endzeit eschatology 2, 19–20, 62, 63, 99, 125, 147–50, 152
    2 Baruch 63, 69–76, 86, 91–5, 96, 97
    4 Ezra 63–9, 75–6, 86, 91–5, 96, 97
    Revelation 76–86
    definition 2–5
    pre-70 texts 87–91, 98
    God's rest 99–125
    post-70 texts 91–8
    Esau 140–1
    unshakeable kingdom 127–34, 140, 143, 145
    1 Enoch 21–30, 89–91, 113, 119–20
    Qumran texts 30–44, 89–91, 120–1

Jubilees 44–54, 88–9, 113, 121–2
Liber Antiquitatum Biblicarum 54–62

"wandernde Gottesvolk, Das" (Gräßer, E.) 7
wicked, destruction of the 35–7
wilderness 35–7, 45–50, 82, 88, 148–9
   forty years 107
   God's rest 102, 104, 105–17
   Kadesh rebellions 107–8, 110
   people's disobedience 105–6, 107–10, 117, 121
   people's failure to enter God's rest 105–11
wisdom 22, 23
world *see also* earth
   coming 70, 75
   continuity between worlds 144
   dualism between heaven and earth 9–15, 127, 141, 143, 147
   heavenly. *See* heavenly realm
   immanent 11, 12
   primordial 2–5
   shaking 2, 5, 7–8, 66–7, 132–4 *see also* unshakeable kingdom
   transcendent 6, 11, 12
   two-worlds concept 64–6, 73–5, 79–85
   worldview 5
οἰκουμένη 8

χρηματίζω (warning) 128–9

Zion 12, 69, 47–8, 72, 73, 92
   revelation of 93–5, 133

Printed in Great Britain
by Amazon